Ionic in Action

Ionic in Action

HYBRID MOBILE APPS WITH IONIC AND ANGULARJS

JEREMY WILKEN

MANNING
SHELTER ISLAND

For online information and ordering of this and other Manning books, please visit
www.manning.com. The publisher offers discounts on this book when ordered in quantity.
For more information, please contact

    Special Sales Department
    Manning Publications Co.
    20 Baldwin Road
    PO Box 761
    Shelter Island, NY 11964
    Email: orders@manning.com

Manning Publications Co.
20 Baldwin Road
PO Box 761
Shelter Island, NY 11964

Development editor: Helen Sturgis
Technical development editor: Gregor Zurowski
Copyeditor: Jodie Allen
Proofreader: Katie Tennant
Technical proofreader: Matthew Merkes
Typesetter: Dottie Marsico
Cover designer: Marija Tudor

ISBN 9781633430082
Printed in the United States of America
1 2 3 4 5 6 7 8 9 10 – EBM – 20 19 18 17 16 15

brief contents

1 ▪ Introducing Ionic and hybrid apps   1

2 ▪ Setting up your computer to build apps   16

3 ▪ What you need to know about AngularJS   35

4 ▪ Ionic navigation and core components   64

5 ▪ Tabs, advanced lists, and form components   94

6 ▪ Weather app, using side menus, modals, action sheets, and ionScroll   126

7 ▪ Advanced techniques for professional apps   163

8 ▪ Using Cordova plugins   186

9 ▪ Previewing, debugging, and automated testing   206

10 ▪ Building and publishing apps   231

contents

foreword   xiii
preface   xv
acknowledgments   xvii
about this book   xix
about the cover illustration   xxii

1 Introducing Ionic and hybrid apps   1

1.1   What is Ionic?   2

1.2   Types of mobile experiences   3

*Native mobile apps   3 ▪ Mobile websites (web apps)   5
Hybrid apps   6*

1.3   Understanding how the Ionic stack works   7

*Ionic: user interface framework   8 ▪ Angular: web application
framework   10 ▪ Cordova: hybrid app framework   10*

1.4   Why Ionic?   11

*Why Ionic is good for developers   11 ▪ Drawbacks of using
Ionic   12*

1.5   Prerequisites for building apps with Ionic   13

*Experience with HTML, CSS, and JavaScript   13 ▪ Experience
with web applications and Angular   13 ▪ Access to a mobile
device   13*

1.6   Supported mobile devices and platforms   14

       Apple iOS   14 ▪ *Google Android   15*

1.7   Summary   15

2   *Setting up your computer to build apps   16*

2.1   Quick-start guide   17

       Setting up your development environment   18 ▪ *Starting a new project   20* ▪ *Project folder structure   21* ▪ *Previewing in a browser   22*

2.2   Setting up previewing environments   23

       Installing platform tools   23 ▪ *Setting up emulators   25 Setting up a connected device   29* ▪ *Adding a platform to the project   30* ▪ *Previewing in an emulator   31* ▪ *Previewing on a mobile device   32*

2.3   Summary   34

3   *What you need to know about AngularJS   35*

3.1   AngularJS at a glance   37

       Views and templates: describing the content   38 ▪ *Controllers, models, and scope: managing data and logic   39* ▪ *Services: reusable objects with methods   41* ▪ *Two-way data binding: sharing between controller and view   41*

3.2   Setting up for the chapter project   41

       Getting the project files   42 ▪ *Starting the development server   43*

3.3   Basics for an Angular app   44

3.4   Controllers: for controlling data and business logic   45

3.5   Loading data: using the controller to load and display data in the view   48

       Filters: convert data to display in the view   51

3.6   Handling click events to select a note   51

3.7   Create a directive to parse a note with Markdown   54

3.8   Using models to manage content editing   56

3.9   Saving and deleting a note   59

       Adding the save() method   60 ▪ *Using Angular forms for validation   61* ▪ *Adding the remove method   61*

3.10   Continuing with Angular   62

3.11   Chapter challenges   63

3.12   Summary   63

4 **Ionic navigation and core components 64**

4.1 Set up chapter project 66
Create a new app and add code manually 66 • Clone the finished app and follow along 66

4.2 Setting up the app navigation 66
Designing good app navigation 67 • Declaring the app views with the state provider 69

4.3 Building the home view 72
Creating a content container 72 • Using CSS components and adding a simple list of links 74 • Adding icons to the list items 75

4.4 Using a controller and model for the reservation view 76

4.5 Loading data into the weather view 80
Adding the template for the weather view 81 • Create weather controller to load external data 82 • Adding a loading indicator to the weather view 84

4.6 Infinite scroll with cards for the restaurants view 86

4.7 Using the slidebox component for app intro tour 89

4.8 Chapter challenges 92

4.9 Summary 93

5 **Tabs, advanced lists, and form components 94**

5.1 Set up chapter project 96
Create a new app and add code manually 96 • Clone the finished app and follow along 96

5.2 ionTabs: adding tabs and navigation 96
Adding tabs container and three tabs to the app 98

5.3 Adding ionNavView for each tab 98

5.4 Loading and displaying current Bitcoin rates 103

5.5 Display a currency's details in the same tab view 107

5.6 Refresh the Bitcoin rates and display help 111
ionRefresher: pull-to-refresh the rates 112 • $ionicPopover: showing help in a popover 113

5.7 Charting historical data 116
Setting up third-party libraries 116 • History tab template using Highcharts and a select box to toggle currency 117 • History tab controller loads data and sets up chart 118

5.8   Currencies tab with list reordering and toggles   121

ionReorderButton: adding reordering to a list   122 ▪ *ionToggle:*
adding toggles to list items   123

5.9   Chapter challenges   124

5.10   Summary   124

6   *Weather app, using side menus, modals, action sheets,*
    and ionScroll   126

6.1   Setting up the chapter project   128

6.2   Setting up the side menu and views   128

6.3   Searching for locations   131

6.4   Adding settings view and data services   133

Create services for locations and settings   133 ▪ *Show favorites*
in side menu list   135 ▪ *Adding the settings template   136*
Settings view controller   138

6.5   Setting up the weather view   139

Get a Forecast.io API key   140 ▪ *Using Ionic CLI proxies   140*
Add the weather view controller and template   141

6.6   ionScroll: building custom scrolling content   142

Using ionScroll with paging   143 ▪ *Creating filters for forecast*
data   148

6.7   Action sheet: displaying a list of options   150

6.8   ionModal: displaying the sunrise and sunset chart   153

Setting up a modal   154 ▪ *Collection repeat: making the sunrise*
and sunset list fast   156

6.9   Popup: alert and confirm changes to favorites   159

6.10   Chapter challenges   161

6.11   Summary   162

7   *Advanced techniques for professional apps   163*

7.1   Set up chapter project   164

Get the code   164

7.2   Custom Ionic styling using Sass   164

Setting up Sass   164 ▪ *Customize Ionic with Sass variables   165*
Using Sass for your own styling   167

7.3   How to support online and offline mode   167

7.4   Handling gesture events in Ionic   169

*Listen for events with Ionic event directives   169 ▪ Listen for events
with $ionicGesture service   171 ▪ Available gesture events   174*

7.5   Storing data for persistence   175

*Using localStorage   175 ▪ Using Web SQL, IndexedDB, and
SQLite   178 ▪ Other options from Cordova plugins   179*

7.6   Building one app for multiple platforms   179

*One size doesn't always fit all   179 ▪ Adapt styling for a
platform or device type   180 ▪ Adapt behavior for a platform
or device type   182*

7.7   Modify default behaviors with $ionicConfigProvider   184
7.8   Summary   185

8   **Using Cordova plugins   186**

8.1   Cordova plugins   187

*Considerations when using plugins   188 ▪ Installing
plugins   188 ▪ Using plugins   189 ▪ Using plugins with
emulators   190 ▪ Plugins and platform limitations   190
Angular and Cordova gotchas   191 ▪ Solutions to common issues
with devices or emulators   192*

8.2   ngCordova   194

Installing ngCordova   194

8.3   Using a camera and photos in the resort app   194

*Setting up the camera project   195 ▪ Adding the camera
plugin   196 ▪ Creating the photo book view   196*

8.4   Using geolocation in the weather app   198

*Setting up the geolocation example   199 ▪ Adding the geolocation
plugin and ngCordova   200 ▪ Requesting a user's location   200
Improving the weather app   202*

8.5   Chapter challenges   204
8.6   Summary   204

9   **Previewing, debugging, and automated testing   206**

9.1   The differences among previewing, debugging,
and testing   207

Why testing is important   208

9.2   Setting up the chapter example   208

9.3   Additional ways to preview apps   209

  Ionic Lab   209 ▪ *Ionic View   210*

9.4   Debugging from a device   212

  Debugging from an Android device   213 ▪ *Debugging from an iOS device or emulator   213*

9.5   Automated testing   218

  Unit tests with Jasmine and Karma   219 ▪ *Integration tests with Protractor and WebDriver   225*

9.6   More test examples   229

9.7   Summary   230

10 **Building and publishing apps   231**

10.1   Building for production: an overview   232

10.2   Building icons and splash-screen assets   233

  Creating the primary icons   234 ▪ *Creating the splash-screen images   235*

10.3   Preparing your app for production   236

10.4   Building Android apps and publishing to Google Play   237

  Setting up for signing your apps   237 ▪ *Build the release app file   238* ▪ *Signing the APK file   238* ▪ *Optimize the APK   238* *Building an updated version of your app   239* ▪ *Creating the app listing and uploading the app to the Play Store   239* ▪ *Updating the app listing or uploading a new version   240* ▪ *Using alternative Android stores   241*

10.5   Building iOS apps and publishing to the AppStore   241

  Set up certificates and ID   242 ▪ *Set up an app ID identifier   242* *Create listing in iTunes Connect   243* ▪ *Build and upload app with Xcode   243* ▪ *Complete the iTunes Connect app listing   244* *Updating the app   244*

10.6   Summary   245

appendix   *Additional resources   247*

  index   249

foreword

This book is the result of nine months of dedicated work by Jeremy Wilken, a top Ionic developer with whom we've had the pleasure of collaborating since we built Ionic and open sourced it in 2013. This book provides an excellent introduction to the Ionic Open Source SDK, and it also offers plenty of rich information for experienced Ionic developers.

Jeremy built three Ionic apps for this book, using just about every Ionic component in existence. Because of that, the book is a solid reference for using the components in an integrated way. The first app, which a resort might use to provide value for guests, incorporates our slidebox, lists, cards, content containers, and basic navigation. The second, a Bitcoin market app, provides real-time currency rates for Bitcoin and uses pull-to-refresh, popovers, tabs, charts, advanced lists, and nested views. The third, a weather app, uses modals, a custom scroll area (paginated scrolling), externally loaded data, side menus, and a search view.

The apps are unique and robust. They are 80% developed for deployment to an app store, with the obvious missing pieces listed at the end of the chapter to challenge readers to complete them.

For experienced developers, the book explains how to target a platform if, for example, they want to use the action sheet in iOS and the popover in Android. The book also provides background about the Ionic ecosystem, explaining how to leverage Cordova and plugins; discussing Ionic's platform services, such as Ionic View; and providing instruction about how to improve Ionic development with advanced techniques and testing. Jeremy provides great examples and insight into how to set up and write your own tests.

Prior to creating Ionic with Max Lynch and Ben Sperry, I joined their company to help develop their already successful products, including Codiqa, which was a jQuery Mobile drag-and-drop interface builder. As we worked on Codiqa, we realized devices and browsers were not being used to their full potential, and users were continually asking for more from our tools. Eventually, we decided to create our toolkit for hybrid applications, in order to push mobile devices to their limits. With the added power of Angular, we've been able to bring hybrid mobile app development to a place where it presents a viable challenge to native application development. Since we released the alpha version of Ionic in 2013, I couldn't be more proud of how quickly the development community has embraced Ionic and helped to grow it even further. The part I'm most excited about is that Ionic is only getting started, and we'll continue to grow and support it, so that developers can build high-performing apps quickly and easily.

You'll find this book to be both an informative introduction to Ionic and an in-depth guide to building better apps, depending on your experience with Ionic and your needs. Thank you for being part of the Ionic community.

Enjoy!

ADAM BRADLEY
COCREATOR OF THE IONIC FRAMEWORK

preface

The importance of mobile may be clear today, but even just a few years ago it was debatable if building mobile apps was worth the time and cost. As of 2015 the number of mobile apps available in the Apple App and Google Play Stores is well over a million. Over six times more phones are sold than desktop/laptop devices, and the number of tablets sold should exceed desktop/laptop devices in 2015. Mobile is here, and here to stay.

Back in 2013, the world of mobile app development was focused primarily on building native apps. These native apps were written in Java or Objective C, and required developers to learn those languages, platform tools, SDKs, and so forth. For a web developer like myself, this presented a barrier to getting into mobile app development. It seemed like the mobile web was focused on building responsive websites, not mobile apps. The idea of a hybrid app (which is a native app built using web technologies) was usually given very little credit due to the quality of older devices and browsers that made hybrid apps sluggish, and design practices that made the apps have a visual disconnect from native apps.

The founders of Ionic saw an opportunity. They realized that mobile devices were improving, quite rapidly in fact, and that hybrid apps could be a serious contender with native apps. They aimed to open the door for developers who want to build native-feeling mobile apps, while using the same languages they already know from web development. Ionic builds on the shoulders of other open source projects, Cordova and Angular. Ionic leverages these projects into a more unified platform for building hybrid mobile apps.

As of version 1.0, it's clear that Ionic has come of age and empowers web developers to build mobile apps. The Ionic team has become fond of calling Ionic the "missing SDK" for hybrid apps. As I've finished this journey of writing *Ionic in Action*, I can see the full vision of Ionic coming to life. The core of what makes Ionic so powerful is the open source components explored in this book. In addition, a platform of services is being built around it for features such as push notifications, analytics, beta testing, and more. I hold open source projects with well-managed development and community input in high regard, and Ionic is certainly in this category (in the top 40 starred projects on GitHub, and it uses Angular, which is in the top 3 as of this writing). Hundreds of thousands of apps have been created with Ionic, and several apps have even been featured in the major app stores.

Writing a book about Ionic was a logical extension of my desire to share my learning experience on how to become a mobile app developer. I started with writing the core parts of this book around a learning pathway that talked about each feature of Ionic and explored them each in isolation. I got up to six chapters done, but it felt like the wrong approach. I like to see something working that I can interact with, and even touch, as is possible in the case of mobile apps.

So after writing the first draft of the three core chapters in the book, I threw them aside and rewrote them from scratch using a very direct, build-the-app-as-you-go approach. It feels much more like the kind of learning path I followed when I built my first Ionic app, and I hope that you find the chapters approachable. In fact, I hope you find that same care applied to all of the chapters in this book.

I learned about Ionic through trial and error, since the documentation has always been a good guide. When I had a project at work that required a mobile app, I was able to put Ionic into service and build a prototype within a day. Working through the early days of Ionic, I regularly updated my app to keep up with the changes and new features, and I was often impressed with the attention to detail and rapid pace of innovation. Over the months of beta releases, Ionic matured its API and design into the polished and consistent form it is today.

The future of Ionic is one that includes even more community-driven contributions and components, more platform services, and continued progress in performance and quality. I can't wait to see what you build, and I'm glad to be with you on your own journey to become a mobile app developer with Ionic.

acknowledgments

In this book I share many things that I've learned over the years, and I owe many for providing training, guidance, and support along the way. While it is impossible to track everyone who has had some impact on my growth that led to this book, I know those who have made the biggest impact are people heavily involved in open source communities. Those who write, maintain, or support open source projects and communities have my highest respect and gratitude.

Thank you, Manning, and the wonderful staff who have worked hard to make this book a reality. They say it takes a village to raise a child, and so it is also with publishing a book. Robin de Jongh was instrumental in getting this book started, and for stimulating my excitement to write. My sincere thanks goes to Helen Stergius for her tireless editing, late-night brainstorming, and positive attitude and energy that pushed me through the major writing phase. I thank the rest of the team who helped bring the book to life through publishing and reviewing, particularly Gregor Zurowski, Katie Tennant, Mary Piergies, Janet Vail, Matt Merkes, Candace Gillhoolley, Kevin Sullivan, Donna Clements, and Jodie Allen.

Many peer reviewers helped by poking holes in some of the weaker areas of early drafts or inspired my confidence to make positive changes over time. Many thanks to Andrea Prearo, Barbara Fusinska, Charlie Gaines, Cho S. Kim, Chris Graham, Gareth van der Berg, Giuseppe de Marco, Jeff Cunningham, Ken Rimple, Kevin Liao, Lourens Steyn, Patrick Dennis, Rabimba Karanjai, Satadru Roy, and Wendy Wise—you suggested many improvements for me to chew on, and the manuscript would not be as strong without your help. Many MEAP reviewers provided some great feedback on the forum. It's pretty neat that people are willing to buy a book and engage with the author on how to make it better.

If you ever have the chance to meet anyone from the Ionic team, you'll find them to be some of the most dedicated and genuine people in tech and open source. I owe the Ionic team a great deal of thanks for making Ionic (and thus the opportunity to write a book on it!), and for their great efforts in reviewing and answering questions along the way. In particular, I'd like to thank Adam Bradley, Ben Sperry, Katie Ginder-Vogel, and Mike Hartington for the many emails, Skype calls, or in-person chats we've had. The Ionic community grows daily due to your tireless efforts and fantastic work. And special thanks to Adam for penning the foreword to my book.

Finally, there's always the underlying support of my wife Linda. In the future, I promise not to write a book when we have a newborn (without your permission of course). It's hard to imagine the amount of time and energy a book requires until you do it, and you've been supportive and understanding when I needed to hide in my office until a draft was done. I love you and our baby always.

about this book

Ionic brings together several existing projects with its own set of tools so web developers can build mobile apps. Ionic has gained a strong following and is a top choice for mobile app developers.

Ionic in Action is a hands-on, example-driven guide to Ionic. During the course of the book, you'll build several nearly complete apps that showcase almost every feature of Ionic. The documentation for Ionic is very good, but it doesn't provide much direction on how to orchestrate a large app.

When you build an app with Ionic, you actually use a combination of technologies (primarily Angular and Cordova). To ensure you're really capable of building mobile apps with Ionic, the book provides chapters on those technologies. There's much more that could be said about Angular and Cordova, which is why entire books have been written about them, but this book tries to do them justice and provides enough foundational knowledge to get you started.

Mobile apps often require access to external data. It's helpful to understand how APIs are able to provide data for web applications. *Ionic in Action* covers how to utilize RESTful APIs through several of the examples.

Who should read this book

This book is intended for web developers who have a foundation in building web applications.

Knowledge of CSS, HTML, and JavaScript is expected. You should understand how to write HTML to structure your content and how to use CSS to modify the styling.

JavaScript experience should include concepts such as asynchronous behavior, objects, and primitives.

No prior knowledge of Cordova or Angular is required. It's helpful to have some background in building web applications in a browser with JavaScript, but this experience can also be gained through careful study of the book examples.

Access to a mobile device is necessary to properly build and test apps. For Ionic, the device needs to be an iOS or Android device. Having one of each is very helpful!

How the book is organized

In the 10 chapters, I cover the entire process from setting up your environment to publishing your finished app:

- Chapter 1 is a detailed overview of Ionic, the other technologies used together to create hybrid apps, and why Ionic is a great choice.

- Chapter 2 gets you through the setup process for all of the tools used in the book, and helps you create your first mobile app using one of the default starter templates.

- Chapter 3 provides a primer for developers who aren't familiar with Angular or who'd like to brush up on their knowledge because Ionic is built with Angular.

- Chapter 4 walks you through creating a mobile app for a fictitious resort that includes basic app navigation and uses a number of visual components such as cards, a list with infinite scrolling, loading indicators to gracefully load data, and a slidebox. You'll learn about the basics of building an Ionic app using a hands-on approach while building your first app.

- Chapter 5 takes you through building another mobile app for tracking Bitcoin currency prices. The Bitcoin app uses tabs, a pull-to-refresh feature, several form components, advanced lists with swipe options, and a chart for quotes over time. The focus in this chapter is how to structure an app using tabs, and how to leverage many more Ionic components.

- Chapter 6 helps you build a weather app. The chapter digs into using the side menu for navigation, modals for presenting tangential information, action sheets to display option buttons, and a custom scrolling behavior. This chapter rounds out your understanding of the Ionic components and primary design elements used in Ionic apps.

- Chapter 7 introduces you to some advanced techniques that are useful for building hybrid apps. You'll learn about how to persist user data, customize Ionic components, work in online or offline mode, configure Ionic's default settings, adapt your apps to have platform-specific functionalities, and handle gesture events.

- Chapter 8 looks at how to use Cordova to allow Ionic apps to support platform features, such as sensor data. The chapter uses two of the apps you built in earlier chapters to demonstrate how to add support for geolocation for the weather app and camera support for the resort app. You'll learn about ngCordova and how to easily integrate with any Cordova plugin.

- Chapter 9 helps you set up testing for your Ionic app. The chapter introduces two primary testing approaches: unit testing for testing your business logic, and integration testing for testing the overall app functionality. You'll also learn about Ionic View and Ionic Lab to help you preview your apps.
- Chapter 10 walks you through the process of submitting your apps to the stores. It covers tips and techniques for preparing your apps for production, adding necessary graphics and assets, and ultimately how to properly build your apps for both iOS and Android.

Code

All of the code for this book is found on GitHub at https://github.com/ionic-in-action. The source code is open source, so you're able to modify it for your own purposes. I only ask that you don't try to publish the example apps to the app stores.

Most of the code is found in code listing blocks, except in cases where the code is short and should already be familiar. The code is well annotated to provide context and descriptions for individual lines. Sometimes code is in bold font to highlight code that has changed from previous steps in the chapter, such as when a new feature adds to an existing line of code.

Author Online

Purchase of *Ionic in Action* includes free access to a private web forum run by Manning Publications where you can make comments about the book, ask technical questions, and receive help from the author and from other users. To access the forum and subscribe to it, point your web browser to www.manning.com/books/ionic-in-action.

This page provides information on how to get on the forum once you're registered, what kind of help is available, and the rules of conduct on the forum. Manning's commitment to our readers is to provide a venue where a meaningful dialog between individual readers and between readers and the author can take place. It's not a commitment to any specific amount of participation on the part of the author, whose contribution to the forum remains voluntary (and unpaid). We suggest you try asking the author some challenging questions lest his interest stray!

The Author Online forum and the archives of previous discussions will be accessible from the publisher's website as long as the book is in print.

about the cover illustration

The figure on the cover of *Ionic in Action* is captioned "Summer Habit of a Moor of Morocco 1695." The illustration is taken from Thomas Jefferys' *A Collection of the Dresses of Different Nations, Ancient and Modern* (4 volumes), London, published between 1757 and 1772. The title page states that these are hand-colored copperplate engravings, heightened with gum arabic. Thomas Jefferys (1719–1771) was called "Geographer to King George III." An English cartographer who was the leading map supplier of his day, Jeffreys engraved and printed maps for government and other official bodies and produced a wide range of commercial maps and atlases, especially of North America. His work as a mapmaker sparked an interest in local dress customs of the lands he surveyed and mapped. This diversity of dress is brilliantly displayed in this four-volume collection.

Fascination with faraway lands and travel for pleasure were relatively new phenomena in the late eighteenth century, and collections such as this one were popular, introducing both the tourist as well as the armchair traveler to the inhabitants of other countries. The diversity of the drawings in Jeffreys' volumes speaks vividly of the uniqueness and individuality of the world's nations 200 to 300 years ago. Dress codes have changed since then, and the diversity by region and country, so rich at the time, has faded away. It is now hard to tell the inhabitant of one continent apart from another. Perhaps, trying to view it optimistically, we have traded a cultural and visual diversity for a more varied personal life—or a more varied and interesting intellectual and technical life.

At a time when it is hard to tell one computer book from another, Manning celebrates the inventiveness and initiative of the computer business with book covers based on the rich diversity of regional life of centuries ago, brought back to life by Jeffreys' pictures.

Introducing Ionic and hybrid apps

1

This chapter covers

- Why you should choose Ionic and how it benefits you
- What Ionic is and how it uses Angular and Cordova
- Why hybrid apps are an ideal choice for mobile development
- Introduction and requirements for Android and iOS platforms

Building mobile apps has become an essential skill for many developers, and with Ionic you'll be able to build hybrid mobile apps that look and feel just like native mobile apps. A *hybrid app* is a type of mobile app that uses a browser window to display its interface. *Ionic* is a combination of tools and utilities that enables developers to quickly build hybrid mobile apps using the same technologies used to build websites and web applications, primarily HTML, CSS (Cascading Style Sheets), and JavaScript. Ionic works by embedding a web application inside of a native app by using Cordova. It's designed to work together with Angular to create a web application for the mobile environment, and includes support for mobile features like user interface controls and responding to touch input.

This book aims to give developers the skills necessary to build Ionic mobile apps. I'll teach you the basics of setting up your projects correctly and how to build rich interfaces, and demonstrate with real-world style examples. I'll help you set up your build, testing, and deployment processes to get your app ready for production. But before we get too far along, we should dig deeper into Ionic and why it's a solid choice for building hybrid mobile apps.

1.1 What is Ionic?

Ionic is a combination of technologies and utilities designed to make building hybrid mobile apps fast, easy, and beautiful. Ionic is built on an ecosystem that includes Angular as the web application framework and Cordova for building and packaging the native app. We'll dig into each in more detail later, but figure 1.1 shows you an overview of these technologies and how they stack. Let's take a moment to cover the basics of how the technology stack works on a device.

In figure 1.1, the stack begins with the user opening the app from the device. Imagine this is an iPhone running iOS or a Nexus 10 running Android. Let's break down each of these pieces in more detail:

- *Device*—This loads the app. The device contains the operating system that manages the installation of apps that are downloaded from the platform's store. The operating system also provides a set of APIs for apps to use to access various features, such as the GPS location, contacts list, or camera.
- *Cordova app wrapper*—This is a native app that loads the web application code. Cordova is a platform for building mobile apps that can run using HTML, CSS, and JavaScript inside of a native app, which is known as a *hybrid mobile app*. It's a utility for creating a bridge between the platform and the application. It creates a native mobile app that can be installed (called the *app wrapper* in figure 1.1),

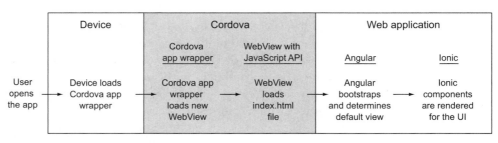

Figure 1.1 **The stack of technologies used with the Ionic framework, and how they fit together**

and it contains what's called a WebView (essentially an isolated browser window) with a JavaScript API that the web application will run inside.

- *Cordova JavaScript API*—This is the bridge that communicates between the app and the device. The app wrapper has access to both the web application and the native platform through the JavaScript API. This is primarily handled behind the scenes, and Cordova ultimately generates the native app for you.

- *Angular*—This is the web application that controls the app routing and function. The Angular web application runs inside of the WebView. Angular is a very popular framework for building powerful web applications. Angular is primarily used to manage the web application's logic and data.

- *Ionic*—This provides the user interface components rendered in the app. Ionic is built on top of Angular, and is primarily used to design the user interface and experience. This includes the visual elements such as tabs, buttons, and navigation headers. These interface controls are the heart of Ionic, and provide a near-native interface inside of a hybrid app. Ionic also includes a number of additional utilities and features that help manage your app from creation to previewing to deployment.

The combination of these technologies makes Ionic a very feature-rich platform for building your mobile apps. Now that you have a bird's-eye view of Ionic and the technology, let's look a little closer at three main types of mobile experiences and why Ionic's approach is beneficial.

1.2 Types of mobile experiences

It's important to understand there are several ways to build applications for mobile devices, and each has its strengths and weaknesses. There are three basic types: native apps, mobile websites, and hybrid apps. We'll look at each of these in detail to clarify the differences.

In figure 1.2, you can see how the three types compare in design and architecture. The figure also shows how each app would access a database or web service API to load data.

1.2.1 Native mobile apps

To create native apps, developers write code in the default language for the mobile platform, which is Objective C or Swift for iOS and Java for Android. Developers compile the app and install it on a device. Using the platform software development kit (SDK), the app communicates with the platform APIs to access device data or load data from an external server using HTTP requests.

Both iOS and Android provide a set of tools to enable developers to leverage the platform features in a controlled manner through predefined APIs. There are tools, both official and unofficial, that can aid in the development of native apps. It's common for developers to use frameworks in their native app to make development easier.

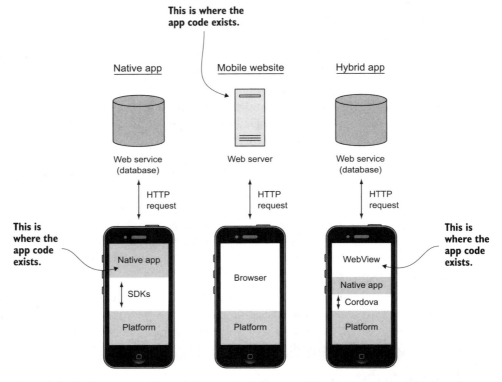

Figure 1.2   Native apps, mobile websites, and hybrid app architectures compared side by side

NATIVE APP ADVANTAGES

Native apps come with a number of benefits over hybrid apps and mobile websites. The benefits revolve around being tightly integrated with the device platform:

- *Native APIs*—Native apps can use the native APIs directly in the app, making the tightest connection to the platform.
- *Performance*—They can experience the highest levels of performance.
- *Same environment*—They're written with native APIs, which is helpful for developers familiar with the languages used.

But there are also a number of disadvantages.

NATIVE APP DISADVANTAGES

The disadvantages of native apps are generally the level of difficulty in developing and maintaining them:

- *Language requirements*—Native apps require developer proficiency in the platform language (for example, Java) and knowledge of how to use platform-specific APIs.
- *Not cross-platform*—They can only be developed for one platform at a time.

- *High level of effort*—Typically, they require more work and overhead to build, which increases costs.

Native apps may be best suited for developers who have a command of Java and Objective C, or for teams with extensive resources and a need for the benefits of native apps.

1.2.2 Mobile websites (web apps)

Mobile websites, or web apps, work well on a mobile device and are accessed through a mobile browser. Web apps are websites viewed on a mobile device in a mobile browser, designed specifically to fit a mobile device screen size. Figure 1.3 shows a couple of examples.

Some website designers develop a second version specifically for use on a mobile device. Perhaps you've used your mobile device to visit a website and were redirected to a version with limited features, such as visiting eBay and ending up on the http://m.ebay.com subdomain. On other websites, such as www.bostonglobe.com, you may

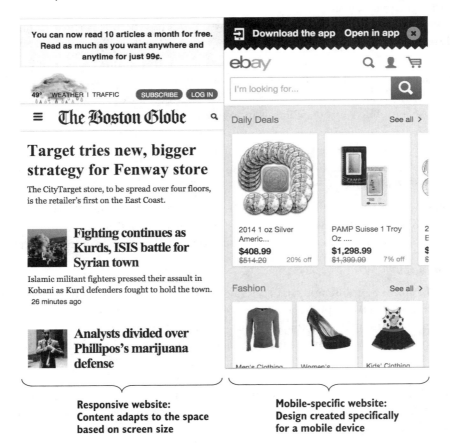

Responsive website:
Content adapts to the space
based on screen size

Mobile-specific website:
Design created specifically
for a mobile device

Figure 1.3   Mobile websites: a responsive site from the *Boston Globe* (left) and a mobile-specific website from eBay (right)

find that the design adjusts to your device's form factor and screen size. This is accomplished with a technique called *responsive design*. The website content will resize and flow according to the browser window size, and some may even be hidden.

MOBILE WEBSITE ADVANTAGES

Mobile websites enjoy a number of benefits, primarily in the level of effort and compatibility on devices:

- *Maintainability*—Mobile websites are easy to update and maintain without the need to go through an approval process or update installations on devices.
- *No installation*—Because they exist on the internet, they don't require installation on mobile devices.
- *Cross-platform*—Any mobile device has a browser, allowing your application to be accessible from any device.

As with native apps, there are also a number of disadvantages.

MOBILE WEBSITE DISADVANTAGES

Mobile websites run inside of a mobile browser, which is the major cause of limitations and disadvantages:

- *No native access*—Because mobile websites are run in the browser, they have no access to the native APIs or the platform, just the APIs provided by the browser.
- *Require keyboard to load*—Users have to type the address in a browser to find or use a mobile website, which is more difficult than tapping an icon.
- *Limited user interface*—It's difficult to create touch-friendly applications, especially if you have a responsive site that has to work well on desktops.
- *Mobile browsing decline*—The amount of time users browse the web on a mobile device is declining, while app use is increasing.

Mobile websites can be important even if you have a mobile app, depending on your product or service. Research shows users spend much more time using apps compared to the mobile browser, so mobile websites tend to experience lower engagement.

1.2.3 *Hybrid apps*

A hybrid app is a mobile app that contains an isolated browser instance, often called a *WebView*, to run a web application inside of a native app. It uses a native app wrapper that can communicate with the native device platform and the WebView. This means web applications can run on a mobile device and have access to the device, such as the camera or GPS features.

Tools that facilitate the communication between the WebView and the native platform make hybrid apps possible. These tools aren't part of the official iOS or Android platforms, but are third-party tools such as Apache Cordova, which is used in this book. When a hybrid app compiles, your web application transforms into a native app.

HYBRID APP ADVANTAGES

Hybrid apps have a few advantages over mobile websites and native apps that make hybrid apps a great platform for building apps:

- *Cross-platform*—You can build your app once and deploy it to multiple platforms with minimal effort.
- *Same skills as web development*—They allow you to build mobile apps using the same skills already used to develop websites and web applications.
- *Access to device*—Because the WebView is wrapped in a native app, your app has access to all of the device features available to a native app.
- *Ease of development*—They're easy and fast to develop, without the need to constantly rebuild to preview. You also have access to the same development tools used for building websites.

Hybrid apps provide a robust base for mobile app development, yet still allow you to use the web platform. You can build the majority of your app as a website, but anytime you need access to a native API, the hybrid app framework provides a bridge to access that API with JavaScript. Your app can detect swipes, pinches, and other gestures just like clicks or keyboard events. But there are a few disadvantages, as you might expect.

HYBRID APP DISADVANTAGES

Hybrid apps have a few disadvantages due to the restrictions that are placed on Web-Views and limitations of native integrations:

- *WebView limitations*—The application can only run as well as the WebView instance, which means performance is tied to the quality of the platform's browser.
- *Access native features via plugins*—Access to the native APIs you need may not be currently available, and may require additional development to make a plugin to support it.
- *No native user interface controls*—Without a tool like Ionic, developers would have to create all of the user interface elements.

With Ionic, you can build hybrid apps so you can leverage the knowledge and skills with which web developers are already familiar.

1.3 *Understanding how the Ionic stack works*

There are several technologies that can be used when building hybrid apps, but with Ionic there are three primary ones: Ionic, Angular, and Cordova. Figure 1.4 outlines how these pieces can work in tandem to facilitate opening the camera from an Ionic app.

Let's break down each of the steps in figure 1.4:

1 The user taps on a button (which is an Ionic component).
2 The button calls the Angular controller, which calls Cordova through the JavaScript API.

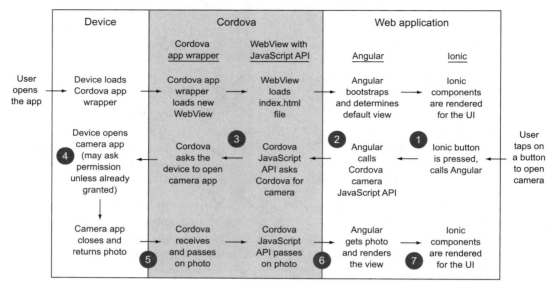

Figure 1.4 **How Ionic, Angular, and Cordova work together for a hybrid app**

3 Cordova communicates with the device using native SDKs and requests the camera app.

4 The device opens the camera app (or prompts for permission if necessary), and the user is able to take a picture.

5 When the user confirms the photo, the camera app closes and returns the image data to Cordova.

6 Cordova passes the image data back to the Angular controller.

7 The visual display of the image is updated inside of Ionic components.

This quick outline of how the pieces communicate can demonstrate how an Ionic app is really a stack of technologies that work in concert. Don't worry if some of these terms are unknown to you—we'll cover them throughout this book. The key here is to see how your app is able to leverage the power of the device. Let's look at each one more closely.

1.3.1   *Ionic: user interface framework*

Ionic's primary feature is a set of user interface controls that are missing from HTML but are common on mobile apps. Imagine a weather app that shows current conditions based on the user's location. Ionic provides a number of user interface components such as a slidebox that allows a user to swipe between several boxes of information like temperature, forecasts, and weather maps. These components are

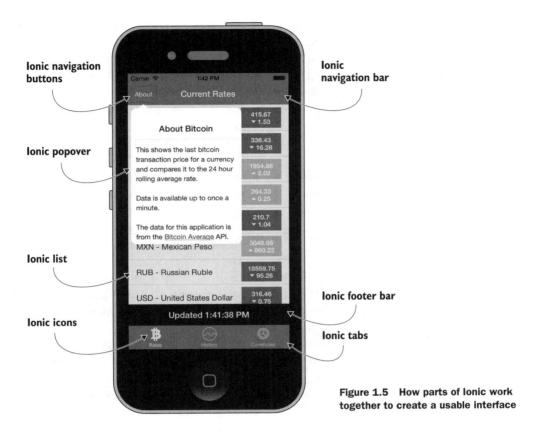

Figure 1.5 How parts of Ionic work together to create a usable interface

built with a combination of CSS, HTML, and JavaScript, and they behave like the native controls you're accustomed to using. Common examples include these:

- Side menus that slide in from the side
- Toggle buttons
- Mobile tabs

In figure 1.5 you can see a screenshot of one of the sample apps you'll build later in the book. It shows how many different Ionic components are used on the screen at once to create a powerful user interface.

Ionic is an open source project that's primarily developed by the Ionic team. Its popularity has grown very quickly since it was launched in November 2013; it has become a primary choice for building hybrid apps. Over 20,000 apps are launched with Ionic each month. Ionic is provided under the MIT license and is found at http://ionicframework.com.

Ionic also has a command-line interface (CLI) tool that provides some helpful developer tools. I'll refer to it as the CLI tool. This tool can help generate starter projects, and preview, build, and deploy your app. I'll demonstrate most of the features of the CLI tool as we go through the examples.

Ionic also includes a font icon library that gives you access to a decent number of useful and common icons for your application. It's optional, but it's provided by default and we'll use it regularly in the examples.

Ionic also has a number of services that aid in mobile app development, such as a visual drag-and-drop app creator and deployment tooling, user tracking and analytics, and push notifications. You can learn more about the full Ionic platform at https://ionic.io.

These user interface controls are the primary features of Ionic, but the Ionic team has worked hard to ensure Ionic's tools and processes work well with Angular and Cordova, which are discussed next.

1.3.2   *Angular: web application framework*

Angular (also known as AngularJS) is a Google open source project that has become quite popular with web application developers. It provides web developers a good application structure and the ability to write complete applications quickly. In the weather app example in this book, you'll use Angular to help manage the user's data and load information from the weather service.

Miško Hevery and Adam Abrons started Angular in 2009. Eventually, Hevery joined Google and brought Angular with him. The project is immensely popular with developers today, and has been adopted by a number of large sites such as www.stackoverflow.com and www.nasa.gov. Angular is licensed under the MIT license and is available at http://angularjs.org.

You no longer have to use a server-based language (that is, PHP, Ruby, or Java) to build complex applications. Today, JavaScript web application frameworks like Angular allow you to build complex applications in the browser. Typically a server application also exists to help manage private data and secure any business logic. This is an obvious advantage for hybrid app developers because the browser is the platform you use to create your apps. If you're familiar with Angular (or other JavaScript application frameworks such as Ember or Backbone), you'll be able to easily apply your knowledge to developing mobile apps with Ionic.

In this book we'll also use additional Angular modules that have been developed by third-party developers. One notable example is a module called `ui.router`, which is an open source Angular module that provides better application routing and navigation than the default Angular routing module offers.

1.3.3   *Cordova: hybrid app framework*

In this book we'll use Apache Cordova as the hybrid app framework. This is the layer that takes care of managing the communication between the browser window and native APIs. The weather-app example needs access to the device's GPS information to know what location to load data for, and Cordova is able to bridge the gap between Angular and the device to retrieve that information.

You may also have heard of PhoneGap. Adobe contributed PhoneGap to the Apache Software Foundation under the name Cordova. Today, PhoneGap is a distribution of Cordova, or, in other words, PhoneGap is essentially Cordova with support for a few additional commercial features from Adobe. For the purposes of this book, we'll use Cordova, but you could use PhoneGap and its commercial features if you desire.

Cordova is an open source Apache project that has a large community around it. Adobe continues to be a major developer of the framework. Cordova is licensed under the Apache 2.0 license.

The core of Cordova provides a lot of features; it also provides a plugin system for developers to create new features such as native API integrations with the phone camera. It's actively maintained with regular releases of improvements and new features. You can find out more about Cordova at http://cordova.apache.org.

Ionic has also sponsored the creation of a project called ngCordova at http://ngcordova.com. ngCordova is a collection of nicely integrated Cordova plugins designed to work well with Angular. Chapter 8 covers more details about Cordova and plugins, and you'll see some examples from the ngCordova project.

1.4 Why Ionic?

Ionic brings a new and important set of improvements to hybrid apps that other tools like jQuery Mobile haven't been able to provide. Until recently, mobile devices were still relatively sluggish and only a native app could deliver the performance and experience many developers wanted or needed. Mobile platform makers hadn't made browsers as fast as the native platforms. All of that has changed as devices have become more powerful, platforms have improved, and new tools like Ionic have made it possible to build amazing hybrid apps.

1.4.1 Why Ionic is good for developers

Ionic is able to provide an experience—built into the hybrid app—that looks, feels, and performs like a native app. The long-standing argument that native apps are the only way to get fast and richly featured apps has been proven wrong. People expect their mobile apps to be fast, smooth, and intuitive, and Ionic apps can deliver:

- *Build apps with the web platform*—Using HTML, CSS, and JavaScript, you can make hybrid apps that behave like native mobile apps.
- *Built with Angular*—For developers familiar with Angular (or even another JavaScript framework like Ember), Ionic is a great choice. Because Ionic is built with Angular, you have access to all of Angular's features and third-party modules. Angular is designed to build major applications, and Ionic extends Angular for the mobile environment.
- *Uses modern techniques*—Ionic was designed to work with modern CSS3 features like animations. Mobile browsers generally have better support for the latest web platform specifications, which allows you to use those features as well.

- *Engaged community and open source spirit*—The Ionic community is very active on forums, with code contributions, and in sharing tips and tricks about the platform. The open source spirit is alive and well within the project.
- *Powerful CLI tool*—With the Ionic CLI tool, you can quickly manage development tasks such as previewing the app in a browser, emulating the app, or deploying an app to a connected device. It helps with setting up and starting a project as well.
- *Ionic services*—Ionic also provides services that make development much easier. The Ionic Creator service allows you to use a drag-and-drop interface to design and export an app. The Ionic View service allows you to deploy an app beta release to customers or test users. In short, Ionic is all about creating not just the basic tools for making hybrid apps, but also the development tools that will help you create them efficiently.
- *Ionic has a dedicated team*—Open source projects can be difficult to select because you can't be sure if they will be properly developed or supported. Ionic has a dedicated team that has a vested interest in keeping the platform on the leading edge.
- *Native-like experience*—With Ionic, you can create a look and feel that's like the native apps, making it easier for your customers to use the app.
- *Performance*—The performance with Ionic is comparable to a native app; the better the app performs, the happier app users will be.
- *Beautiful, flexible design*—The user interface components have been carefully designed to implement native style guidelines, but also allow for easy customization of any visual aspect of the app.

With Ionic, you can craft feature-rich apps for your customers that take you far less time and effort to create. This can provide great value for you, your team, and your app users.

1.4.2   *Drawbacks of using Ionic*

Ionic isn't always the right solution for your needs. It's important to evaluate the needs of each project to ensure Ionic is the right solution for you:

- *Limited platforms*—Ionic 1.0 only fully supports iOS and Android platforms. Other platforms such as Windows Phone or Firefox OS may be fully supported in the future but aren't guaranteed. Apps may still function on other platforms, but Ionic isn't actively supporting them.
- *Older platforms not supported*—Ionic supports iOS 7+ and Android 4+ properly. Older versions may work properly and aren't actively tested. This can be a challenge if your app needs to run on old or low-spec devices.
- *Not equal to native*—The native device APIs are only available if Cordova supports them. If you need deep integration with the device, it may be more difficult to achieve.

- *Not geared for heavy graphics*—This is a limitation of hybrid apps in general because they run in the browser. If you have a game app or heavy graphic requirements, the hybrid app environment has fewer abilities compared to a native app environment.

There may be situations where your app requirements force you to choose something other than Ionic, but even in those cases Ionic can be a very useful tool during the early prototyping phase.

1.5 Prerequisites for building apps with Ionic

To build hybrid apps, you should have a few skills that aren't covered in this book. You don't need to be an expert in any of the following areas, but you should be prepared to use them all together.

1.5.1 Experience with HTML, CSS, and JavaScript

If you've built a website, you've used the web platform. The browser is like the operating system that you'll use to develop the sample mobile apps in this book. HTML, CSS, and JavaScript are the key languages the browser understands. HTML gives structure to the content, while CSS provides the design. JavaScript then provides the interaction and logic necessary for the web application.

You'll need to be familiar with JavaScript syntax and concepts such as asynchronous calls, events, prototypical inheritance, and variable scoping.

1.5.2 Experience with web applications and Angular

You should have a fundamental understanding of web applications, because we'll build them inside of the sample mobile apps. There are a number of technologies and libraries that developers use to build web applications, and familiarity with the concepts will help you greatly.

In this book, web apps will be written in JavaScript using the Angular framework. Ionic is built specifically to work with Angular, and developers who have experience building applications with Angular will be able to apply their experience easily. You might have experience with another framework, such as Ember or Backbone, that can provide a foundation as you learn the Angular-specific approach.

We'll cover a bit about Angular in chapter 3 to get you up and running, but this isn't a book about Angular. You'll want to refer to the books *AngularJS in Action* (http://manning.com/bford) and *AngularJS in Depth* (http://manning.com/aden) to learn everything you want about Angular beyond the scope of this book.

1.5.3 Access to a mobile device

Having a mobile device is extremely important when building a mobile app. I recommend that you have at least one device for every platform to test on an actual device. There are emulators that let you see what your apps should look like on a mobile device, but they aren't full substitutes for the real thing.

You'll have to register these devices with your developer accounts as well, so it's not practical to borrow. If you need a device, you can check for a refurbished or used item online and use it just for development testing. The more types of devices you can test your app with, the better.

These three prerequisites will help you be more successful at designing, testing, and building mobile apps across multiple platforms. Let's take a look at the mobile platforms Ionic supports.

1.6 *Supported mobile devices and platforms*

A number of mobile platforms—OS, Android, Windows 8, Firefox OS, Tizen, Blackberry, and more—are in use. With Ionic, you can build for both iOS and Android. Support for Windows 8 and Firefox OS is planned for the future, but isn't currently available.

While it may be possible to develop an app by previewing only on a simulator, devices can act differently in the real world. Let's take a closer look at these two primary platforms and requirements.

1.6.1 *Apple iOS*

Apple makes the popular iPhone and iPad devices, and they share a common platform called iOS. Apple has strong control over the entire experience from the devices to the software to the apps, essentially making it a closed system. This has made iOS a strong platform from the perspective of users and developers.

Apple provides Xcode as the primary development program for iOS and OS X development. Xcode is free and available in the App Store if you don't already have it downloaded. We'll cover setting up for iOS development in the next chapter.

Xcode comes with a set of simulators that allows you to simulate different versions of iPhones and iPads. The simulators are fairly good at giving a realistic experience, which is helpful when targeting multiple versions of iOS with the same app.

Apple has one major requirement for building iOS mobile apps: you need a Mac computer. Apple has only designed its development tools to work on Apple's operating system, OS X, and it's also recommended that you run the latest version.

For those of you who aren't using a Mac, it's worth considering purchasing one if you plan to do iOS development. If you just need to build mobile apps, you'll be able to take advantage of any of the Mac computers. Any new Mac will have enough processing power to manage the simulation and build process. If you consider purchasing a used machine, you should verify that it's able run the latest version of OS X.

If you don't have a Mac, there are some options that can help build your apps. Ionic is building a service that will allow you to build mobile apps for any supported platform even if you don't have a Mac.

The Apple Developer Program has two types of membership: iOS and OS X development. You'll need to sign up at http://developer.apple.com and join the iOS program. It costs US $99 per year, but you only need to sign up when you're ready to sign and deploy your app to the App Store. You can download Xcode and work through this entire book without an account until the point when I show you how to deploy an app to the App Store.

1.6.2 *Google Android*

Google created Android as an open source mobile platform, and has allowed mobile device makers to integrate Android into their devices. Compared to Apple's approach, Android has a very diverse set of devices because Google doesn't control every device Android is installed on. Older devices may also have Android forks specifically designed for a mobile carrier. This open system has encouraged adoption and also has been the leading platform in emerging markets by allowing lower-cost devices due to the absence of licensing fees for the operating system.

Android provides a number of tools for developing that are freely available for download from Android's site, http://developer.android.com/. Google has also been working on additional tools that are being built into Chrome, Google's browser, to provide useful development support for hybrid app developers. We'll cover how to set up your computer for Android development in the next chapter. The Android SDK has a simulator that can emulate the screen size and resolution of most Android devices.

Android development is supported on Mac, Linux, and Windows computers. You can review the exact requirements for Android developer tools at https://developer .android.com/sdk/index.html.

Google also has a Developer Program, which has a one-time fee of US $25. Just like with iOS, you don't have to sign up until you're ready to publish your app into the Play Store. You can register at https://play.google.com/apps/publish/signup/.

There are a few other Android app stores, notably the Amazon Web Store, which may also charge for a developer program. These aren't covered in this book. But you'll be able to build and deploy apps for any Android-based device, even if the app is distributed through a different store.

1.7 *Summary*

Throughout this chapter we've looked at details about how Ionic provides a powerful set of tools for building hybrid apps. Let's review the major topics covered in this chapter:

- Ionic is a solid choice that benefits developers, managers, and users.
- Hybrid apps are an advantage for developers who are already familiar with the web platform, and don't require learning additional programming languages.
- Hybrid apps use a WebView inside of a native app to run web applications that have access to native APIs.
- Ionic is designed to work with Angular for web application development and Cordova for integration with the device platform.
- Android and iOS are supported and require developer subscriptions. iOS development tools require a Mac.

In the next chapter, we'll review how to set up your computer to develop Ionic apps and set up a simple app to get started.

Setting up your computer to build apps

You're probably ready to get started with some code and actually build a mobile app. I'll walk you through the steps to get all of the tools needed to set up Ionic and then help you create a new sample project. By the end of the chapter, you'll have a sample app running on your computer that you can set up and preview on a connected device or a simulator. The steps in this chapter will be applied to future chapters, so you may find it a useful reference.

This chapter has two parts for setting up your development environment. The first part is a quickstart guide to getting the basics installed, running your sample app, and previewing it in a browser. This is great for getting up and running and

Figure 2.1   You'll be able to preview a sample app in a browser, an emulator, and a connected device.

being able to develop quickly. Think of this as setting up the development environment. The second part is a guide to setting up ways to view your app on an emulator or on a connected device like those shown in figure 2.1. This is like setting up the previewing environment. If you're anxious to start building apps, feel free to skip the second part of this chapter and come back later when you need it. The emulator and connected devices aren't necessary until you're ready to test your app in a true mobile environment or need to use mobile features like the camera or GPS.

In this book the command line will be your friend. On Windows you'll use the command prompt, which can be found in the program list. On OS X you'll use the Terminal, which can be found in the Launchpad or by typing terminal in Spotlight. I recommend adding a shortcut on your desktop for Windows or adding it to the dock on OS X because it will get a lot of use. Linux users may find they need to install additional dependencies, and should consult the documentation for their flavor of Linux to install any missing packages.

2.1   Quick-start guide

In this section you'll get the essential development environment set up, set up your first app, and preview the app in a browser. Because you're building a hybrid app, the browser is the easiest way to preview it.

The majority of your development time will be spent using the browser for previewing and developing your app. As your app matures, you'll likely begin to use an emulator to simulate a real mobile device, or build the app on a connected mobile device. Figure 2.2 shows a typical workflow during development, and this section covers the browser preview, while the next section covers the other two options.

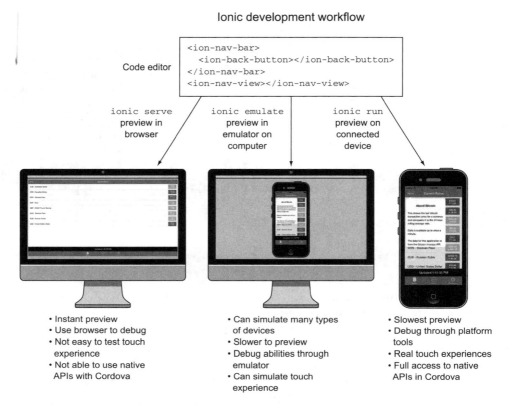

Figure 2.2   Typical workflow, and reasons why you would preview in a browser, emulator, or device

2.1.1   *Setting up your development environment*

To begin building mobile apps with Ionic, you need to ensure you have some required software set up. I'll walk you through how to install and set these up on your computer. In table 2.1, you can see the list of software you need to have installed on your machine to get started.

Optionally, I recommend the use of Git for source code versioning to make it easier to follow along with the source code. This isn't required, but I'll provide you with the

Table 2.1   Software required for your development environment

Software	Homepage
Node.js	http://nodejs.org
Ionic CLI	http://ionicframework.com
Cordova	http://cordova.apache.org

Git commands along the way to follow along more easily. If you're not familiar with Git or if you don't have it installed, you can find more details at http://git-scm.org.

If you already have these installed, you can jump to the next section. Otherwise, let's review the installation instructions.

INSTALL NODE.JS

Node.js (often referred to as Node) is a platform that runs JavaScript outside of the browser. It allows developers to create applications written in JavaScript that can then execute anywhere. Ionic and Cordova are both written on top of Node, so it's the first installation requirement.

Node can be installed on your machine by going to http://nodejs.org and downloading the package for your platform. If you already have Node installed, you should go ahead and install the latest stable version.

You can validate that Node installed correctly by opening a terminal in OS X or the command prompt on Windows and executing the following to check the version of Node:

```
$ node -v
v0.12.0
```

If you have any issues with installing Node, you can review the documentation on the Node website. Now we'll use Node's package manager to install Ionic and Cordova.

INSTALL IONIC CLI AND CORDOVA

You can easily install Ionic and Cordova in a single command. This command uses the Node package manager (npm) to install and set up your command-line interface (CLI) tools. Make sure Git is already installed first:

```
$ npm install -g cordova ionic
```

This may take a few minutes, depending on the speed of your connection. On a Mac, you may have trouble installing global modules without using sudo. In this case, I'd recommend setting your file permissions correctly for npm so you don't allow Node modules to run as the root user. You can read about how to solve this permission problem at mng.bz/Z97k.

Ionic and Cordova will be installed in such a way that they're available from the command line. Both of these tools execute using Node, but are aliased so you can run them with just the cordova or ionic commands. You can test that they're correctly installed by running the following commands and ensuring they execute without errors (in this book I've been using the following versions):

```
$ cordova -v
4.2.0
$ ionic -v
1.3.14
```

Setting up your development environment is important, so make sure each of these are installed and up to date. You should keep Ionic updated, and it will alert you when updates are available. Update Cordova when there are new features you need or bug fixes. Sometimes updating Cordova may require updates to your project, so it should be done only when necessary, and always review the Cordova documentation about possible required changes. To update Ionic or Cordova, you can respectively run the following commands (Ionic will inform you when an update is available):

```
$ npm update -g ionic
$ npm update -g cordova
```

At this point you have everything you need, so let's start setting up your sample app.

2.1.2 *Starting a new project*

Ionic provides a simple `start` command that allows you to set up a new project, shown in figure 2.3, in seconds. Ionic provides a set of starter templates that you can use to begin; we'll use the `sidemenu` template here. Run the following commands to create a new project and then to change into the new directory:

```
$ ionic start chapter2
$ cd chapter2
```

It may ask if you want to create an Ionic account, which you can ignore for now. The account helps you use their services, which we won't be using yet, and you can always create an account later.

> **Ionic command-line utility**
>
> There are a number of commands available with the Ionic utility. To see the available commands, you can look at the help details by running `ionic --help`.
>
> To see more details about what the utility can do and more documentation, you can view the source code on GitHub at https://github.com/driftyco/ionic-cli.

Ionic will create a new folder called chapter2 that will be used to set up the new project using the `tabs` template. Let's take a moment to understand what each folder is for.

```
● ● ●    jeremy@jeremy: ~/www/ionic-in-action/chapter2 — ..tion/chapter2 — zsh — 102×28
→ ionic-in-action git:(master) ionic start chapter2
Running start task...
Creating Ionic app in folder /Users/jeremy/www/ionic-in-action/chapter2 based on tabs project

DOWNLOADING: https://github.com/driftyco/ionic-app-base/archive/master.zip

DOWNLOADING: https://github.com/driftyco/ionic-starter-tabs/archive/master.zip
Initializing cordova project.
Fetching plugin "org.apache.cordova.device" via plugin registry
Fetching plugin "org.apache.cordova.console" via plugin registry
Fetching plugin "https://github.com/driftyco/ionic-plugins-keyboard" via git clone
→ ionic-in-action git:(master) ✗ cd chapter2
→ chapter2 git:(master) ✗
```

Figure 2.3   Using the ionic `start` command will generate a simple project scaffolding.

2.1.3 *Project folder structure*

The project folder contains a number of files and directories, which of each have a unique purpose. Here are the files and directories you should see in a new project:

- .bowerrc
- .gitignore
- bower.json
- config.xml
- gulpfile.js
- hooks
- ionic.project
- package.json
- plugins
- scss
- www

This is the generic structure of any Ionic app. The files and directories that are set up and required by Cordova are config.xml, hooks, platforms, plugins, and www. The rest are created by Ionic. Ionic uses both Bower and npm to load some of the dependencies for the project.

Bower and npm

Both Bower and npm are package management tools that help to download additional files used by a web application. Bower is positioned to help you add additional front-end files to your project, such as jQuery or Bootstrap, and npm is designed to add packages for Node.js projects or Node applications.

With Ionic, the front-end Ionic code is loaded with Bower, and Gulp dependencies are loaded with npm. Gulp is a popular build tool for JavaScript, and we'll discuss Gulp and its role later.

You can find information about Bower at http://bower.io and npm at https://npmjs.org.

The config.xml file is used by Cordova when generating platform files. It contains the information about the author, global preferences, platform-specific preferences, enabled plugins, and more. The default config.xml file generated will use Ionic as the author and HelloWorld as the app name. You can read about all of the options at https://cordova.apache.org/docs/en/edge/config_ref_index.md.html.

The www directory contains all of the web application files that will be run inside of the WebView. It's assumed that there will be an index.html file inside; otherwise, you could structure your files however you like. By default, Ionic sets up a basic AngularJS application that you can build from.

We'll cover these files and directories in more detail as they're used. Now that you have your files generated, you can preview your sample app.

2.1.4   *Previewing in a browser*

You can preview your app in the browser, which makes it very easy to debug and develop without having to constantly build the project on a device or emulator. Typically you'll develop your app using this technique, and then test in the emulator and on a device when the app is more complete. The following command will start a simple server, open the browser, and even autorefresh the browser when you save a file change:

```
$ ionic serve
```

It may prompt you to choose an address, and in most cases you should select localhost. It will open the default browser on your computer on port 8100. You can visit http://localhost:8100 in any browser, but it's best to preview using a browser used by the platform you're targeting because that's the browser the WebView uses.

Because you're viewing the app in a browser, you have access to the developer tools you'd use for building websites. As you develop, you'll want to have the developer tools open to aid in development and debugging, as you see in figure 2.4.

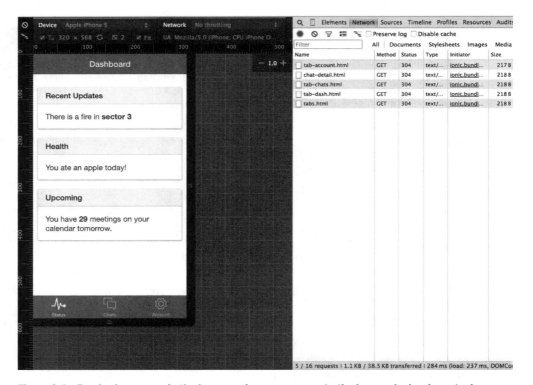

Figure 2.4   Previewing an app in the browser gives you access to the browser's developer tools.

Does it matter what browser I use to preview?

While you're free to use any browser for previewing your app, you should really consider using Chrome or Safari. iOS uses Safari for the WebView and Android uses the Android browser for its WebView. When possible, using the same browser on your computer will simulate the mobile environment most effectively. The Android browser isn't the same as Chrome, but Chrome is the closest choice.

The browser on your mobile device, and used in the WebView, isn't identical to the browser on your computer. But they're certainly related and tend to support the same general features.

Safari for Windows shouldn't be used for previewing, because it was discontinued by Apple and is no longer supported.

2.2   Setting up previewing environments

This section will guide you in setting up both emulators and connected devices for previewing your mobile app. Both allow you to preview the app like it's intended to be used, not just in a browser but inside a mobile device. An emulator is a virtual device, which actually runs the mobile platform (Android, for example) in a container and can execute your app like a real physical device. A connected device is any physical device that you connect directly to your computer with a USB cable, and you're able to install your app directly onto it.

To get everything set up, you need to do the following:

- Install platform tools needed for building apps.
- Download and set up emulators for previewing.
- Set up a connected device for previewing.
- Set up the project for each supported platform and preview.

The following sections contain a lot of detail about getting started, particularly with Android. Don't get too worried about the apparent complexity, since much of this is a one-time setup. Once you have the tools set up, you'll be able to reuse them for any future projects. You can build prototypes of your app using just the tools we've covered so far in this chapter and come back to this section at a later time when you're ready to start testing on a device.

2.2.1   Installing platform tools

You need to install additional software to emulate and deploy to connected devices. You only need to set up the software for the platforms you wish to support. Table 2.2 has the required software for Android and iOS development. Ionic version 1.0 only supports Android and iOS fully; other platforms such as Windows Phone or Firefox OS may be supported in future versions.

Table 2.2   Android and iOS software for emulating and deploying to devices

Platform	Software	Where to find
iOS	Xcode	Search for "Xcode" in App Store on Mac
Android	Android Studio	http://developer.android.com/sdk/index.html

OS X ONLY: INSTALL XCODE FOR IOS

Apple requires Xcode for the emulation and distribution of iOS apps. It's only available for Macs, so if you plan to support iOS, then you need to have a Mac.

You can download Xcode by opening the App Store and searching for "Xcode." It's an official Apple app (figure 2.5), and it's quite large (over 3 GB), so be sure to have enough free space.

INSTALL ANDROID STUDIO

Android development can be done on any Windows, Mac, or Linux computer. Android runs on Java, which is cross-platform as well. Android provides two options to choose from: Android Studio or the Android stand-alone SDK Tools. Android Studio is a full IDE with the SDK built in, versus just having the SDK itself. You can download either tool from http://developer.android.com/sdk/index.html.

You really only need the SDK. Android Studio is a great IDE for someone building native Android apps, but we won't use it in this book. I'd recommend only installing

Figure 2.5   Xcode is free and available for download through the App Store on your Mac computer.

the stand-alone SDK Tools for your platform. Additional installation instructions can be found at http://mng.bz/flIn.

When you install the stand-alone SDK on Mac or Linux, make sure you add the directory to your path so you can easily execute Android commands. To verify the installation was successful, you can run the following command to see the Android help:

```
android -help
```

Now you're ready to set up emulators.

2.2.2 Setting up emulators

Emulators allow you to run a virtual device on your computer that simulates the actual environment of a mobile device. The virtual device will run the platform inside of the emulator—for example, inside of an Android emulator you can run the actual Android operating system and install your app for development.

You'll want to use an emulator when you're ready to test various types of devices quickly or you need to test your app on a device you don't have access to. It's slower to preview in an emulator compared with the browser, so you'll likely emulate when your app is already functional in the browser.

Emulators require installation and some configuration, and can require some time to download. Let's go over how to set up both Android and iOS emulators.

SETTING UP AN IOS EMULATOR

Emulators are referred to as *simulators* in Xcode. To begin setting up your iOS simulator, open Xcode and then Preferences. In the Downloads tab, you'll see a list of available optional packages, which include documentation and iOS simulators, as shown in figure 2.6.

I suggest downloading only the most recent simulator at this point. Later you can install the emulators for all versions of iOS that you plan to target for testing. The documentation also isn't necessary because you can find it all online should you need it. Because these simulators and documentation are very large, save yourself the time and disk space and download only what you need.

Once the download is complete, your iOS simulator will be set up and ready to use. You can reset the emulator if you ever need to by having the simulator open and going to the iOS Simulator in the top menu and choosing Reset Content and Settings.

> **Which versions of Android or iOS should I use?**
>
> Ionic provides support for iOS 7+ and Android 4+ (with limited support for Android 2.3). Generally it's a good idea to target the lowest version possible to increase the potential use base. Setting a minimum version number in the native app project will prevent devices running older versions from being able to install your app.
>
> But there may be reasons to limit support to newer versions if your app uses additional plugins or features that aren't available on older versions.

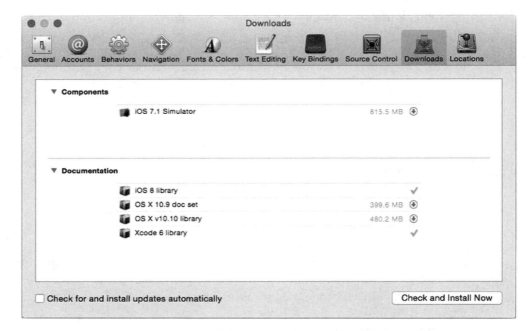

Figure 2.6   In Xcode Preferences, use the Downloads tab to download and install iOS simulators.

SETTING UP AN ANDROID EMULATOR

Android emulators are much more free-form than iOS emulators—they allow you to build your own device by declaring the device specifications. Luckily there are some presets that help guide you through this process, but due to the wide variety of Android devices available, setup is a bit more complex than for iOS.

You need to set up the SDK packages, so run `android sdk` in the command line. The SDK Manager will appear. It allows you to download the platform files for any version of Android, which is a bit more than you need. For the time being, I recommend you download just the most recent release packages and core tools. You need to choose the following items, as shown in figure 2.7:

- Tools:
  - Android SDK Tools
  - Android SDK Platform-tools
  - Android SDK Build-tools (choose the most recent version)
- Android 4.4.2 (API 19, when paired with Cordova version 4.2):
  - SDK Platform
  - ARM EABI v7a System Image

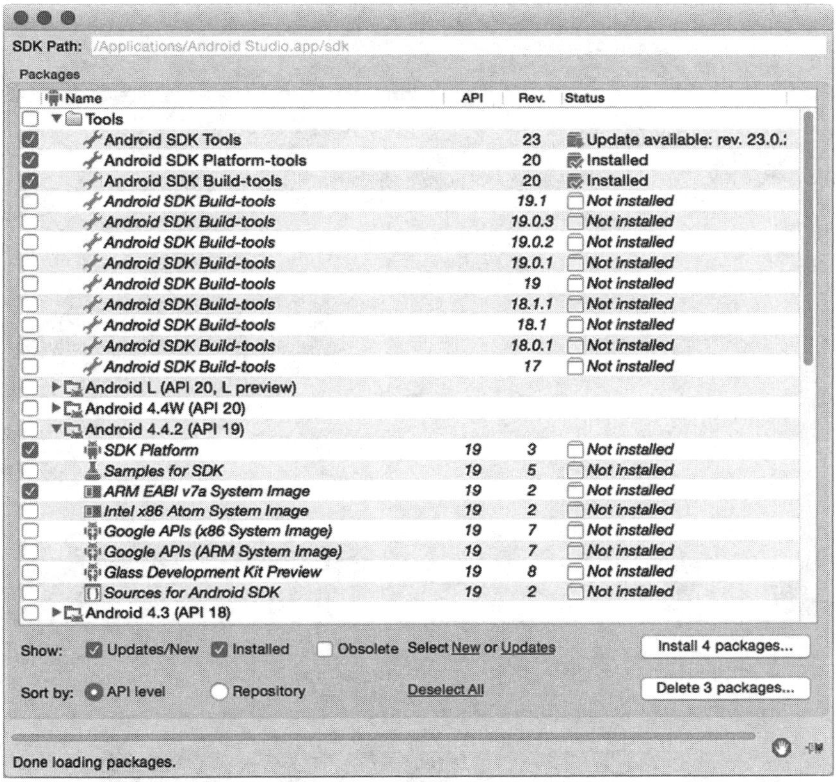

Figure 2.7   Choose the SDK Tools, Platform-tools, and the most recent Build-tools packages, as well as the most recent stable release of Android SDK Platform and the ARM System Image.

Cordova sets a default API level (here, API 19 with Cordova 4.2.0), but that may change over time. You may get a notice later on to install a missing SDK platform for another API level if support changes.

Now you have to define emulator device specifications. This gives you control over the exact device features such as RAM, screen size, and so on. Open the Android Virtual Device (AVD) Manager by executing the following command, also shown in figure 2.8:

```
android avd
```

Choose the Device Definitions tab so you can set up a device based on a known device configuration, as shown in figure 2.9. I recommend using a Nexus 4 or Nexus 5 device, because they're developed by Google and very popular.

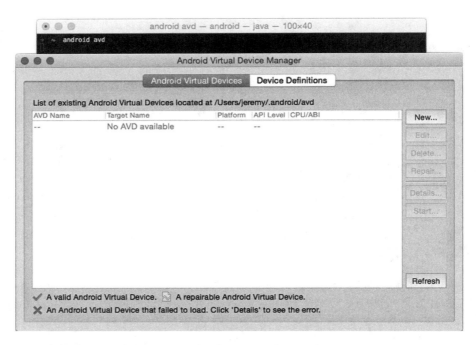

Figure 2.8   Open the AVD Manager with the command `android avd`.

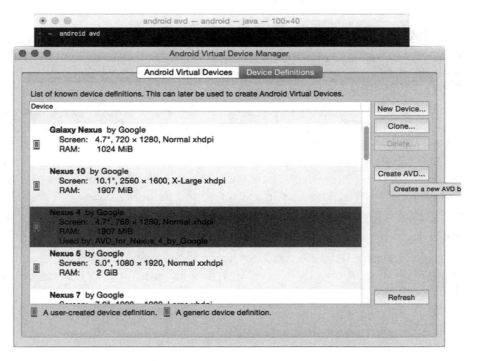

Figure 2.9   Choose a device definition that you want to base your configuration on and then click Create AVD.

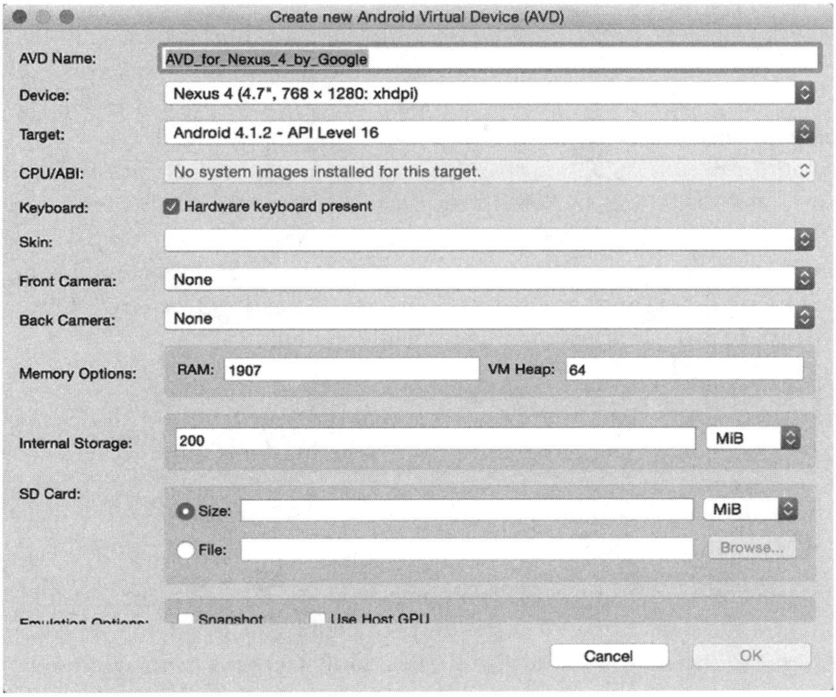

Figure 2.10 Create a new device based on Nexus 4 by Google. This device has the same basic features as an actual phone, though the cameras are not enabled.

Once you've selected the device from the list, click Create AVD and it will open a form with additional details that you can specify about the device. Here you can decide what version of the Android platform to run, the screen size and resolution, and more. Choose the presets like those shown in figure 2.10.

Once you've finished, click OK and it will save your device. You can create or delete devices as needed, just make sure to always have one set up for emulating. The first time it runs, it may be a bit slow because it will have to do some extra things to set up and boot.

Now that you've got an Android device setup, you can use it in your projects when you want to emulate for Android. When you send an app to your new emulator device, it will boot this device for you.

2.2.3 Setting up a connected device

If you have an Android or iOS device, you'll want to be able to connect and deploy your apps to it. You can set up any number of connected devices that you have access to, in case you have both new and older devices that you want to be able to test. You'll want to test on devices when possible before you attempt to deploy to a store, and whenever you need to verify the functionality behaves as you expect with a touch environment and that any native plugins work as expected.

SETTING UP AN iOS DEVICE

To connect your iOS device and deploy your app, you have to have an Apple Developer account with iOS. You'll connect your iOS device to your Mac and open Xcode. Choose Window > Organizer from the top menu to open the Devices Manager.

Apple requires security profiles to be set up so that your phone is verified to be connected for deploying your apps. You must connect your account in Preferences > Accounts, and it will help you set up certificates and provision profiles. Xcode should guide you through the steps for your device because they may vary. For additional assistance, refer to Apple's documentation at https://developer.apple.com/library/ios/documentation/ToolsLanguages/Conceptual/Xcode_Overview/. Once the profiles are set up, your device should be available to deploy.

SETTING UP AN ANDROID DEVICE

The first step is to enable developer settings on your Android device. By default, Android devices aren't able to connect to debugging tools unless directly selected by the device owner.

Start by enabling the developer mode on your device, as follows:

1　Open the Settings view and scroll to the last item, About Phone.
2　At the bottom of the About Phone view, there should be a Build Number item—you must tap on it seven times to enable the developer mode. As you get closer to seven taps, the device should notify you how many taps are left.
3　Once this is complete, you can go back to the Settings view and you'll see a new Developer Options item.

Then, to enable USB debugging, you need to do the following steps:

1　Choose the Developer Options item in the Settings view.
2　Scroll down until you see the USB debugging option.
3　Toggle it on—it may prompt you to confirm your choice—and then your device should be ready for debugging when it's connected to your computer.

Now your device is set up to debug, and when it's connected to your computer, the system can detect it for building and deploying to the device.

2.2.4　Adding a platform to the project

Before you can preview your app in an emulator or on a device, you need to set up the project to support the platform(s) of choice. Again, you open the command line to use the `ionic` tool. These two commands will create project files for iOS and Android, respectively:

```
$ ionic platform add ios
$ ionic platform add android
```

You can add only one platform per command, so if you plan to support multiple platforms, you'll have to add them individually. You can see how each platform triggers a different set of tasks that are required to set up the project for that platform.

Inside the platforms directory, there will now be a new folder for each platform added with platform-specific files inside. Currently, they just generate the base app files, but eventually you'll modify these files and use them to generate the final app.

2.2.5 *Previewing in an emulator*

Now that at least one platform has been added to your app project, you can use one of the platform's emulators to preview your app. If you haven't already set up an emulator, you'll need to do that first. Emulators are great for testing in a more real-world environment, but are slower to use during development. Launching and previewing in an emulator takes some processing time to set up and begin, especially the first time. If you're on a Mac and emulating on iOS, you'll also need to install `ios-sim`:

```
$ npm install -g ios-sim
```

Now you can run the app in an emulator using the `emulate` command:

```
$ ionic emulate ios
$ ionic emulate android
```

The emulator should open after running a number of tasks. You'll see a lot of output in the command line as it builds and generates the necessary files, but as long as it ends with a success message, the emulator will launch and load your app.

When emulating Android, you can use `--target=NAME` to run the app in a specific device you created; otherwise, the default emulator is used. iOS lets you change the hardware once the emulator has opened from the Hardware top menu.

If you already have the emulator up and running, you can run the `emulate` command again without closing the emulator. This is faster than exiting the emulator and relaunching it every time you change files, because the emulator doesn't have to reboot itself each time.

Ionic has a very powerful feature that allows you to reload the app instantly using live reload like you saw earlier in the browser. The feature is a huge timesaver, and also can output the console logs to the Terminal so you can read them. See the blog post about the feature at http://mng.bz/gKJ8.

To emulate with live reload, run the commands with the extra flags `-l` and `-c` to start live reload and console logging. This allows you to see the logs like you'd see in the browser console in the Terminal, and allows the app to reload any time you make a file change for faster previewing. For example:

```
$ ionic emulate ios -l -c
$ ionic emulate android -l -c
```

To preview on a specific emulator from the command line, you'll have to add another parameter to the command that declares the emulator to use. For Android, you use `--target=[emulator name]` where you pass the name of the emulator from the AVD Manager. In iOS, you can run `ios-sim showdevicetypes` to see a list of devices, and then use `--devicetypeid [device type]` where you specify the device type from the list `ios-sim`, printed in the console.

2.2.6   *Previewing on a mobile device*

Nothing beats the real thing. If you have an Android or iOS device, you'll most likely want to deploy your app on it at some point. While that's very useful, it's also slow and more difficult to debug. But Ionic also provides the same live reload feature found in the previous section. The quick way to preview using the command line is as follows:

```
$ ionic run ios -l -c
$ ionic run android -l -c
```

If your device isn't connected and paired yet, the commands will fail to run properly.

PREVIEW ON AN IOS DEVICE

In your project, make sure you've added iOS as a platform, navigate to the platforms/ ios directory, and open the file with the extension .xcodeproj. This opens the Xcode project for your app, and you can then choose the device as an option to deploy, as shown in figure 2.11.

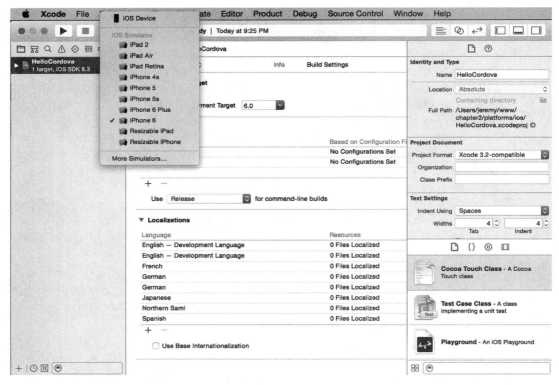

Figure 2.11   You can choose the device or emulator that you wish to deploy from Xcode by opening the project.

You can deploy that app to your phone as many times as you want. Each deploy will override the existing version. You can also uninstall the app just like any other app by pressing on it until the icon shakes, and tapping on the X in the corner.

DEPLOY TO AN ANDROID DEVICE

As long as you've already added Android to your project, you can deploy to a connected Android device with a few steps. Ensure USB debugging is enabled, and if it isn't you can refer back to section 2.2.3 on how to do this.

If you're on Windows, download the appropriate USB driver for your device from https://developer.android.com/tools/extras/oem-usb.html. If you're on OS X, you don't need to do anything. If you're on Linux, you should consult the steps at https://developer.android.com/tools/device.html.

To confirm the device is connected, run `adb devices` from the command line. You should see a list of devices like that shown in figure 2.12, and if you've set up any emulators, they should appear as well.

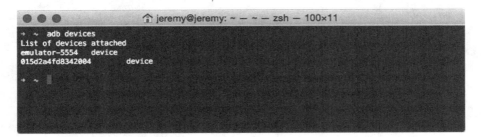

Figure 2.12 Android devices listed by running `adb devices` from the command line. Emulators are prefixed with `emulator`, while actual devices are a hash.

Now you have to build the Android project, which will generate a .apk file, and then you'll install it onto the device. You need to locate your app inside the platforms/android/ant-build directory, and in it the filename that ends with –debug.apk:

```
ionic build android
adb -d install platforms/android/ant-build/HelloCordova-debug.apk
```

You'll be able to find the app HelloWorld in the app pane. Opening it will display the same app that ran in the emulator, as shown in figure 2.13.

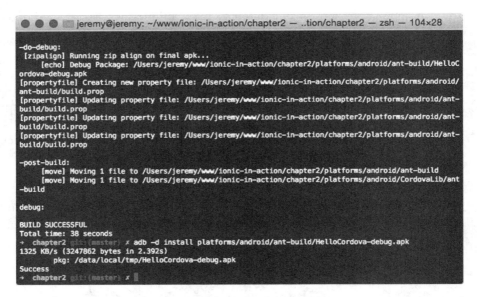

```
-do-debug:
    [zipalign] Running zip align on final apk...
       [echo] Debug Package: /Users/jeremy/www/ionic-in-action/chapter2/platforms/android/ant-build/HelloC
ordova-debug.apk
[propertyfile] Creating new property file: /Users/jeremy/www/ionic-in-action/chapter2/platforms/android/
ant-build/build.prop
[propertyfile] Updating property file: /Users/jeremy/www/ionic-in-action/chapter2/platforms/android/ant-
build/build.prop
[propertyfile] Updating property file: /Users/jeremy/www/ionic-in-action/chapter2/platforms/android/ant-
build/build.prop
[propertyfile] Updating property file: /Users/jeremy/www/ionic-in-action/chapter2/platforms/android/ant-
build/build.prop

-post-build:
     [move] Moving 1 file to /Users/jeremy/www/ionic-in-action/chapter2/platforms/android/ant-build
     [move] Moving 1 file to /Users/jeremy/www/ionic-in-action/chapter2/platforms/android/CordovaLib/ant
-build

debug:

BUILD SUCCESSFUL
Total time: 38 seconds
→ chapter2 git:(master) x adb -d install platforms/android/ant-build/HelloCordova-debug.apk
1325 KB/s (3247862 bytes in 2.392s)
       pkg: /data/local/tmp/HelloCordova-debug.apk
Success
→ chapter2 git:(master) x █
```

Figure 2.13   Using the Ionic build and Android deployment tools, the app is built and installed
onto a connected Android device.

2.3   Summary

This chapter covered the steps to set up your development environment and build out
a sample app. While the app was very basic, the rest of the steps were important since
they'll be used frequently as you begin to develop your own apps. Let's review the
major topics covered in this chapter:

- Some software setup is required to begin developing hybrid apps.
- The command-line utility for Ionic provides many features such as tools to start
  a project, build a project, and preview the app in a browser.
- Previewing apps in a browser is the primary environment for development and
  debugging.
- Emulators are great for previewing your app, and we covered how to set them
  up.
- You can preview the app on a connected mobile device with the proper setup.

In the next chapter, you'll learn about Angular because it's vital for developing apps
with Ionic.

What you need to know about AngularJS

This chapter covers

- How AngularJS apps are built and structured
- The fundamentals of AngularJS that power many Ionic features
- How to use controllers, filters, directives, scope, and more

AngularJS is a web application framework, and its popularity has made it one of the most-used JavaScript tools available today. Ionic is built on top of Angular, so it's important to have a grasp of how it works. Instead of having to build an entire web application framework for Ionic, it uses Angular and extends it with a large number of interface components and other mobile-friendly features.

This chapter will walk you through the core of what Angular is and cover most of the fundamentals you need to know to be effective. If you're already quite comfortable with Angular, then you can skim the chapter or jump ahead. This chapter is for those who are new to Angular or have minimal experience and need a good primer.

We'll look at controllers, which are aptly named because they're designed to control your data. Then we'll discuss scope and how it works as a glue between the controller and the user interface, which is called a view. By looking closer at views, you'll see how they're built using templates and scope to create the interactive visual experience. Along the way, we'll also look at some other features such as how to use filters to transform data, how to build and use directives to enhance regular HTML elements, and how to work with an external data source to load and save data for your applications.

This chapter will teach you about Angular by building a basic web application, as shown in figure 3.1. You can work through the examples or look at the complete example available on GitHub at https://github.com/ionic-in-action/chapter3. To see the end result, the application demo is also available at https://ionic-in-action-chapter3.herokuapp.com/.

Figure 3.1   The chapter application will have a list of notes and a way to view and edit notes.

By the end of this chapter, you'll have a general understanding of how Angular works. There's too much involved to properly cover everything Angular has to offer. Other books and material can provide you deeper Angular training, but we'll cover the primary features used in this book.

Before we jump into the code, let's take a moment to talk about Angular in general and what problems it helps to solve when you're building web applications.

3.1 AngularJS at a glance

Before you build an application with Angular, let's take a look at the parts that make up a typical application built with Angular, starting with the views and templates used to display content and then looking at how data is loaded by controllers into the view. Figure 3.2 illustrates the way these pieces create the list of notes in your application and demonstrates how they're connected.

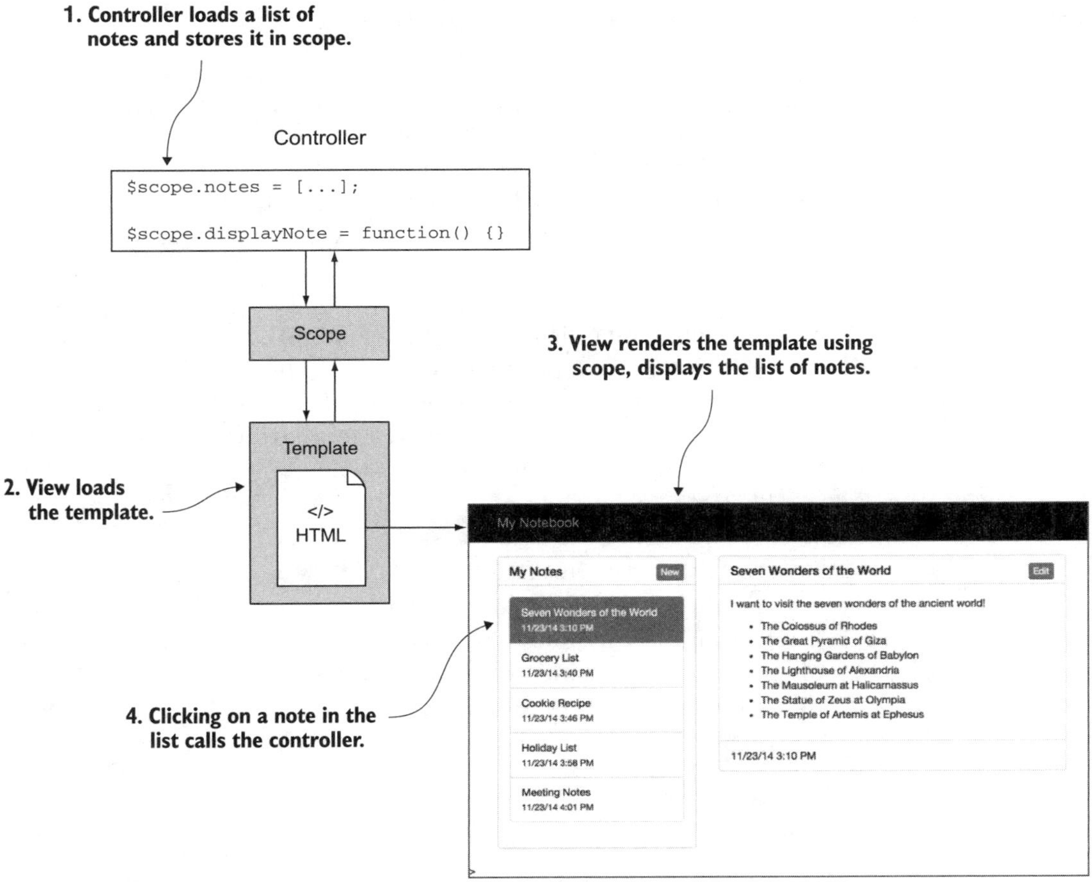

Figure 3.2 How the list of notes is rendered from loading data in the controller to displaying in the view

3.1.1   *Views and templates: describing the content*

Angular works very closely with HTML, and often you'll be creating templates. A template is a block of HTML that's loaded into the application when needed. Angular enhances the HTML with new features and abilities by extending HTML's vocabulary.

A view is the use of a template to display data. A view will always have a template (which is the HTML markup) but also includes the data used. A view will transform the template into the final visual experience for the user, which means it will modify the template based on the data. A snippet of the template from the example in figure 3.2 is as follows:

```
<ul class="list-group">
   <li class="list-group-item"
      ng-repeat="note in notes"
      ng-click="displayNote($index)"
      ng-class="{active: note.id == content.id}">{{note.title}}<br />
   <small>{{note.date | date:'short'}}</small></li>
</ul>
```

ngRepeat lets you create a <li> for each note in the notes array.

ngClick calls the displayNote() method when <li> is clicked.

ngClass allows you to conditionally show a class.

Display date and use filter to display it using short date format (defined by Angular).

This sample template shows just one `<li>` element inside of a `<ul>`, but has several attributes that are called *Angular directives*. A directive modifies the behavior of the element it's placed on. In this case, `ngRepeat` will loop over a JavaScript object or array and create a `<li>` element for each. `ngClick` is like the JavaScript `onClick` event handler, and it will call a function called `displayNote()` when clicked. When this template is rendered, it will create a new list item element for each note in the `notes` array.

The double curly braces (`{{}}`) indicate that some data is to be displayed here. This concept is called *data binding*, and the syntax is known as an *expression*. Anything between the braces is the expression, which is evaluated by Angular against the current model data. Therefore, the content of `note.title` will be injected into the `<li>` element where the double curly braces wrap it.

The template is the HTML with any additional directives or expressions. The view takes data and renders the template for final display based on the values in the data. Assuming the `notes` array has five notes, the `<ul>` element will contain five list item elements, like you see in the screenshot of the view in figure 3.2.

Angular comes with many directives, and they all start with ng. Some help to modify the display (`ngShow`, `ngClass`), while others are used with forms (`ngModel`, `ngForm`), and yet others are useful for listening to events such as clicks (`ngClick`, `ngMouseover`). Angular also has some directives that sit on top of HTML elements, such as inputs, text areas, and anchor tags, that provide additional features that HTML doesn't have by default. For example, Angular is able to enhance an `<input type="text">` element by adding support for additional attributes that can do custom validation. We'll use more directives in the example later, but the full list is available in the Angular documentation.

What is the difference between ngApp and ng-app?

When people write about Angular, they can refer to directives as `ngApp` or `ng-app`. In reality, they're talking about the same thing, but there's a reason why both exist.

When you see `ngApp` or `ngClass`, this is the JavaScript version of the name. JavaScript syntax rules don't allow a hyphen to be used in a variable name, so instead the convention is to use camel case but start with a lowercase letter. The documentation uses this style and it's used in this book as well.

When you see `ng-app` or `ng-class`, this is the HTML version of the name. HTML is case-insensitive and allows hyphens in tag or attribute names. The convention is to use a hyphen to increase the readability of the directive in the markup and follow normal conventions in HTML attributes.

Now let's discuss how data is connected to the view and displayed.

3.1.2 *Controllers, models, and scope: managing data and logic*

Controllers are functions that are attached to a Document Object Model (DOM) node and are used to drive the logic of your application. A controller is essentially a function object in JavaScript that can be used to communicate with the scope and respond to events.

The *scope* is like a shared context between the controller and view. Think of it as the connection between what happens in the controller and in the interface, and when the scope is updated in the controller it also updates in the view. You can see a diagram of how these pieces work together in figure 3.2, where the arrows indicate both the view and controller communicate using the scope as the hub.

The scope has two key roles: to store data and give access to controller methods. Data that's stored on the scope is called the *model*. A model is any JavaScript value (usually an array or object, but it can be simple like a number or string) that you store on the scope, and it's shared between the controller and views through the scope.

Let's take an isolated example of a controller that would pair with the view and template from earlier:

```
angular.module('App')
.controller('Controller', function ($scope) {        ◁─┐  Declares controller
  $scope.notes = [                                        and uses $scope
    { id: 1, title: 'Note 1', date: new Date() },         service to access scope
    { id: 2, title: 'Note 2', date: new Date() }
  ];                                                    Creates array of note
  $scope.getNote = function (index) {                   objects for notes model,
    $scope.content = $scope.notes[index];               which ngRepeat will display
  };
});                                                     Adds a method to update the
                                                        content value, which is triggered by
                                                        an ngClick directive in the view
```

This controller sets the `notes` model with an array of items onto a special object called the `$scope`. This is the object that Angular provides for each scope where you can store values to share between the controller and view (which become models). The view would display the array of notes in the list using ngRepeat. The getNote() method is available for you to declare which of the notes should be stored on the content model. The view is able to call this function because it's also attached on the scope.

Everything in this controller is isolated from the rest of your application, except for any child scopes. This is important because it limits the visibility of code and variables. A common challenge for new Angular developers is accidentally putting things into different scopes and having trouble accessing values in a different scope, which isn't possible by default.

Angular scope is also hierarchical. Scopes can be nested, just like the DOM. In fact, a scope is reflective of the DOM structure on the page. A scope can be attached so that it's only visible to an HTML element and its children, just like how a CSS class can be used to target styles of the element it's placed on or its children.

Hierarchy becomes particularly important if you want to communicate between scopes, because a child scope can look upward to its parents (just like how JavaScript has prototypical inheritance, if you're familiar with that concept). Some directives in Angular create child scopes for you, which can cause some confusion about which scope is where. If you look for a value on a child scope and it doesn't exist, it will actually check each parent scope for that value until it either finds the value or runs out of parent scopes to check.

The root scope (with the special $rootScope object to access it) is the first scope created by an Angular application to which all other scopes are attached. This means anything you put on the root scope is available to any scope, which might sound helpful but isn't advised. You want to keep your scopes clean and focused instead of piling everything onto the root scope. JavaScript in general has this type of a problem, where often applications use the global scope to store variables. Imagine you have a value called id; if you placed a value id in a child scope, it would conflict and cause you to lose access to the root scope value. This becomes a problem as you incorporate more code, because the more people who work on an application or the more external tools you incorporate, the more difficult it is to be aware of all that happens in the application to avoid these kinds of naming collisions.

Controllers aren't for everything

There are a few things you shouldn't do with a controller because they can make your code hard to maintain and test later. The primary offense is doing document object management (DOM) manipulation in a controller. Imagine you're building a slide-show. The controller shouldn't handle the task of changing the DOM or styling for the slideshow features because that would be best placed in a custom directive.

You should also avoid using the controller to format or filter data; instead use form controls and filters.

3.1.3   *Services: reusable objects with methods*

Angular has a notion of a service that's a JavaScript object that can be shared through the entire application. Angular provides a number of services by default, and you can create your own. If you've dabbled in Angular at all, you've certainly used some of the built-in services.

One very common service is $http, which is Angular's service for handling HTTP requests. It has a number of methods such as get(), post(), and other HTTP actions. Services can be very complex (like $http), or they can be simple objects with data. You'll see some examples in this book of simple services that only are used to share data between different parts of an application.

Services are lazy-loaded by Angular, meaning they aren't loaded into memory until they're used. They're also singletons, meaning that if you change a value on a service in one place, it will be reflected in another. You'll see this in action in the examples for chapters 5 and 6, where you'll be able to make changes in one place and see them reflected in another instantly.

Ionic exposes a number of features as Angular services. We'll work with some in the next few chapters, but keep in mind that just about anything you include in your controller is a service.

3.1.4   *Two-way data binding: sharing between controller and view*

One of the most powerful features about Angular is two-way data binding. You've seen how a view binds data into the template, but it also works in the opposite direction. The view can change values on the scope, which values are immediately updated in the scope and reflected in the controller. This is particularly helpful with forms, such as when a user types into a text input and the value of the scope changes as the user types. You don't have to do anything special to enable two-way data binding—it happens automatically for you.

In the application in this book, you'll see two-way data binding happening when you set up the editor. As you type into the editor box, the contents will be previewed on the right. You'll also see this in action in most of the Ionic apps you build.

That sums up the key concepts of Angular that help provide the basic background you need to get started. Let's see how these concepts really work in the chapter project.

3.2   *Setting up for the chapter project*

In this chapter, you'll build an Angular app from a base HTML page. I've already done some work by creating the design and markup for the foundation so we can focus just on the features Angular builds.

This application is a simple note-storing application, where you can load and modify a list of simple notes. The features for the app include

- Store notes in JSON file
- View, create, edit, and delete notes

- Use Markdown formatting in notes
- Editor and preview of Markdown side by side

The application has been set up with the base HTML and CSS required. It also contains a simple RESTful server written with Node to allow you to manage the list of notes, and this is provided so we can focus on Angular and not the API. We'll focus solely on how to add Angular into this base and cover the major features of Angular along the way.

3.2.1   Getting the project files

Throughout this chapter, you'll be able to follow along using Git tags to check out specific versions of the code. You can also follow along by writing the code yourself from the book examples. Even if you aren't familiar with Git, you can run the commands to follow along, or use the second option and download the base application files and code.

Using Git, you can get started with this chapter base by cloning the `chapter3` repository, and then checking out the `step1` tag as follows:

```
$ git clone https://github.com/ionic-in-action/chapter3.git
$ cd chapter3
$ git checkout step1
```

If you don't want to use Git, you can also download and extract the base application files at https://github.com/ionic-in-action/chapter3/archive/step1.zip, as shown in figure 3.3.

You can use the same step to get the code for every step; just change the number of the tag in `step1` to the current number.

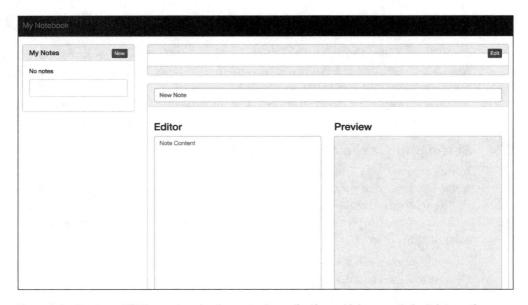

Figure 3.3   The base HTML template for the example application, which currently isn't interactive

3.2.2   *Starting the development server*

Now that you've got the project files downloaded onto your computer, you need to get your development server set up. For the web application to work properly, you need to have a server running like it would in a production environment. While I don't want to dig into the details around this server, you should know a few things if you haven't used Node for a development server before.

In the server.js file that you see in the project is a simple RESTful server based on the popular Express.js framework. The primary reason for this is that you want to have a way to keep track of your notes over time, and the RESTful API allows the application to read, create, edit, and delete notes in your list. The server also takes care of loading files into the browser over HTTP, which is essentially what the `ionic serve` command does for your Ionic apps.

I've commented the server with some notes, and if you're interested you can dig into it more. I won't cover it in detail here, but it's important to know a few things about it:

- The server runs on port 3000, which means you have to visit http://localhost:3000 to view the web application.
- The server accepts incoming requests, and depending on the URL and HTTP method used, it will modify the list of notes.
- The server uses a JSON file (data/notes.json) as a database to keep it simple. In real-world applications, you'd use a more robust database solution.

The server won't run until you've downloaded some Node packages that it requires. This is easy to do by running the following command to use Node Package Manager (npm) to install the required files. First navigate to the directory in the terminal, and then run

```
$ npm install
```

This will take a few moments, as npm looks at the list of dependencies (found in package.json) and downloads them from GitHub. It will log the progress of the downloads and inform you when they're completed.

Now you can start the server, and it must continue to run in the command line. It will start the server and listen for requests on port 3000. At any point you can stop the server by pressing Ctrl+S or just closing the command-line window as follows:

```
$ node server
```

At this point, you can visit http://localhost:3000 in your browser and you should see a base template layout like you see in figure 3.3. You'll be modifying the HTML and adding JavaScript to bring this base layout to life as a note-taking application.

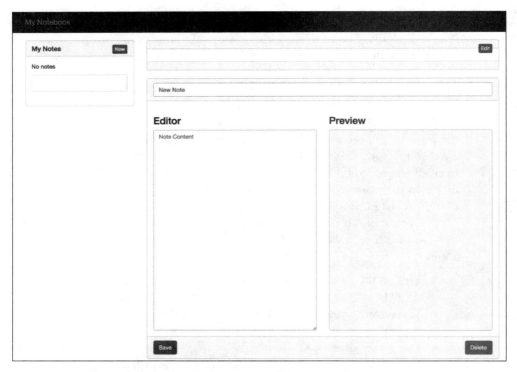

Figure 3.4   When Angular is added to the page, it still appears the same. You have to tell Angular to do some things before the content will change.

3.3   *Basics for an Angular app*

The fundamentals of Angular start with creating an Angular application in your JavaScript and then adding a reference to it in your HTML. Angular works closely with the page DOM, so you actually restrict an Angular application to a DOM element and its children. In this case this will be the <html> element, so that Angular has access to the entire page. Ionic often uses this on the <body> element. In figure 3.4 you'll see the same content in the browser as before, but it will have Angular installed and ready to use.

You can get the code for this step if you've cloned the repository from GitHub by running the following in your command line:

```
$ git checkout -f step2
```

This will reset any changes you've made and set the code to the step2 tag.

To create an Angular application, you use the ngApp directive on an element and declare the name of the application. Open the index.html file and add the ngApp directive as follows:

```
<html lang="en" ng-app="App">
```

At this point, you're attaching an Angular application called App to the root HTML element. This gives the Angular app access to the entire DOM, but you also could have attached it to the </body> tag. I recommend putting it on the <html> or <body> element.

You haven't yet declared this app in JavaScript, so let's do that now. Angular has a module system, which is a mechanism to help encapsulate program code into individual pieces. When you declare a new module, you provide a name and then an array with a list of dependencies (this chapter has none). Ionic itself is an Angular module, which you'll declare as a dependency in other chapters. Angular modules are declared in the following way. Create a new file in js/app.js and add the following line to it:

```
angular.module('App', []);
```

Lastly, you need to add a </script> tag to the index.html file to load the Angular module. In the index.html file, right before the closing </body> tag, add a new </script> tag as follows:

```
<script src="js/app.js"></script>
```

You need to make sure this is after the Angular library because JavaScript files are loaded and executed in the order they're declared on the page.

You've just declared and attached the most basic of Angular applications to your page. The angular.module() method creates the module and attaches it to the DOM with ngApp. This is the most basic Angular application, and in fact it does nothing yet. All Angular apps are declared in this basic way.

3.4 *Controllers: for controlling data and business logic*

Let's get some of the business logic wired up into the application. Here you'll add a controller to manage business logic that controls the various parts of the application. This step won't change the way the application appears in the browser just yet, because a controller is about managing data and not the visual aspect of the application. But you need the controller in place before you can start to manage the visual elements.

The result of adding a controller will give the controller a particular region on the page that it has access to, as you can see later in figure 3.5. For example, you need to be able to manage how you load the data and attach it to the scope. You can reset the project to step3 if you're using Git:

```
$ git checkout -f step3
```

Listing 3.1 declares a basic controller. You first have to reference the App module and then declare a controller with the controller method. It passes the name of the controller and the function that contains the controller logic. Create a new file in js/editor.js and add the code from the following listing.

Listing 3.1   Editor controller (js/editor.js)

References App module
to attach controller to
this module

```
angular.module('App')                                    ◁
.controller('EditorController', function ($scope) {       ◁
  $scope.state = {
    editing: false                    Declares controller with name
  };                              EditorController and passes a function
});                                   that has dependencies listed
```

Creates
model value
and stores
it on $scope

This is a very simple controller that currently only creates a simple model called
state. The $scope service is injected so that you can set the state property. Remember, values on $scope are called *models* and are also available for the view.

Services starting with $

You'll notice that Angular services start with a $ symbol, and the same holds true for
Ionic's services. When you see a service beginning with $, it's a convention to designate it as part of the core of Angular or Ionic.

Services that we create in the examples in this book are never prefixed, but I have
capitalized them. There's no requirement for how you name services, but the core
follows the convention of prefixing with $.

Now you need to add the file to the index.html file to include it in the application.
Add a </script> tag to the bottom of the HTML right before the closing <body>
element:

```
<script src="js/editor.js"></script>
```

The last step is to attach the controller to the DOM. This will create a new child scope
for this controller to use. This is done by using a special HTML attribute, called an
Angular directive, to declare where the controller should be attached. In this case,
you'll want to attach it to the div with a class of container on line 25 of index.html:

```
<div class="container" ng-controller="EditorController">
```

Here you use the ngController directive and declare the name of the controller
you've created in the JavaScript file. This will attach the controller to the DOM and
make the controller able to manage anything inside of this element. You can see in
figure 3.5 where the controller's scope is available, which is most of the page except
for the top title bar.

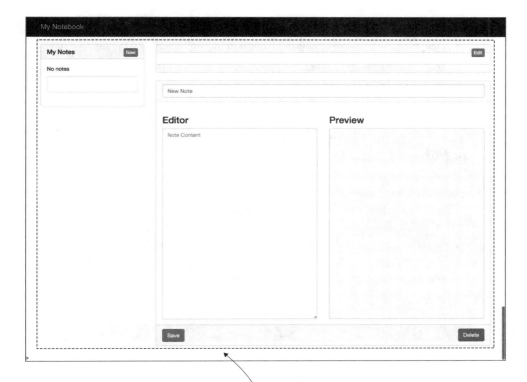

The controller's scope is limited to anything inside of the dashed line.

Figure 3.5 The controller's scope can only apply to markup inside of the dashed line. The header is outside of the scope because of where you've attached the controller.

More about the server in this project

The included server does two things: it serves the static files for your application and has a RESTful API. The topic of building a RESTful API is beyond the scope of this book, but I wanted to take a moment to go over the basics of this implementation. This server runs using Node, which you've already installed. Node allows you to do some pretty interesting things such as work with the computer's file system and respond to HTTP requests.

Node has modules that can be included in a program so you can reuse features. In this case, I've used a very popular Node module called Express. Express has a lot of the built-in features for building an HTTP server. I also used the file system module to maintain a list of notes in a JSON file. These are things you can't do with JavaScript in a browser, but Node makes them possible.

(continued)

You can look at the server.js file inside of this project to see the server code. This is a fully featured server, and it's impressive how easy it is to create with Node. You can learn more about Express at www.expressjs.com.

3.5   Loading data: using the controller to load and display data in the view

Let's start loading the data and getting it to display in the application. On the left the application will show a list of the notes that have already been created. I've seeded this project with a few notes to get you started. Because you've already created your controller, you can update the controller to load data into the app. To do this, you'll use the Angular $http service, which allows you to make HTTP requests to load data from the Node server. Figure 3.6 shows where the application will display the list of notes. You can reset your project to step4 if you're using Git:

```
$ git checkout -f step4
```

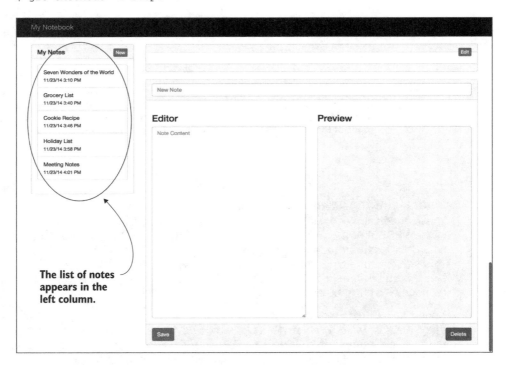

Figure 3.6   The data will be loaded and then displayed in the list on the left, showing the five default notes.

Now you need to modify the controller to add the HTTP request to the notes service, and assign the resulting data to the scope. Open the js/editor.js file and update it to the following code.

Listing 3.2   Editor controller loading notes from service (js/editor.js)

```
angular.module('App')
.controller('EditorController', function ($scope, $http) {    ◁─┘  ❶ Injects $http service into controller
  $scope.editing = true;

  $http.get('/notes').success(function (data) {              ◁──┘  ❷ Uses $http.get to load notes; on success, handles data returned
    $scope.notes = data;                                     ◁───
  }).error(function (err) {
    $scope.error = 'Could not load notes';                   Attaches returned data from http to $scope
  });
});
```

Handles error, stores error

This now will make an HTTP request to http://localhost:3000/notes to load the default list of notes from the data/notes.json file as soon as the controller loads. You can inspect the network requests in your browser inspector tools to see that the request returns the array of notes. Angular takes care of automatically parsing the JSON into a JavaScript object if it can detect the response body as a valid JSON string. This makes it easy to load JSON data without having to handle the parsing yourself.

In your controller function, you can declare any number of parameters for the function, and Angular will try to locate a service by that name and inject it into the controller. For example, you're able to inject the $http service into your controller ❶ and then use it to load data ❷. This is called *dependency injection* (DI), and it's a powerful feature of Angular to be able to make services available for your controllers to use. Angular services aren't global and can't be used without first being injected.

Imagine you have a menu at a restaurant that represents all of the Angular services available. Dependency injection is like a waiter who comes to your table and takes your order for a particular item on the menu. He goes to the kitchen, has the item prepared, and returns with it for you. Similarly, the DI system looks at your requested services, does any work to set them up, and returns the services to your function for you to use. You're able to inject the default Angular services or any other services that you create yourself.

In the code there are two methods chained to the $http.get() method. The code inside of the success() function will run when the data has loaded, while the code inside of the error() function will run if there was a problem getting the data (for example, the HTTP request failed because the server was down).

Angular and asynchronous methods

JavaScript is single-threaded, which means it can only execute one task at a time. Certain tasks, such as loading data from a server, can take a reasonably long time. In synchronous programming this would block other tasks' code from running until it was finished, likely causing the interface to freeze during this time. Fortunately, JavaScript doesn't do this. JavaScript supports many asynchronous tasks, which solves this problem.

When JavaScript runs an asynchronous task, it begins with the first part of the task, and then sets it aside to continue running other tasks. When the asynchronous task finishes, it alerts JavaScript, and the rest of the task is queued to execute. This frees up JavaScript to continue processing tasks. HTTP requests in JavaScript (also called AJAX or XHR requests) are one example of an asynchronous function because there's a lot of time spent waiting for the server to respond.

There are two primary ways to handle asynchronous functions: callbacks and promises. Angular uses promises for asynchronous method calls, but both may be used depending on the structure of the application or modules you're using.

To get more details about promises with Angular, I recommend looking at this blog post from Xebia's blog: http://blog.xebia.com/2014/02/23/promises-and-design-patterns-in-angularjs/.

You can't yet see any of the data on your screen, so you need to update the template file to show the list of notes in the left column. This will require template binding and several Angular directives to manage the display of this data from the $scope. Open the index.html file and look for the markup shown in the following listing, and add the bold parts into the template.

Listing 3.3 Notes list template (index.html)

```html
<div class="col-sm-3">
  <div class="panel panel-default">
    <div class="panel-heading">
      <h3 class="panel-title"><button class="btn btn-primary btn-xs pull-
      right">New</button> My Notes</h3>
    </div>

    <div class="panel-body">
      <p ng-if="!notes.length">No notes</p>
      <ul class="list-group">
        <li class="list-group-item" ng-repeat="note in
      notes">{{note.title}}<br />
        <small>{{note.date |
      date:'short'}}</small></li>
      </ul>
    </div>

  </div>
</div>
```

ngRepeat loops over every note and displays the note title.

ngIf conditionally includes or removes element from DOM depending on if there are notes.

Binding shows date, but also formats date using short format date filter.

Here the template displays the list of notes once the controller has loaded them. While the list is loading or if no notes are found, the ngRepeat list would be empty and the ngIf would display the "No notes" message. The expression is evaluated every time the notes model is updated, so as soon as the notes model has at least one item in the array, the expression !notes.length will return false to hide the paragraph element. This is a simple way to use Angular's directives to modify the template based on values attached to the $scope.

ngRepeat will loop over every item in an array (or property of an object) and create an element for each item. In this case, there will be a <li> element for each note in the array, and it will display the title and date the note was last saved.

You can explore the large number of directives that Angular provides to see all of the features. You'll use a number of them in Ionic apps, but I'll provide some detail about any new ones as they're used.

3.5.1   *Filters: convert data to display in the view*

The note.date data binding in the template is followed by | date:'short'. This is called a *filter*, which will modify the display of the binding without changing the value on the scope. For example, here we have a date object, and using the Angular date filter, the display formats it to a human-readable format while retaining the original date object on the scope.

Filters are used in expressions by adding the pipe character and then the filter. Filters can be chained together—in other words, you can add more than one filter. For example, a filter could sort an array (using the orderBy filter) and then another filter could reduce the array to 10 items (using the limitTo filter). The expression with the filters would appear like this:

```
{{notes | orderBy:'title' | limitTo:10}}
```

Angular has a handful of filters by default, such as a currency filter to format a number as a currency value (like $100.00 for US dollars or €34 for Euros) based on browser settings. Filters can also be used as a service, but that's less common.

3.6   *Handling click events to select a note*

Now you need to be able to view these notes individually. You'll want to click on a note in the list on the left and have that note appear on the right. Figure 3.7 shows how the click will select the note and then display it on the right. You can set your Git repository to this step by checking out the step5 tag:

```
$ git checkout -f step5
```

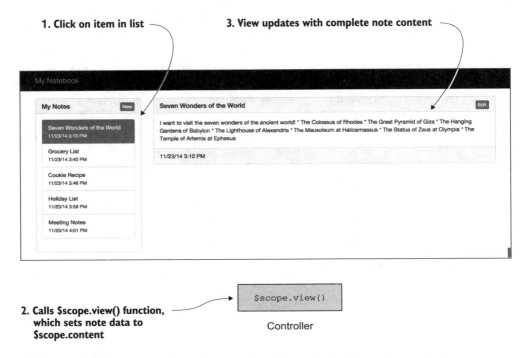

Figure 3.7   Clicking on an item calls the controller and updates the view with the selected note.

You'll use ngClick to handle when a user clicks on the item, and then assign the data from the note to a new model for display. Look at the template again, and modify the section with the list of notes to add the click handler, found in the bold portion of the following listing.

Listing 3.4   Adding `ngClick` to note list (index.html)

```
<ul class="list-group">
  <li class="list-group-item" ng-repeat="note in notes" ng-
    click="view($index)" ng-class="{active: note.id ==
    content.id}">{{note.title}}<br />
  <small>{{note.date | date:'short'}}</small></li>
</ul>
```

> ngClick and calls view() passing index; adds ngClass to add active class if note is selected

Each note in the list can now be clicked, and on click, Angular will try to call the $scope.view() function. The ngClass directive is a useful way to conditionally apply a CSS class to the element. In this case the active class is used to highlight the item after you've clicked on it to view the note.

The $index value is passed to the view function, and it's a special variable that ngRepeat provides. It helps you know what the index of the array item is, and in this case the index of the note that has been clicked.

You haven't created the view function yet, so let's address that now. Open the editor controller and add the view function found in the following listing into the controller function.

Listing 3.5 View function in the editor controller (js/editor.js)

Declares new $scope method
called view and accepts index
of clicked item

```
$scope.view = function (index) {
  $scope.editing = false;
  $scope.content = $scope.notes[index];
};
```

Sets a new model for
content model to contain
note that was clicked

Sets editing state to
false because you want
to just view an item

Now the `click` event will fire the `view()` method in the controller when the note is clicked. The `view()` method sets a new `content` model that contains the data from the note that was clicked, using the index value that was passed. The method also sets the `editing` model to `false` because any time you view an item, it should reset to the display mode and not the editing mode. The editing mode will be wired in a few more steps.

Next is handling the `click` event and setting the `content` model with the note data that was selected. But you aren't able to see the note yet in the view, so you need to update the template to display the selected note properly.

You've created a new `content` model that contains the note, but you have to update the template to show the note. You can set your Git repository to this step by checking out the `step6` tag:

```
$ git checkout -f step6
```

Now you need to modify the right column of the application to display the two panels properly. So far the right shows two panels, and you need to configure it so only one of the panels appears at once. The first panel is intended for when you want to view a note, and the second panel is for when you want to edit a note. You've already set a `$scope.editing` property that you'll use to determine which panel to show. Open the index.html file again and modify the right column content by adding the bold portions from the following listing. You can find this HTML inside of the first `div` with the `panel` class.

Listing 3.6 Modify template to view a note (index.html)

ngHide hides top panel if
condition is true, in this
case when editing is true

Binds title
into panel
header

```
<div class="panel panel-default" ng-hide="editing">
  <div class="panel-heading">
    <h3 class="panel-title">{{content.title}} <button class="btn btn-
primary btn-xs pull-right">Edit</button></h3>
  </div>
```

```
        <div class="panel-body">{{content.content}}</div>
        <div class="panel-footer">{{content.date | date:'short'}}</div>
    </div>
    <form name="editor" class="panel panel-default" ng-show="editing">
```

ngShow hides bottom
panel if condition is
false, in this case when
editing is false

Binds note date and
passes it through date
filter to use short format

When you run the application now, you're able to click and view each note individually. The template will now react to the changes made in the view() method, which set the content and editing models. When the editing model is true, the editing panel will appear; otherwise, the note panel will display. The ngShow and ngHide directives are useful to toggle the display of elements like those shown in listing 3.6.

You've added the bindings for the note title, content, and date. The date has the date filter applied just as you did earlier. Now you need to create a new directive that will parse the note content to display it properly.

3.7   *Create a directive to parse a note with Markdown*

At this point you can view your existing notes, but the formatting isn't quite right in the notes. This application will support writing notes with Markdown, which is a simple way to write text that can be easily converted into HTML markup. You can learn more about Markdown at http://daringfireball.net/projects/markdown/. Figure 3.8 shows the area that will be formatted using Markdown. You can set your Git workspace to this step by checking out step7:

```
$ git checkout -f step7
```

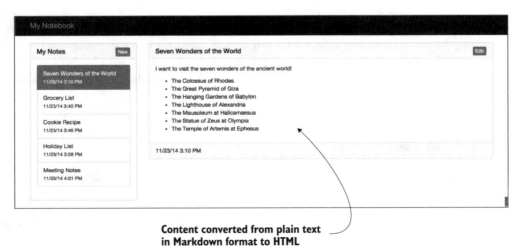

Content converted from plain text
in Markdown format to HTML

Figure 3.8   Note content written in Markdown format will now be parsed and converted into HTML.

You'll create a simple Angular directive that can convert the plaintext with Markdown syntax into HTML. To do this you'll use the popular JavaScript Markdown library called Showdown. It's already included by default in the application file.

To create the directive, open the app.js file. Directives aren't part of a controller, so organize the code so it's stored in the main app file (in a larger app you'd want to separate this into its own file). In the following listing you can see the directive you'll use to convert Markdown to HTML.

Listing 3.7 Markdown-to-HTML directive (js/app.js)

```
angular.module('App', [])
.directive('markdown', function () {
  var converter = new Showdown.converter();
  return {
    scope: {
      markdown: '@'
    },
    link: function (scope, element, attrs) {
      scope.$watch('markdown', function () {
        var content = converter.makeHtml(attrs.markdown);
        element.html(content);
      });
    }
  }
});
```

- **Directives return an object to define directive settings**
- **Converts Markdown into content variable**
- **Declares directive and names it 'markdown'**
- **Creates Showdown converter to use later**
- **Declares custom scope that expects a value to be assigned to a Markdown attribute**
- **Uses scope watcher to update any time model changes**
- **Injects converted HTML content into element**
- **Declares link function that actually manages conversion from Markdown to HTML**

This directive will automatically convert the Markdown to HTML any time the content changes, which will become helpful when you're editing. The directive works by first creating a new Showdown converter service. The directive is then defined, and in this case the directive will have its own isolate scope nested inside of the controller scope. I've defined Markdown as a property of the scope, and I'll demonstrate how that value gets populated in the next section.

The link function is used by Angular as part of the rendering process. It will use the $scope.$watch feature, which allows you to listen for when the Markdown content is changed. When it detects a change, the plaintext content is passed to the Showdown converter and then injected into the element as HTML. The source content in the scope will remain the plaintext version, but it will always appear as the converted HTML.

Let's put the directive into action and see how to pass it the Markdown content. It will take your note content, parse it using Showdown, and inject the resulting HTML into the element. Open the index.html file and modify the existing content binding as follows:

```
<div class="panel-body" markdown="{{content.content}}"></div>
```

Notice how this is an HTML attribute like the other directives you've used. You assign the `content.content` model to the markdown attribute to pass the content of the model to your directive's isolated scope. This directive is used as an attribute on the element that you want to inject the content into. The HTML is injected inside the `div` element, and any time the `content.content` model is changed, your scope `$watch` function will fire to reconvert the new content.

Directives are a very complex topic, and we've only scratched the surface of what you can do with them. There are also different ways this directive could have been built, which makes the directive feature in Angular quite powerful, but also somewhat difficult to grasp.

Will I need to write my own directives?

You're not required to write your own directives. Directives exist for any situation where you want to modify an element in the DOM, but you can often manage the same logic using a controller. But there are many good reasons why you'd want to create custom directives.

Directives are easier to test when they're written well. Directives encapsulate both the functionality (they can include a controller or link function) and the template (they can include template fragments). This makes them modular and isolated from other aspects of your code, making the tests focused on just the directive.

They're also reusable and reduce code that would otherwise have to be written in multiple places. Regardless of where in the application you want to reuse the directive, it would have a consistent behavior. If you put that logic into a controller and want to use it again in another controller, you'll either have to write the same code twice or work out how to share scopes.

You could build Angular and Ionic apps without your own directives. I recommend beginners not focus on directives until they're comfortable with Angular in general. If you're comfortable, then a few ways to identify when something should be a custom directive is to look for cases where code is being duplicated or where the DOM is being manipulated from the controller.

At this point, the viewing of existing notes is complete. Next we'll focus on making the editor work.

3.8   *Using models to manage content editing*

The editor will have two primary functions: to edit existing notes and to create new notes. To begin you'll set up the editor so it can create a new note when the application first loads, or when a user clicks the New button. Figure 3.9 shows the changes you'll make in this section. You can set your Git repository to the code for this section by checking out the step8 tag:

```
$ git checkout -f step8
```

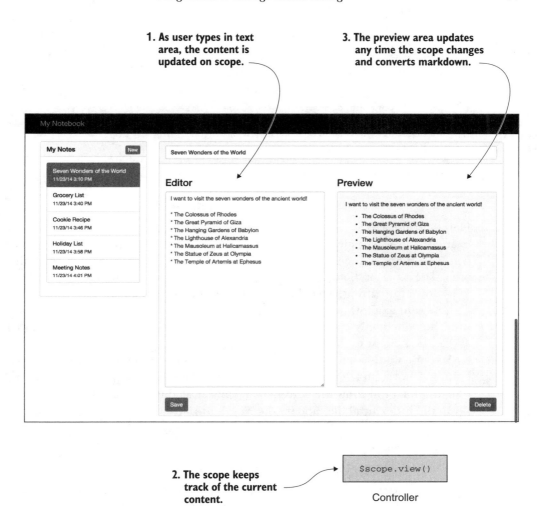

Figure 3.9   The model is modified by a user using the text area, and the preview area is instantly updated with changes.

To begin, you need to add some models to the form so you can use the form controls to update the data. You also want to have the right side of the editor show a preview of the content as you type, so you'll add the Markdown directive here as well.

Open the index.html file and modify the markup inside of the form to reflect the bold portions from the following listing.

Listing 3.8   Updating the editor with models (index.html)

```
<div class="panel-heading">
  <h3 class="panel-title"><input type="text" class="form-control" ng-
    model="content.title" placeholder="New Note" required /></h3>
```

Attaches
title model
to input

```
    </div>
    <div class="panel-body">
      <div class="row">
        <div class="col-sm-6">
          <h3>Editor</h3>
          <textarea class="form-control editor" rows="10" ng-
      model="content.content" placeholder="Note Content" required></textarea>
        </div>
        <div class="col-sm-6">
          <h3>Preview</h3>
          <div class="preview" markdown="{{content.content}}"></div>
        </div>
      </div>
    </div>
  </div>
```

Attaches
content
model to
text area

Uses Markdown directive
to preview content

Here you use `ngModel` to link the model values to the input and text area, so any changes a user types into those fields will instantly change the `content` model. Once you have these changes, you can reload the page and start to type in the editor text area. The `preview` field should update immediately with the content, and if you use Markdown formatting, it will be converted in the preview area.

You want to allow users to click the New button to create a new note, because right now the editor only appears when the application first loads. To do this you need to add a `click` event to the New button.

You also want to allow notes to be edited, so you need another button that will start editing a note after it's opened. This will be done by simply changing the `editing` model, which will show the editing panel and hide the note panel.

In the index.html file, update the New button using the bold code as follows:

```
<h3 class="panel-title"><button class="btn btn-primary btn-xs pull-right" ng-
    click="create()">New</button> My Notes</h3>
```

Then update the Edit button using the bold code as follows:

```
<h3 class="panel-title">{{content.title}} <button class="btn btn-primary btn-
    xs pull-right" ng-click="editing = true">Edit</button>
```

The New button will try to call the `create()` method from the controller, which you'll define next. The Edit button doesn't call a method, but will actually update the value of the `editing` model to set it to `true`. You could also have written this as a function, but because you can use expressions in your template, this does the trick.

Now you need to define the `create()` method in your controller, so open the editor controller and add a new method, as shown in the following listing.

Listing 3.9   Create note controller method (js/editor.js)

```
$scope.create = function () {
  $scope.editing = true;
  $scope.content = {
    title: '',
    content: ''
  };
};
```

Ensures
editing
state is
set to true

Resets content model
with blank values

Creates method and
attaches to scope so
it can be called from
ngClick in template

When the Edit button is clicked, the `create()` method will fire. It changes the `editing` model to be true and then resets the `content` model for a blank note. This will cause the editor to appear and a blank note to be displayed in the form, which is your new note.

3.9 *Saving and deleting a note*

Now you're able to create and edit notes, but you aren't able to save them yet. You need to add a `save()` method to the controller and have the Save button call it. But you also only want to save the item if the note is valid, which means it needs both a title and some content. Figure 3.10 shows the Save and Delete buttons when you're editing an item, and how they call the controller methods to handle the `click` event. You can set your Git repository to the code in this section by checking out the `step9` tag:

```
$ git checkout -f step9
```

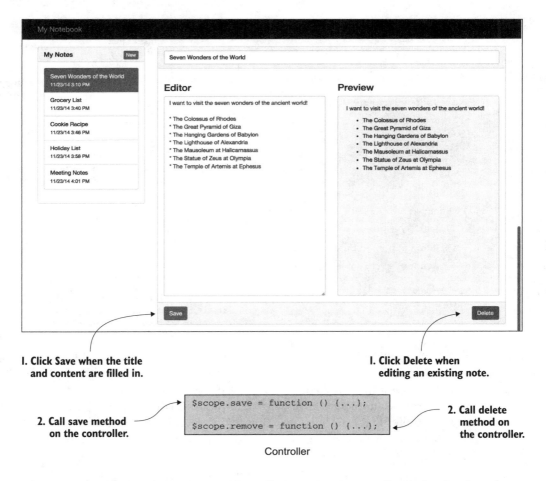

Figure 3.10 The Save and Delete buttons call a method stored on the controller that handles the `click` event.

3.9.1   *Adding the save() method*

Saving a note requires using the $http service again to send the note to the service. The service uses the POST method to create a new note and the PUT method to update a note. $http.post() and $http.put() both accept a second parameter, which is the data to be sent to the service. Otherwise, the syntax is the same as $http.get().

Before you can save a note, you have to determine if the note is new or already exists. To do this, look for an id on the content. New notes aren't given an id until they've been saved, so if it exists you need to update it. Once you know if the note is new or existing, you can call the correct service endpoint.

Open the editor controller and add the save() method from the following listing.

Listing 3.10   Save controller method for saving notes to service (js/editor.js)

Sets date value of last-edited date for this note

Checks if this note has an id so you can either update an existing note or create a note

Attaches save() method to scope

Because this is a new note, give it a unique id based on current timestamp

```
$scope.save = function () {
  $scope.content.date = new Date();

  if ($scope.content.id) {
    $http.put('/notes/' + $scope.content.id, $scope.content).success(function
      (data) {
        $scope.editing = false;
    });
  } else {
    $scope.content.id = Date.now();
    $http.post('/notes', $scope.content).success(function (data) {
      $scope.notes.push($scope.content);
      $scope.editing = false;
    });
  }
};
```

Sends a PUT request to notes API to update note and disable edit mode when completed

Sends a POST request to notes API to create a new note and then adds note to notes list before disabling edit mode

The save() method starts by updating the date value with the current timestamp because you want to store the time it was last saved. It then sends either a PUT or POST request, depending on if the note is new or existing, by checking if an id exists. When the request has completed, both types of requests will disable the editing mode to view the saved note. If the note is new, then it's also given an id and then added to the notes array in your controller. This is important to keep both the application and the service layer in sync with one another; otherwise the new note would be stored into the service layer but not shown on the left notes list.

3.9.2   Using Angular forms for validation

Before you save an item, you'll use Angular's built-in form features to help validate the form and disable the Save button if it's invalid. Angular extends the default form features you know about in HTML with a large set of features, and one particularly useful feature is automatic validation.

Notice on the form controls that you have the `required` attribute. Angular will look for that and automatically set some values on your scope to track if the forms are valid. In this case, a note requires both a title and content, so if either is blank the entire form is invalid.

Angular uses the normal HTML form element or the `ngForm` attribute to enhance forms. In this case you're using a normal form element and have given it a name of `editor`. The form then adds a new property by the same name to the scope, and has a number of values such as `$valid`, `$invalid`, `$dirty`, or `$pristine`. These values can help you understand if an input is valid or has been modified.

You'll use the validation to disable the Save button until the form is valid, and add a `click` event to the Save button. In the index.html file, locate the Save button and add the following bold directives to the element:

```
<button class="btn btn-primary" ng-click="save()" ng-
    disabled="editor.$invalid">Save</button>
```

`ngClick` should be familiar by now. It will call the `save()` method in the controller and take care of saving the note. But it will not fire while `editor.$invalid` is true. The `ngDisabled` directive looks at the form validation and disables it while both form controls are empty. Angular is aware of validation attributes, such as `required`, and when an `ngModel` is attached to a form field, the form can provide automatic validation.

3.9.3   Adding the remove method

The last feature to create is a way to delete a note. The Delete button shows only when you've selected an existing note to edit. To get the changes in your Git repository for this section, check out the `step10` tag:

```
$ git checkout -f step10
```

First, you'll add the `remove()` method, which will handle calling the service to delete the note and then remove it from the application. Using the code in the following listing, you can update the editor controller.

> **Listing 3.11   Method to delete a note (js/editor.js)**

```
$scope.remove = function () {                           ⟵── Declares remove() method
  $http.delete('/notes/' + $scope.content.id).success(function (data) {   ⟵ Makes delete request to notes API
    var found = -1;
    angular.forEach($scope.notes, function (note, index) {     ── Loops through notes to find index of deleted note
      if (note.id === $scope.content.id) {
        found = index;
      }
```

```
  });
  if (found >= 0) {
    $scope.notes.splice(found, 1);
  }
  $scope.content = {
    title: '',
    content: ''
  };
  });
};
```

If note was found, removes it from notes list in Angular app

Resets content model for a new note

The `remove()` method sends an HTTP `delete` request to the notes service based on the `id` of the note, and then when it has returned it will remove the item from the `notes` array in the controller. To delete the note from the `notes` model, it loops over every note, looking to see if the deleted `id` matches a note, and only if found does it splice (remove) that item from the array. It also resets the `content` model so it's ready for a new note.

The last change is to add `ngClick` to the Delete button to call the `remove()` function. You'll also use an `ngIf` to conditionally show the Delete button only when you're editing an existing note, because you shouldn't be able to delete a new note that hasn't been saved. The following snippet shows the Angular directives used on the Delete button in bold:

```
<button class="btn btn-danger pull-right" ng-click="remove()" ng-
    if="content.id">Delete</button>
```

The button will now display only when editing an existing note, and when clicked it will call the `remove()` method to delete the note from the model.

This now completes your Angular notebook application. In a whirlwind tour of Angular through building this application, we've scratched the surface of many of the core pieces of Angular. As we move from just Angular to building Ionic apps, you'll continue to see these features used. There are more concepts we won't cover, because it takes far more pages than I can devote here.

3.10   *Continuing with Angular*

Learning Angular is important to building Ionic apps, so if this is your first look at Angular, I want to encourage you to spend time with it. I believe the best way to learn Angular is to interact and build with it.

There are many opinions about how to best work with Angular. While there are certainly some best practices that have been discovered, there are also many opinions. Take care not to be overwhelmed by the vast number of posts online that discuss the "right" way to build Angular applications. They likely have good points, but also may have opinions that don't fit your programming style or needs.

You can continue learning about Angular with *AngularJS in Action* (http://manning.com/bford/) or *AngularJS in Depth* (http://manning.com/aden/) from Manning. The Angular website (https://angularjs.org or https://angular.io) is the primary resource for documentation, and also includes a good getting-started guide.

There are also many good recorded talks on YouTube that range from beginning with Angular to very specific, advanced topics; see, for example, https://www.youtube .com/user/angularjs.

Even while you could create a fairly good Ionic app without knowing the inner details of Angular, your ability to develop a great Ionic app increases as you learn and expand your Angular skills.

3.11   Chapter challenges

Now that you've seen the fundamentals of Angular in action in this chapter, here are a few challenges for you to dig into to improve your understanding:

- *Show errors*—Notice that you set the value of $scope.error in the $http.get() method, but never did anything with it. Modify the template so that an error message will show when the value of $scope.error is set.
- *Handle other* $http *errors*—The $http methods all can handle error situations, and in the example in this chapter only the get() method is set up to do this. Improve the example by adding error handling for the other methods as well.
- *Use* ngResource—Instead of $http, you could use the ngResource module, which is an abstraction for interacting with a RESTful API that makes it easier to create services based on $http. You'll need to include the module by adding the files to the application (you can use a browser or download from Angular's site) and work out how to include another module in your application.

3.12   Summary

In this chapter we've covered many aspects of Angular through the example notebook application. Let's review the major topics covered in this chapter:

- Angular extends HTML with additional features that are made available through the many directives it provides or that you can create yourself.
- Templates are HTML and may contain Angular directives or expressions. These templates are converted into a view that users interact with.
- Controllers are used to hold the business logic of your application. They're functions that can have any number of servers injected into them using Angular's dependency injection system.
- Scope is the glue that holds the controller and views together, and powers the two-way data binding in Angular. When data changes in the view or controller, the data is automatically synced to the other.
- Filters are ways to transform data in a template without modifying the source model stored in the scope.
- Directives are powerful, and you can create your own when you're comfortable with Angular. They aren't required, but should be used when appropriate.

In chapter 4, you'll build your first Ionic app from the ground up and learn about many features that you'll use in your apps.

Ionic navigation and core components

4

This chapter covers

- Managing the user state and navigation for the app
- Displaying icons, lists, and cards to cleanly organize content
- Loading data from external sources and showing a loading screen
- Using infinite scrolling to continuously load data
- Using a slideshow component as an app intro

In this chapter I'll show you how to create a fully functional mobile app for a fictitious resort in Hawaii. The core feature of this app is managing user app navigation. I'll also introduce you to some of the Ionic components throughout this chapter, such as loaders, content containers, and a slideshow.

This chapter is laid out to provide a walk-through of the process to build the complete app. The complete example is available on GitHub if you'd like to take a look at the whole app first. You can find it at https://github.com/ionic-in-action/chapter4. You can also preview the app at http://ionic-in-action-chapter4.herokuapp.com.

A vital part of any mobile app is managing the users' ability to navigate through the app. You'll first set up the necessary foundation for the application navigation. Then you'll build from that foundation and add new views that introduce additional Ionic user interface components. All of the components will work together to provide a mobile app that shows the current weather details, a visitor's reservation details, and upcoming events at the resort. It will also include an introductory tour of the app using a simple slider, which you may have seen in other mobile apps. At the end of the chapter, I'll provide a list of several suggested challenges to improve the app and practice what you've learned.

Figure 4.1 outlines the basic app flow. This provides a general idea of what users will be able to do and where they can navigate. There are notes about the basic features for each of the views. Some type of wireframing like you see in figure 4.1 is helpful in the planning stages of any mobile app.

Now let's get you started with building this app!

User opens the app and goes to the tour

Intro view
• Use slidebox
• Only show on first use
• Use button to skip

Home view
• Link to other views
• Use list component
• No back button
• Use icons

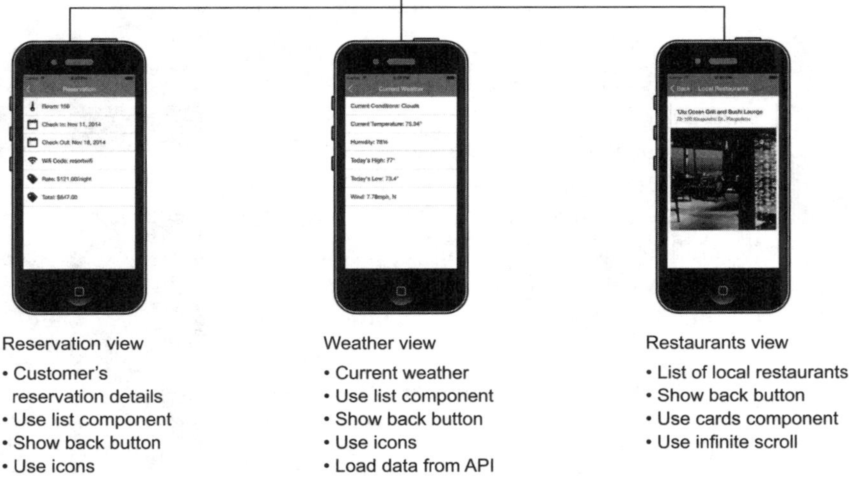

Reservation view
• Customer's reservation details
• Use list component
• Show back button
• Use icons

Weather view
• Current weather
• Use list component
• Show back button
• Use icons
• Load data from API

Restaurants view
• List of local restaurants
• Show back button
• Use cards component
• Use infinite scroll

Figure 4.1   Resort app wireframe showing the views and user flow

4.1 Set up chapter project

For this chapter, you have the option to follow along by creating and writing all the code for a new app, or cloning the app from GitHub and checking out the app at various points along the way. Either way, you'll get to see and run the code for a particular step, so the choice is yours. The Git option is faster if you don't want to copy all of the code from the book into your project.

4.1.1 Create a new app and add code manually

To create a new project for the app using the Ionic command-line interface (CLI) utility, open the command line and execute the following command (remember, you can refer to chapter 2 if you need a refresh on how projects are set up):

```
$ ionic start chapter4 https://github.com/ionic-in-action/starter
$ cd chapter4
$ ionic serve
```

4.1.2 Clone the finished app and follow along

To check out the finished app and use Git to follow along for each step, use the following command to clone the repository and check out the first step:

```
$ git clone https://github.com/ionic-in-action/chapter4.git
$ cd chapter4
$ git checkout -f step1
$ ionic serve
```

4.2 Setting up the app navigation

Before you build the resort app, take a look at figure 4.2. It shows the various places in the app that a user will be able to go. You'll build out each piece individually, but here you can see them all together.

Your first task is to get the app navigation set up, and then you'll work on adding the content into each view. Ionic is built to work with a third-party routing framework called ui-router, which is like the central brain for navigation. In case you're not familiar with ui-router, I'll show you the key features you'll need. Ionic layers on top of ui-router in some ways, so you don't often have to worry about the inner workings unless you develop your own custom navigation techniques.

Figure 4.2 All completed app views

I talk about navigation and routing, which are two different but related concepts. I use the term *navigation* as the act of a user moving around inside of an app (a user tapping a button to go to another place), and the term *routing* as the application's internal process to decide what to do when a user navigates (the application deciding where to go when a button has been tapped). In other words, navigation is the user action and routing is the application logic that responds to user input.

> **Why Ionic uses ui-router and not ngRoute**
>
> There's an official router for Angular (ngRoute) that isn't used by Ionic. The primary reason is that ngRoute doesn't support some important features that the ui-router project supports, such as named views, nested views, and parallel views. An example would be allowing a tabbed interface that's actually multiple views. These features are built into the core of Ionic, through the `ionNavView` directive. Ionic is built to work only with ui-router, so attempting to use ngRoute will cause issues with your app.
>
> There are a lot of aspects of ui-router that aren't covered in this book, and it's best to refer to the website https://angular-ui.github.io/ui-router/ for more detailed information about some interesting features that might be useful in advanced use cases.

In the wireframe in figure 4.1 and in the app overview in figure 4.2, you can see there are really five potential places, or views, for a user to be:

- Intro
- Home
- Reservation
- Weather
- Restaurants

Traditional websites have pages, but in a mobile app there are no distinct pages. As a user navigates inside of an app, it's less obvious that the view changes, compared to a website where you can watch the URL change in the address bar and see the page reload. I like to think of a view as a well-defined visual experience, just as you see in the preceding list with five very distinct places the user can see in the app. Before you set up navigation in the app, let's talk about how to design the app navigation for users.

4.2.1 Designing good app navigation

Mobile app navigation is somewhat like traveling to a new city. Imagine you arrive by train in this new city, and you walk out of the train station near downtown. You may have some idea what you'd like to do or how to get around (such as visit some museums), but you first have to rely on the street signs to understand where you are in relation to your destination. Because you're familiar with street signs and common city rules, you're able to find your way to your destination. In your app, you're responsible for providing the street signs for your users.

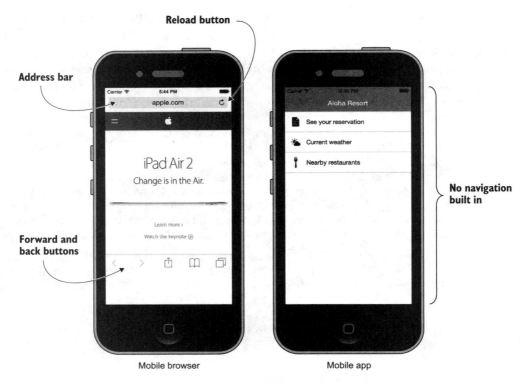

Figure 4.3   Browsers have navigation aids like an address bar and reload and back buttons. Apps have no buttons, so the developer must provide navigation options.

Even though you're building a web application inside of your hybrid app, the user experience isn't the same as it is for a web application viewed in a browser. Users can't navigate in the same manner because hybrid apps don't have the browser window and features such as the address bar or back or reload buttons, as shown in figure 4.3. This means it's up to you, the app developer, to provide the ability to navigate the app.

When you consider the navigation, you should consider the flow like in figure 4.1 to understand how a user moves from view to view. There may be multiple ways that a user can get to a given view, but it should always be clear and intuitive for the user. There are many ways to create a navigation flow for users, from custom interactions to the more common features Ionic provides by default. It's better to use common navigation techniques, such as buttons, than to create experiences that a user will have to learn how to use.

I recommend you look at four or five of the apps you use on a regular basis and try to understand the navigation flow they use, and what techniques they provide to the user. Do they use buttons? Is there a side menu or tabs to help get to key parts of the app? Do you ever get lost, and if so, can you see why? Thinking critically about these items will help you while you design your apps.

4.2.2 *Declaring the app views with the state provider*

Now it's time to dig into some code. Your first task is to add the Ionic navigation components into the app HTML markup. Then you'll declare one view to start with. The result will look like figure 4.4, which is mainly the content container with no content and the navigation bar (navbar). If you're following along using Git, you can check out the code for this step:

```
$ git checkout -f step2
```

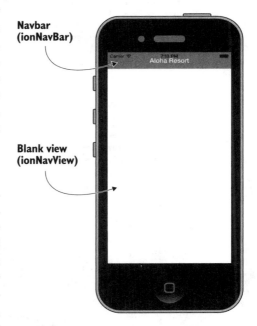

Figure 4.4 A basic app with navigation and a single view with no content

ionNavView and ionNavBar are the foundational Ionic components for the navigation. ionNavView acts like a placeholder for different view content to be loaded into the app, and ionNavBar shows a header bar that will update as a user moves from view to view. These two components are designed to work together, but you could use ionNavView without using ionNavBar if you didn't want a top navbar.

If you're familiar with frames in HTML, ionNavView is similar in the sense that it allows content to be loaded inside. But ionNavView isn't an actual frame. If you want to understand more about Angular and templates, refer back to chapter 3. Remember that Angular has a way to take markup (that is, the template) and inject it into the view (in this case, inside of ionNavView). Without ionNavView, the app wouldn't know where to load the content, so you'll always need at least one ionNavView in your app if you use navigation.

ionNavBar will place a top bar in the app, which is found in many apps. It's like a title bar. Think of it like a place where you can put the current view's title and also use it to place buttons, such as a back button. You'll use the ionNavBackButton component in this app because the app users will need a way to go back. In figure 4.1 the bottom-row views will all have a back button to return to the home view. The home view will not show a back button, because it's the top-level view and the back button will not display.

Take the index.html file in listing 4.1 and add in the navigation components. These components can't run without some JavaScript that you'll add from listing 4.2, but first focus on the components in the markup. This code shows only the contents inside of the </body> tag of the page, but you'll need to retain the rest of the markup in the HTML file.

Listing 4.1   App navigation components in markup (www/index.html)

```
<body ng-app="App">
  <ion-nav-bar class="bar-positive">
    <ion-nav-back-button class="button-clear">
      <i class="icon ion-ios-arrow-left"></i> Back
    </ion-nav-back-button>
  </ion-nav-bar>
  <ion-nav-view></ion-nav-view>
</body>
```

Declares ionNavBar;
also gives it a style
with bar-positive class

Declares ionNavView,
where each view
content will display

Uses arrow back
icon for back
button

Where Angular app
is attached to page

Declares ionNavBackButton, which will
show and hide if there's a way to go back

So far, you're just declaring placeholders for content. You haven't actually declared any views, but when you do, these components will automatically know what to do with the information. It's likely that many apps you build will have markup similar to listing 4.1 as the foundation for the app navigation.

You can see there are classes on some of the components, and this is common. Ionic allows you to customize the display of many components by using CSS classes. We'll cover these options in more detail later.

If you run this code, you'll notice it doesn't really do anything yet. That's because you haven't declared any views. What you actually need to declare is a list of states for the application. States are a concept given to you from the ui-router. A state is the current representation of the application that's visually represented in the view, which would contain details such as the URL associated with the view, the name of the controller for the view, and the template attached to the view. In this book, you'll declare states that are typically linked to a view (the home view in figure 4.1, for example, is a state). For a more in-depth discussion about states, you can refer to the ui-router details at https://github.com/angular-ui/ui-router/wiki.

If you recall, we talked about how routing is the concept for declaring what paths through the application a user can navigate. You could think of it like a folder tree, where states can be organized as children of other states.

Right now you've created the home state, but you haven't yet declared any of the other files inside of that directory to view. The states you declare include a way to route the user to a particular place in the app, which can be done using URLs or using the name of a state. In this book we'll usually use the state name for navigation.

Let's have you add some states to the app, as shown in listing 4.2. You'll add these states into the app.js file, which contains the Angular app definition. You'll use the $stateProvider service to declare your states, and the $urlRouterProvider to help provide a fallback in case an invalid request is made. The code in the following listing will be added right after the first line (as shown).

Listing 4.2   Declaring app states (www/js/app.js)

```
angular.module('App', ['ionic'])
.config(function ($stateProvider, $urlRouterProvider) {
  $stateProvider.state('home', {
    url: '/home',
    templateUrl: 'views/home/home.html'
  });
  $urlRouterProvider.otherwise('/home');
})
.run(function($ionicPlatform) {
```

Declares first state for home view

Adds new config method and injects $stateProvider

Angular module definition, already in file

Angular run method, already in file

Declares a fallback URL to go to if app can't find requested state

Tells state to load a template from a given URL when view is active

Gives state a URL that can be used with anchor links

All right, you've got the first state declared, and it's called home. It's very simple—it will only try to load a template from the URL provided in templateUrl. As you add more states to the app in this chapter, you'll see other configuration values that can be provided. You can always review the full set of options based on the ui-router documentation. The examples in this chapter will demonstrate the most common variations.

The otherwise() method is important because it catches situations where the application is unable to find the requested route, much like a 404 error page on a website. If a user tries to request a state that doesn't exist, the otherwise() method will be used to display the home view. It's always a good idea to declare an otherwise() method in case your app has a routing problem, so it can always have something to show instead of a blank page or error. You might consider making a special error view that people can use to send you feedback.

You might have noticed there's a template declared, but you haven't yet created this file. It's time to add this last file to make the first view work correctly and see how the view gets loaded into the app. I prefer to organize all of my views into a folder called views, so create a new file at www/views/home/home.html and put the contents from the following listing inside.

Listing 4.3   Add template for home view (www/views/home/home.html)

```
<ion-view view-title="Aloha Resort" hide-back-button="true">
</ion-view>
```

Uses ionView to declare a view template; title is used in navbar and hide-back-button will disable back button

Now you can run the code and see that it runs correctly. You should see the app running with a blue navbar and the title "Aloha Resort." The rest of the view is blank, for the moment. You'll add that in next. It should look like you see in figure 4.4.

Note the `hide-back-button` attribute. This attribute tells `ionNavBar` that this view doesn't want the back button to show. There are other `ionView` attributes that you may use that you can find in the documentation.

Now this isn't terribly impressive just yet! Let's move on to the next part where you'll get the home view set up. Along the way we'll talk about the content area, how to use icons, and lists.

4.3   Building the home view

The example so far has a blank view with a title, so now you need to add more content into this view. The primary feature of this page is to provide a list of links that will take users to the weather, restaurants, and reservation views. If you're following along using Git, you should check out the next step:

```
$ git checkout -f step3
```

In listing 4.3, there's a very basic and very blank view. Inside of this view, you'll put a few things. You'll add `ionContent`, which is a generic wrapper for content but has a lot of features you might not notice immediately. Then you'll create a list of navigational links for each of the views. Lastly, you'll add some icons to make them a little nicer on the eyes. You can preview the result in figure 4.5.

4.3.1   Creating a content container

`ionContent` is the most commonly used content container. It provides a number of features:

- *Sizes content area to device*—It will determine the appropriate height for your content container based on the device.
- *Aware of header and footer bars*—It knows if there are header or footer bars, and will adjust its size and position accordingly.
- *Manages scrolling*—It has a number of configuration options to manage scrolling. For example, you might want to lock scrolling to be one direction only (horizontally), or no scrolling at all.

There are a lot of options with `ionContent`, but they're primarily related to managing the scrolling experience. In most cases you'll not need any of those options, but you

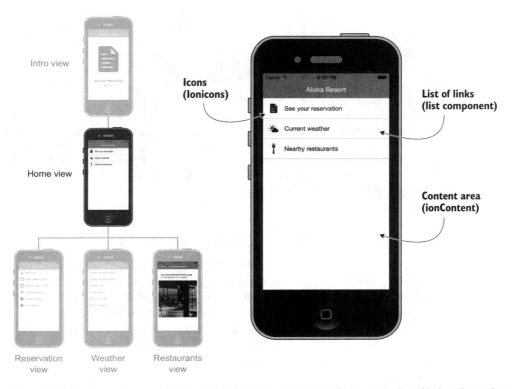

Figure 4.5 The home view with icons and a list of links, and content is correctly placed below the navbar

can see the various options in the documentation. Let's add this tag to the home view. Open the home view file again and add the code like you see in the following listing.

Listing 4.4   Adding `ionContent` to home view (www/views/home/home.html)

```
<ion-view title="Aloha Resort" hide-back-button="true">      ←— ionView
  <ion-content>                              ←—                      declared earlier
  </ion-content>                                  ionContent that
</ion-view>                                        will hold content
                                                   for view
```

That's it? Yes! In this case `ionContent` is pretty easy to use, and because you plan to use the default features, you don't have to make it any more complex than this. The content area will now resize and take the navbar into consideration when it calculates the size and position of the content. Without `ionContent`, the content would start in the top left corner behind the navbar, which is obviously not desirable.

> **Is your content in the wrong place?**
>
> The vast majority of the time, you'll use `ionContent` to wrap your content. If you ever run into trouble where your content is misplaced on the screen, start by double-checking that you have `ionContent` in the right place.
>
> There are some situations where you don't want to use `ionContent`; you'll see one example of this in chapter 5 where tabs shouldn't be inside of `ionContent`. Sometimes you may have to add some CSS to make things display like you want if you don't use `ionContent`. For example, if you use `ionHeaderBar` without `ionContent`, the content will be positioned under the `ionHeaderBar`. Ionic tries to make the design and components work in most cases, but some nonstandard use cases require extra CSS.

4.3.2   *Using CSS components and adding a simple list of links*

Now that you have a content container, you'll want to add a list of links. Ionic comes with a lot of components that are simply CSS classes applied to elements. If you're familiar with front-end interface frameworks like Bootstrap or Foundation, you'll be quite familiar with the method of adding classes to create visual components. Some of the components are mobile-focused designs for several form elements like checkboxes, a range slider, buttons, and more.

Ionic has a list component, which is a pair of classes for a list and each list item. The list component has a number of style configurations; you'll start with the most basic and then add icons.

Let's add a basic list of links to the app, as shown in listing 4.5. While you can use a normal unordered list element, I'll actually show you how to use a `div` to wrap a list of anchor tags. This is important to note because the CSS styling applied is very complete and will allow you to use the class on different elements.

> **Listing 4.5   Adding a list to the home view (www/views/home/home.html)**

```
<ion-view title="Aloha Resort" hide-back-button="true">      ionView and ionContent
  <ion-content>                                              declared from earlier
    <div class="list">                              ◁
      <a href="#/reservation" class="item">
        See your reservation                          Adds list class to a
      </a>                                            container element to
      <a href="#/weather" class="item">              designate a list container
        Current weather
      </a>
      <a href="#/restaurants" class="item">           Adds item class to an element
        Nearby restaurants                            to create a list item, in this
      </a>                                            case a link to another view
    </div>
  </ion-content>
</ion-view>
```

Using a CSS component normally means just following the component guideline and giving elements the proper CSS classes. We'll look at more-complex lists in the next chapter, but for displaying a simple list of items, this suits our needs quite well. The documentation also shows a number of different list item display types, such as having dividers, thumbnails, or icons.

The list has some links to different URLs that you haven't yet defined. You'll add each view individually, and then the app will be able to navigate to that view. With the item class on the anchor tag, it adopts the list item display. These three links are related to the three views (refer to figure 4.1 to see the app flow).

CSS and JavaScript components

In the Ionic documentation, you'll see that the components are split into two distinct categories: CSS and JavaScript. If you look closely, you'll notice that some components appear on both lists, such as header bars and lists. You might wonder why are there two, and is one better than the other?

Some components are CSS-only (buttons), others are JavaScript-only (infinite scroll), while some are both (tabs). CSS components provide a visual display to a component but have no real configuration or interactivity. JavaScript components provide more intelligent and interactive components, which may or may not build from a CSS component.

Some component types are implemented as CSS and JavaScript, such as tabs. You can consider using just the CSS features if you don't need the features provided by the JavaScript version. While Ionic is very fast, any time you can reduce the use of JavaScript, it can help keep the overhead low.

Also when a component has both CSS and JavaScript versions, you can use the same CSS classes on the JavaScript components to modify the appearance. For example, in this chapter, `ionNavBar` is using the CSS class to adjust the color.

4.3.3 Adding icons to the list items

The last thing you need to do for this view is add some icons. Ionic comes with a set of icons, called Ionicons, that are bundled by default. Icons are used in many places, so you'll see them frequently. You can view the available icons at http://ionicons.com. The icons are actually a font icon, which are custom fonts that replace standard characters with icons and use CSS classes to display the icons. If you'd like to use another font icon library (such as Font Awesome), you should be able to include that without conflicts.

The list component has a special display mode that uses icons. Using an extra CSS class and adding an icon element will generate the desired effect of having the icon displayed to the left of the text in the list item. Let's say you'd like the icon to be to the left of the text. You can finish the home view as you see in the following listing by adding some icons and updating the list item with a new class.

Listing 4.6   Add icons to home view (www/views/home/home.html)

```
<ion-view title="Aloha Resort" hide-back-button="true">
  <ion-content>
    <div class="list">
      <a href="#/reservation" class="item item-icon-left">
        <i class="icon ion-document-text"></i> See your reservation
      </a>
      <a href="#/weather" class="item item-icon-left">
        <i class="icon ion-ios-partlysunny"></i> Current weather
      </a>
      <a href="#/restaurants" class="item item-icon-left">
        <i class="icon ion-fork"></i> Nearby restaurants
      </a>
    </div>
  </ion-content>
</ion-view>
```

Adds item-icon-left class to get desired styling

Adds italics element using icon class with icon designation to transform it to icon

This is the most common way to include an icon, but because it's inside of a list, you need to use the special item-icon-left class to get the display you desire. You could also use item-icon-right to have the icons float to the right side.

Icons are often declared like this: <i class="icon ion-calendar"></i>. By default the italics element is an inline element that would modify the text inside. But you have no text inside, just two CSS classes. The first class, icon, gives the element the base CSS styles for an icon, and the second class, ion-calendar, provides the specific icon to display. Together, the inline element becomes an icon. You can see the icon and the entire home view in figure 4.5.

Now the home view is how you want it, so let's move on to the reservation view, and you'll learn how to display information using a controller.

4.4   *Using a controller and model for the reservation view*

Very often you'll need to add custom logic to your controller to handle loading data or interactions. The home view has no custom logic because it just shows a static list of links. But for the reservation view, you'll want to be able to load a user's specific data and display it. Because this is just an example, you don't have a real hotel database to use for loading data, but you can still use a controller to contain your data. If you're new to Angular, it's best to review the section in chapter 3 about controllers before continuing with this chapter. If you're following along using Git, you can check out the code for step4:

```
$ git checkout -f step4
```

Declaring a controller with Ionic follows the same pattern as for any Angular controller, like you saw in chapter 3. Remember, Ionic is built on top of Angular, so instead of having to provide its own framework, it uses Angular. You'll create this new controller, and inside it will contain the model for the reservation view. The result of these changes is shown in figure 4.6.

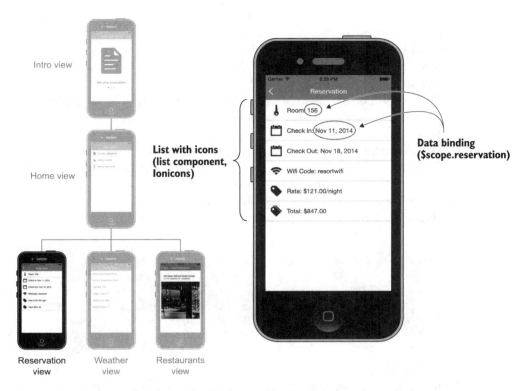

Figure 4.6 The reservation view, using bindings and loading data from the controller

You'll recall from chapter 3 that to create a model in Angular, you attach a value onto the $scope object. You'll attach an object with the properties describing a user's reservation details, such as the dates of arrival and departure, room number, and so forth. Take a look at the controller in the following listing. Add it to the views directory under www/views/reservation/reservation.js.

Listing 4.7   Reservation controller (www/views/reservation/reservation.js)

```
angular.module('App')                                          References App module
.controller('ReservationController', function ($scope) {
  $scope.reservation = {
    checkin: new Date(),
    checkout: new Date(Date.now() + 1000 * 60 * 60 * 24 * 7),
    room: 156,
    rate: 121,
    wifi: 'resortwifi'
  };
});
```

Setting dates for stay, automatically calculating today to next week

Setting other static values for reservation

Attaching model object called reservation to $scope

Declares controller, providing name and function; takes list of items to inject like $scope

This controller doesn't do a whole lot, but it does provide a place for you to hold your data and use Angular's binding features. You didn't do this on the home view because the list of items on the home view is very simple and unchanging. In this example, you can see how this information would change from user to user, and would be loaded here in the controller.

This controller needs a template like the home.html file to display information. The reservation view will have a list, similar to the home view, and include some icons in the template.

The major difference between this template and the home template is that you'll bind data from the controller into the template. The bindings will also use Angular filters, which is a very useful way to convert data from the model to a different display format. You'll also get to see a little bit of Angular expressions in action.

Listing 4.8 has the reservation view for the controller you just built.

Note about file organization

Now you may begin to see more clearly why I prefer to organize my files together by views—it helps to keep related parts together. Many Angular tutorials lump the JavaScript files in one place and the HTML templates in another, making it hard to keep track of related items. Later you'll also place CSS files in the folder for a view. Keeping all the files related to a single view in one location has improved my workflow greatly. I no longer spend precious time trying to find where the related code exists.

You're not required to follow my conventions, but they're my preferred conventions based on my years of building applications with Angular, and they're the conventions used in this book.

Listing 4.8   Reservation view template (www/views/reservation/reservation.html)

```
<ion-view view-title="Reservation">          ⟵  Declares view with title Reservation
  <ion-content>
    <div class="list">                       ⟵  Wraps list with list component class
      <div class="item item-icon-left">
        <i class="icon ion-key"></i> Room: {{reservation.room}}
      </div>

      <div class="item item-icon-left">
        <i class="icon ion-calendar"></i> Check In: {{reservation.checkin |
      date:'mediumDate'}}
      </div>

      <div class="item item-icon-left">
        <i class="icon ion-calendar"></i> Check Out: {{reservation.checkout |
      date:'mediumDate'}}
      </div>
```

Adds content wrapper to help with content display

A list item using a filter in binding, in this case formatting date

A list item with an icon; binds room value into template

```
        <div class="item item-icon-left">
          <i class="icon ion-wifi"></i> Wifi Code: {{reservation.wifi}}
        </div>
        <div class="item item-icon-left">
          <i class="icon ion-pricetag"></i> Rate: {{reservation.rate |
    currency}}/night
        </div>
        <div class="item item-icon-left">
          <i class="icon ion-pricetags"></i> Total: {{reservation.rate * 7 |
    currency}}
        </div>
      </div>
    </ion-content>
</ion-view>
```

A list item using a binding with an expression and filter

At first glance this may appear very similar to the home view, but you've used Angular bindings to add data from your model in the controller ($scope.reservation) and display it in the template. Binding is very common in Angular, and you'll likely use this frequently. Anything between the {{}} is evaluated as a special type of concept called an *Angular expression*. Angular expressions allow you to bind data from the $scope and even write math expressions that will be evaluated automatically. Refer to chapter 3 for a deeper explanation of Angular expressions and data binding.

Let's take a closer look at the example {{reservation.rate * 7 | currency}}. First there are two key parts, separated by the pipe character (|). On the left is the expression, and on the right is a filter. In the expression, you're able to do math by multiplying the daily rate by 7 to get the weekly rate. When an expression has a variable name, such as reservation.rate, it tries to resolve the value by looking at the $scope for that property. If it doesn't exist, the expression will fail and display nothing. Using a filter is optional, but here you use the built-in Angular currency filter, which takes a value and formats it for the local currency of the browser. It doesn't change the value of the reservation.rate property to include the currency sign; it just transforms it for the display.

While there are many other tricks and possibilities with expressions, the most common use is simply binding data to the view. You'll see them again in action with the weather view. Before we move to another view, you need to add this view to the application's state provider. At this point you have the files in place but haven't told the application about it. Open the app.js file again where you declared the first state, and add a new state as shown in the following listing. This will be placed right after the existing home view, and be sure that there's no semicolon between them.

Listing 4.9 Declaring the reservation state (www/js/app.js)

```
.state('reservation', {                              ⟵── Declares new state called reservation
    url: '/reservation',                             ⟵── Routes app using /reservation URL
    controller: 'ReservationController',             ⟵┐ Declares name of controller
    templateUrl: 'views/reservation/reservation.html'  ┘ used for this view
});
```

Declares view file to load ⟶

Great, now you have the view declared and everything should work, right? Not just yet—one easy-to-forget step is left. You're still building web applications, so you created a new JavaScript file but haven't yet added it to the index.html file to load. If you see errors in the JavaScript console that say the `ReservationController` is undefined, then either you haven't included that file in the app or there's a syntax error somewhere. Add this line to your index.html, right before the `</head>`:

```
<script src="views/reservation/reservation.js"></script>
```

Now you can run the app and tap on the reservation link to view the reservation details. It should appear like in figure 4.6. You'll notice the back button appears, and as you navigate to child views the back button will automatically show and hide. You've hidden it from the home view, so the child views like reservation will show the back button. Just a note: If you refresh the app while still on the reservation view, the back button will not appear. This is because it's like your first visit to the app, and there's no place to go back to in the history. If you get stuck, you can change the URL in the browser address bar to http://localhost:8100 to start over.

4.5   *Loading data into the weather view*

When you're at a tropical resort, it's good to know that the weather forecast is sunny and warm. You came for the beach, so it had better be beach weather! In this next view, you'll load weather data from an external service. There are many services that provide this data, but here you'll use Open Weather Map, which has a free and open API. Other services exist but may require an account or payment to load data. If you're following along using Git, check out `step5` for this section:

```
$ git checkout -f step5
```

Like the reservation view, you'll need an Angular controller. This controller will take care of loading the data from Open Weather Map, and then store it on your model so the view can bind data. You'll use the `$http` service from Angular to handle the data loading. I've also created an API that will proxy the request to Open Weather Map, and in case Open Weather Map goes down, my API will still run for you.

The view will be another list of items, such as current temperature and conditions, today's highs and lows, and wind speed and direction. I'll show you how you can use `$scope` methods in your template expressions to calculate information. In this case you'll take the wind direction that's given to you in number of degrees and convert that into a compass value such as North, East, South, and West.

Loading data from an external website can take some time. So far a view is displayed immediately upon navigation to that view, but in this case you can't show the weather data until it has loaded. This may take under a second, or in some cases a few seconds, depending on the speed of the connection, the server response speed, and other variables (many out of your control). To provide a better experience, I'll show you how to use the `$ionicLoading` service to display a loading indicator while the data loads.

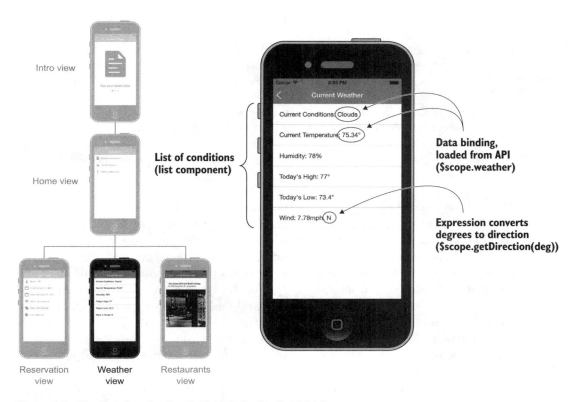

Figure 4.7   Weather view: loading (left) and after loading (right)

Figure 4.7 shows the result of the loading component in action and then a display of the local weather details.

You'll start by adding the template file, then add the controller and data-loading steps, and lastly implement the loading component.

4.5.1   Adding the template for the weather view

The template for the weather view is fairly simple—you just want to show a list of weather conditions. You'll create a list and bind the values for the data into it. This will be mostly familiar except for one new type of Angular expression that we'll cover.

Create a new file for the weather view at www/views/weather/weather.html, and add the code from the following listing.

Listing 4.10   Weather view template (www/views/weather/weather.html)

```
<ion-view view-title="Current Weather">        ◁——  Declares view and title for navbar
  <ion-content>                                ◁——  Wraps content in container
    <div class="list">
```

<table>
<tr><td>

Adds list items that bind to data properties of weather object

</td><td>

```
    <div class="item">Current Conditions:
    {{weather.weather[0].main}}</div>
    <div class="item">Current Temperature: {{weather.main.temp}}&deg;</div>
    <div class="item">Humidity: {{weather.main.humidity}}%</div>
    <div class="item">Today's High: {{weather.main.temp_max}}&deg;</div>
    <div class="item">Today's Low: {{weather.main.temp_min}}&deg;</div>
    <div class="item">Wind: {{weather.wind.speed}}mph,
    {{getDirection(weather.wind.deg)}}</div>
      </div>
    </ion-content>
</ion-view>
```

</td></tr>
</table>

> This item has two bindings; second one calls a method on the scope

Here you've created a new view and given it a title of "Current Weather," and used the content container to manage the position of the content area. The listing also uses the list CSS classes again, just to keep it simple, as a way to list the weather details.

This template has more complex bindings because the data returned by the Open Weather Map is formatted as a JSON string that's parsed into a JavaScript object by Angular. You can view the standard output of the weather data by viewing the Open Weather Map API in your browser at http://api.openweathermap.org/data/2.5/weather?q=London,uk. You can replace the London,uk value with any city to load data matching that query. If you review this output from the API, you can see the object and array items that you have to navigate to access specific data values. My API for this chapter is at https://ionic-in-action-api.herokuapp.com/weather and only returns weather information for one location. (If you're interested in how my API was built, you can view the source file at https://github.com/ionic-in-action/apis.)

I want to point out one more expression that's a little different from the rest. If you look at the last list item, you'll see {{getDirection(weather.wind.deg)}}. This expression will actually reference a method attached to the $scope in your controller. You haven't written this yet, but the method is called getDirection and takes a single parameter, which is the wind direction in degrees. You can use methods like this in an expression as part of your logic when necessary.

4.5.2   *Create weather controller to load external data*

Now you need to set up the controller and load some data. You'll use the $http service from Angular to load data from a URL. You'll inject the $http service into the controller, get a URL, and then handle the success or failure of the HTTP request. Open a new file for the controller at www/views/weather/weather.js and put the contents of the following listing inside.

Listing 4.11   Weather view controller (www/views/weather/weather.js)

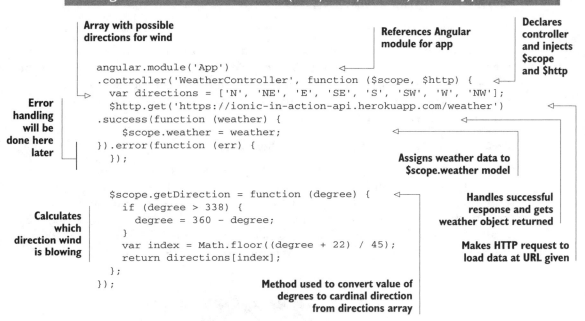

Array with possible directions for wind

References Angular module for app

Declares controller and injects $scope and $http

Error handling will be done here later

Calculates which direction wind is blowing

```
angular.module('App')
.controller('WeatherController', function ($scope, $http) {
  var directions = ['N', 'NE', 'E', 'SE', 'S', 'SW', 'W', 'NW'];
  $http.get('https://ionic-in-action-api.herokuapp.com/weather')
  .success(function (weather) {
    $scope.weather = weather;
  }).error(function (err) {
  });

  $scope.getDirection = function (degree) {
    if (degree > 338) {
      degree = 360 - degree;
    }
    var index = Math.floor((degree + 22) / 45);
    return directions[index];
  };
});
```

Assigns weather data to $scope.weather model

Handles successful response and gets weather object returned

Makes HTTP request to load data at URL given

Method used to convert value of degrees to cardinal direction from directions array

This controller will now automatically load the weather data every time a user loads the view. It's loaded into the $scope.weather model, so your template can then bind to that data. You can use the browser developer tools to inspect the response from the API to see what's been sent back. This is the most basic way to load data into your application from a URL.

We aren't handling the error yet in case the API doesn't send back data. This will be added in the next section, but you should always have an error handler with $http.

Then the getDirection method takes the number of degrees for the wind direction and returns one of the user-friendly values from the directions array. This would be more appropriately done as an Angular filter, but for the purposes of this example I used this approach.

You need to add this new view to the list of states, and also include the </script> tag for the new controller. Open the main app file and add another state to the end of the state list, as shown in the following listing.

Listing 4.12   Declare the weather view state (www/js/app.js)

```
.state('weather',
    {
  url: '/weather',
    controller: 'WeatherController',
  templateUrl: 'views/weather/weather.html'
});
```

Declares weather state; adds it to existing list

Adds URL, controller, and template values to define state

Then also add the </script> tag to load the weather controller into the index.html file, right before closing the </head> tag:

```
<script src="views/weather/weather.js"></script>
```

Now you can preview using `ionic serve` to view the app in its current state. Choose the weather link and it will open the weather view. You'll notice the view will load and the bindings will be empty for a brief moment until the data has loaded. This isn't very pretty, and could confuse users. Adding a loading indicator is important for the user experience, so let's do that now.

4.5.3　Adding a loading indicator to the weather view

The loading screen prevents a user from using the app until the loading has finished, so it's important to consider when this is appropriate or when it might unnecessarily stop the user from interacting with the app. If your app can't continue until data is loaded, then it's likely this component will come in handy. For example, if you're loading account data when the app opens, the loading component can display because the user can't act on the data yet. You can see the default display in figure 4.8.

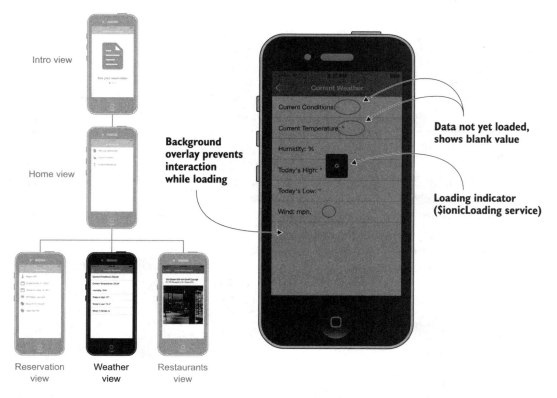

Figure 4.8　Weather view with loading indicator active while data is loaded from API

The loading component has two methods: `show()` and `hide()`. You'll have to tell the loading component when to use `hide()` because it will not automatically know when loading is finished. You can view all of the configuration options in the documentation.

In the example here, you'll want to show the loading indicator while the HTTP request is waiting to finish. You need to tell it to show right before you make the request, and then tell it to hide when the response is returned. The loader won't hide automatically because it's unable to determine when it's the correct time to hide automatically.

The loading component is implemented in the controller using JavaScript only, so open the weather controller again and update it as shown in the following listing (you'll only modify the relevant parts).

> **Listing 4.13 Add loading component to weather view (www/views/weather/weather.js)**

```
                                                                 Injects $ionicLoading
                                                                 service into controller
.controller('WeatherController', function ($scope, $http, $ionicLoading) {  ◁┘
  var directions = ['N', 'NE', 'E', 'SE', 'S', 'SW', 'W', 'NW'];

  $ionicLoading.show();                                         ◁─┐  Shows loading component
  $http.get('https://ionic-in-action-                              │  and calls it right before
    api.herokuapp.com/weather').success(function (weather) {      │  HTTP request starts
    $scope.weather = weather;
    $ionicLoading.hide();                                       ◁─    When response
  }).error(function (err) {                                            is successful,
    $ionicLoading.show({                                              hides loading
      template: 'Could not load weather. Please try again later.',   component
      duration: 3000
    });
  });
});
```

If there's an error, uses loader to display a message and closes after three seconds

Take a look at the updated controller now, and you'll notice how the loading component is shown and hidden based on when you tell it. You have to first inject the loading service (`$ionicLoading`) into your controller. Because Ionic's services are built on top of Angular, they're injected just like any other Angular service (like `$http`).

`show()` is used right before an asynchronous command is executed. HTTP requests made by JavaScript are always asynchronous, and the success or error methods allow you to choose what to do when the HTTP request has finished. Hopefully it will be successful and you just `hide()` the loading component, but in case of an error, you reconfigure the loading component to show an error message.

The second `show()` method will automatically close after three seconds because you're using it here to display an error. It accepts an object containing configuration values to modify the behavior, which you may wish to use to customize the loading message, for example.

There's only one loading component that can exist, so even though you call the show method twice, it just updates the already visible component with a new configuration. It doesn't create two loading components. This is important in cases where you have multiple asynchronous events happening; you'll have to design logic to properly choose when to hide the component. For example, if you're displaying a chart that has to load data from two separate HTTP requests, you'll have to decide if both requests have to finish before you hide the loading component, or if you want to hide it as soon as the first request finishes so you can chart the data immediately and add the second set of data when it finishes later.

You should also consider using other components to give users feedback about errors when they occur—we'll cover some in the next few chapters. You may want to do different things depending on the type of error; for example, if the weather API sends back a message saying it's temporarily down, you could try to reload the data again after waiting a moment.

Next up is the restaurants list view, and we'll spend some time looking at using cards and the infinite scrolling component.

4.6   *Infinite scroll with cards for the restaurants view*

In the restaurants view, you want to show a list of local restaurants that the resort guests might enjoy. To achieve this, you'll load a list of restaurants from an external website, display the name and image of each restaurant using the cards component, and use infinite scroll to allow more places to be loaded as a user reaches the bottom of the list.

Cards are really just a variation on lists, as you'll see in listing 4.14. The card component is used fairly often in many apps because it's good at displaying each item in a clean format with some nice visual depth. It's best used for displaying a piece of data with some visual separation from the rest of the content. If you're following along using Git, you can check out the step6 code:

```
$ git checkout -f step6
```

In this example you'll load the data from an API made just for this book, which contains actual restaurant data. You can see the view in figure 4.9, which has a list of cards, and as you scroll to the bottom, the infinite scroll loading indicator will appear while more items are loaded.

Each restaurant will display inside of its own card, which gives a nice visual experience. You can review all of the ways you can style cards in the documentation, but here you'll use a title and image in the cards. Start this view by creating the template in www/views/restaurants/restaurants.html as shown in the following listing.

> **Listing 4.14   Restaurants view template (www/views/restaurants/restaurants.html)**

Creates list of cards and ngRepeats over restaurants

```
<ion-view view-title="Local Restaurants">          ◁——— Declares view
  <ion-content>
    <div class="list card" ng-repeat="restaurant in restaurants">
```

```
    <div class="item">
      <h2>{{restaurant.name}}</h2>
      <p>{{restaurant.address}}, {{restaurant.city}}</p>
    </div>
    <div class="item item-image">
      <img ng-src="{{restaurant.image_url}}" />
    </div>
  </div>
  <ion-infinite-scroll on-infinite="getRestaurants()" ng-if="total > page"
    immediate-check="false"></ion-infinite-scroll>
  </ion-content>
</ion-view>
```

Card items show name and location of restaurant

Cards can use other list styles like image

Infinite scroll element will call getRestaurants() when within a certain distance of bottom, until reaches end of list

By adding the `card` class to the list item, you're able to create the card display. Each card is its own list, but you use `ngRepeat` to create a new card for each restaurant. The major difference here is the inclusion of the `ionInfiniteScroll` component.

Infinite scroll works by a fairly simple rule: If the component is within a certain distance of the view area (by default 1%), then it will call the method declared with the `on-infinite` attribute. Because initially the view won't have any restaurants, it will

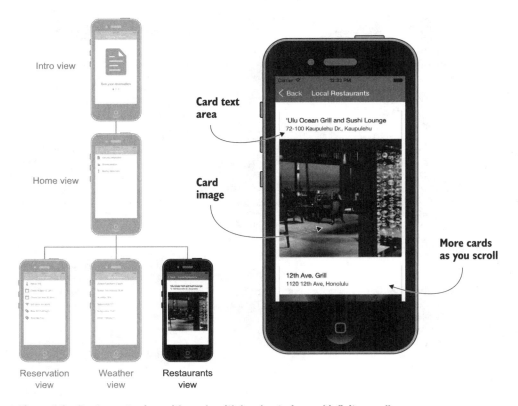

Figure 4.9 Restaurants view with cards with local eateries and infinite scroll

show a loading indicator and make a call to the getRestaurants() method to load the initial set. Once the request for data is complete, the infinite scroll component will hide the loading indicator and be pushed down the view below the list of items. Only when a user scrolls to the bottom will it be triggered again. Due to a quirky behavior of infinite scroll, it can actually call the method twice on loading. To fix this, disable infinite scroll from loading initially by setting the immediate-check attribute to false, and you'll have the controller load the data.

The infinite scroll component will continue to request data as long as it returns and any time it becomes visible. But when there are no more items to load, you want to stop the component from loading anymore. The ngIf statement is how you'll disable infinite scroll when you reach the end of your available data from the service. You'll handle the logic in this controller, but the API is returning a value that indicates how many pages of data are available so you can check that against how many have already loaded.

Now you need to add a controller for your view. This controller will need to handle the loading of the restaurants data, and it will also inform the infinite scroll component when new data is loaded so it can hide itself. The code in the following listing shows the controller code you should put into www/views/restaurants/restaurants.js.

Listing 4.15   Restaurants view controller (www/views/restaurants/restaurants.js)

```
angular.module('App')
.controller('RestaurantsController', function ($scope, $http) {

    $scope.page = 0;
    $scope.total = 1;
    $scope.restaurants = [];

    $scope.getRestaurants = function () {
      $scope.page++;
      $http.get('https://ionic-in-action-api.herokuapp.com/
       restaurants?age=' + $scope.page).success(function (response) {
        angular.forEach(response.restaurants, function (restaurant) {
          $scope.restaurants.push(restaurant);
        });

        $scope.total = response.totalPages;
        $scope.$broadcast('scroll.infiniteScrollComplete');
      }).error(function (err) {
        $scope.$broadcast('scroll.infiniteScrollComplete');
        console.log(err);
      });
    };

    $scope.getRestaurants();
});
```

Creates controller and inject services

❶ Creates some scope variables for view

❸ Increments page value and makes an HTTP request for data

❷ Defines method that will load restaurants

❹ Takes list of restaurants and adds them to restaurants array for ngRepeat

❺ Updates total pages based on value sent by API

❻ Broadcasts event that will tell infinite scroll component everything is done

❼ Handles errors by broadcasting infinite scroll and logging error

❽ Loads first page of restaurants from API on loading

Listing 4.15 started with three variables ❶: page, `total`, and `restaurants`. You use the page variable to track the last page that was requested from the API, and `total` stores the total number of pages available from the API (which you get after the first API call). You also set a blank array for `restaurants`, which will be used by ngRepeat to create the list of restaurants.

Like the weather controller, you need to call your API to load data. It's inside of a scope method called getRestaurants() ❷ because you'll be calling it repeatedly. Every time infinite scroll needs to load more data, it calls getRestaurants(). It first increments the page value ❸ and makes the HTTP request. Once the data is returned, you push each of the results into the `restaurants` array ❹ to add them to the end. It also sets the `total` value ❺ with the number of pages available.

When infinite scroll is triggered and calls getRestaurants(), it doesn't know when the HTTP request has finished loading. You're able to tell it everything is done by using the `$scope.$broadcast('scroll.infiniteScrollComplete')` call ❻, which sends a message to the component to complete. When this event is called, infinite scroll will stop showing the loading animation; otherwise, if you fail to call it, the animation will continue to run. You also handle possible errors ❼ by logging the error to the console and also telling the component to complete. The last thing you do is kick off the initial load of data ❽ by calling getRestaurants().

Before you can see this in action, you need to add your view to the states. Like usual, the app.js file must be updated with a new state for the restaurants view:

```
.state('restaurants', {
  url: '/restaurants',
  controller: 'RestaurantsController',
  templateUrl: 'views/restaurants/restaurants.html'
});
```

Also, the new controller file needs to be loaded in the app index.html file:

```
<script src="views/restaurants/restaurants.js"></script>
```

Now you can run the app and view the list of restaurants displayed in a card list. The last goal is to add an introduction to the app, which will include a set of slides that give a brief introduction and tour of what the app is about. Let's look at how to use a slidebox component and build out this tour!

4.7 Using the slidebox component for app intro tour

The resort wants to make sure that the first time someone uses the app, the user is able to see a quick tour of what the app can do. There are many ways to do this, but here you'll use the ionSlideBox component to show a simple slideshow of the three primary features. If you're following along using Git, you can check out the code for step7 to complete the example:

```
$ git checkout -f step7
```

Slideboxes are used in many places and many ways. They're great for showing items in a list that you can swipe between, such as a list of images for a product, or to have a rotating view of suggested items. The slidebox is able to automatically run like a slideshow or allow a user to swipe between items.

The $ionSlideBoxDelegate service can be used to programmatically control the slidebox. For example, you could have a button that could use the slidebox service to force the slidebox to go to a particular slide. This service isn't used here, but it's helpful in cases where you need to add more control to how the slidebox operates. It's also possible that you might use the slidebox multiple ways on the same view, and in that case you can control each way independently. The slidebox service is able to name each slidebox instance and then target each individually.

In this example, the tour will show three slides using the slidebox. You'll apply a little bit of extra CSS to make the display work as intended, because by default things will only size to the default size of the content and you want the slides to be full-screen. You can see the slidebox in action in figure 4.10.

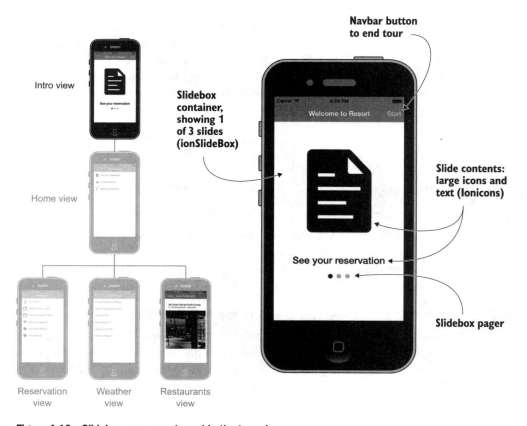

Figure 4.10   Slidebox component used in the tour view

Let's take a look at how to add a slidebox, which in many cases uses just markup to display the component. The following listing shows the template for your view that you should put into a new file at www/views/tour/tour.html.

Listing 4.16   Tour view template (www/views/tour/tour.html)

Declares view and gives ID so you can target CSS →

```
<ion-view view-title="Welcome to Aloha Resort" id="tour-view">
    <ion-nav-buttons side="right">
      <a class="button button-clear" href="#/home" nav-clear>Start</a>
    </ion-nav-buttons>
```

Adds button to navbar that allows user to go to home view

ionSlideBox acts as content wrapper and slidebox container using pager →

```
    <ion-slide-box show-pager="true">

      <ion-slide>
        <span class="icon icon-slide ion-document-text"></span>
        <h3>See your reservation</h3>
      </ion-slide>
      <ion-slide>
        <span class="icon icon-slide ion-fork"></span>
        <h3>Find local restaurants</h3>
      </ion-slide>
      <ion-slide>
        <span class="icon icon-slide ion-ios-sunny"></span>
        <h3>Get the weather</h3>
      </ion-slide>
    </ion-slide-box>
</ion-view>
```

Each ionSlide is automatically added as a new slide to slidebox

The names of the tags for the slidebox are very clear, which helps developers understand what's happening. The slidebox will have three slides, and each contains an icon and a header tag with some information about the app. The slidebox will only be as large as the content inside of it is calculated, and right now because the icon and header tags are standard HTML elements, they'll only make the slidebox as tall as the text itself.

You'll want to enhance this with some CSS styling. In this example there's an id added to the ionView, which will be used next when you add some CSS. I find it helpful to prefix CSS by view so I can ensure that my styles won't affect other areas of the app. But you can write your CSS selectors however you prefer.

Now it's time to add that CSS to the app. You have three style blocks to add to give the tour the design you want. Create the www/views/tour/tour.css file, and add the contents of the following listing.

Listing 4.17   CSS for tour view (www/views/tour/tour.css)

```
#tour-view .slider {
  height: 100%;
}
```

Styles to make slider full height

```
#tour-view .slider-slide {
  padding-top: 100px;
  text-align: center;
}
```
Provides padding for top of slide and center content

```
#tour-view .icon-slide {
  font-size: 20em;
  display: inline-block;
}
```
Makes icons large and displays them as inline blocks

Make sure you add a reference to it in the www/index.html file to load the styles, as follows:

```
<link href="views/tour/tour.css" rel="stylesheet">
```

The CSS here makes the icons large and centers the content, as well as makes the slidebox full height. This is helpful so a user can swipe on the whole screen (except the header bar) to change the current slide; otherwise, the user would have to swipe on only the content itself. You could improve or modify this styling to suit your own needs, and depending on the content that you displayed it might change dramatically.

The last step for the app is to update the state with the new tour view, and then you want to change the default state to the tour for when the app is first opened. Open again the app.js file and you'll add a new state, and change the default `otherwise` route as shown in the following listing.

> **Listing 4.18   Tour state and update default route (www/js/app.js)**

```
.state('tour', {
  url: '/tour',
  templateUrl: 'views/tour/tour.html'
});

$urlRouterProvider.otherwise('/tour');
```
Adds tour state with route and template

Changes the otherwise route to go to the tour state

With that, the app is complete! If you launch the app from scratch, it will now first take you to the tour, and then you can go to the home view. If you've been using the live reload feature this entire time, you may not be redirected to the tour. If that's the case, clear the value after the pound symbol in the URL so it's just /#/. This will reset the route and take you to the tour.

4.8   *Chapter challenges*

Now that you've learned a lot about how to build a navigable interface for your mobile app, here are a few challenges to improve the chapter example into a more comprehensive app:

- *Add a new state*—Try to add a new state to the app. For example, add another state with a view containing directions to the resort.
- *Improve the design*—Get creative and improve the display of the weather view. Look at weather apps for some inspiration.

- *Implement the wind direction filter*—In the weather view, replace `getDirection()` in the scope with a filter that can take a degree number and return a string.
- *Cache weather data*—Instead of always requesting new weather data, find a way to cache and only reload the weather if it's more than 15 minutes old. Consider using `localStorage` to store the data.
- *Create a weather service*—This demo uses `$http` in the controller to load data. Try to build an Angular service for loading of weather data so the controller doesn't use `$http` directly.

4.9 Summary

In this chapter we covered the primary means for navigation inside Ionic apps and a number of the components available. Let's review the major topics covered in this chapter:

- Ionic apps are built around the idea of states. States are declared in the `config()` method using `$stateProvider`.
- Ionic loads your templates inside of the `ionNavView` component when the state changes.
- The `ionNavBar` tag automatically can update the title of the navbar based on the current view.
- The list and card components are mobile-friendly ways to display lists of content.
- You can load data using the `$http` service into your controller, and use the `$ionicLoading` service to show a loading indicator while it loads.
- The `ionSlideBox` is a fully featured slideshow component for a mobile interface, and you used it in this chapter as an app introductory tour.

In chapter 5 you'll learn about using tabs for your app navigation, along with a number of other Ionic features, such as pull-to-refresh, advanced lists, and forms.

Tabs, advanced lists, and form components

5

This chapter covers

- Using the tabs component with individual navigation histories
- Displaying a list of items that can be toggled and reordered
- Setting up pull-to-refresh to reload data
- Using several mobile form input controls

This chapter continues our look at many of Ionic's features, and just like in chapter 4, you'll build a complete app from start to finish. You'll build a mobile app to show current market and historical chart data for Bitcoin in many different currencies. The interface will leverage the Ionic tabs component to have three tabs: to view current market rates, to view a chart of historical rates, and for currency management.

You'll learn more about how to have a navigation window inside each tab. This is important when you want to create rich experiences with tabs that maintain the user interface state between tabs. Also when you load data from an external source, the data is cached even if you change between tabs, improving speed and avoiding unnecessary HTTP requests.

What is Bitcoin?

Bitcoin is a popular digital cryptocurrency. It has a buy and sell price, much like a stock or commodity, and is exchanged via digital marketplaces. For the purposes of this chapter, you're mostly interested in the current price of Bitcoin compared to traditional currencies (such as US dollars or Euros), and also in visualizing the price history over the past month.

You can read more about Bitcoin and the technology that powers it at https://bitcoin.org.

In figure 5.1 you see the app that you'll create. You'll show the current rates for Bitcoin in several currencies, which will compare the price over the past 24 hours to indicate if it's trending positively or negatively. Then you'll show the historical price, averaged hourly, over the past month. You'll use a third-party library to generate the chart. Lastly, the currencies that are displayed in the app can be configured by toggling them to show or hide them, as well as reordered so your favorite currencies are at the top.

The entire example is available on GitHub at https://github.com/ionic-in-action/chapter5. The example is also live at https://ionic-in-action-chapter5.herokuapp.com.

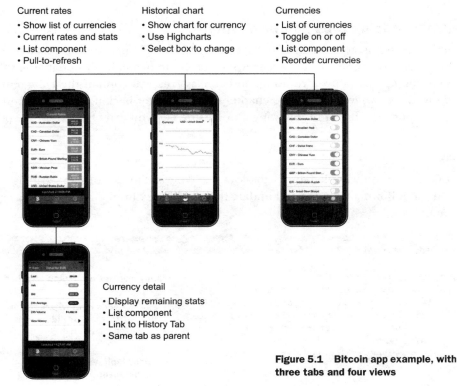

Current rates
- Show list of currencies
- Current rates and stats
- List component
- Pull-to-refresh

Historical chart
- Show chart for currency
- Use Highcharts
- Select box to change

Currencies
- List of currencies
- Toggle on or off
- List component
- Reorder currencies

Currency detail
- Display remaining stats
- List component
- Link to History Tab
- Same tab as parent

Figure 5.1   Bitcoin app example, with three tabs and four views

5.1   Set up chapter project

You can follow along in this chapter either by creating a new Ionic app and adding the code from the listings in this chapter, or by cloning the finished app from the *Ionic in Action* GitHub repository and following along with each step. At the end, use ionic serve to preview the app in a browser.

5.1.1   Create a new app and add code manually

To create a new project for the app using the Ionic command-line interface (CLI) utility, open the command line and execute the following command (remember, you can refer to chapter 2 if you need a refresher on how projects are set up):

```
$ ionic start chapter5 https://github.com/ionic-in-action/starter
$ cd chapter5
$ ionic serve
```

5.1.2   Clone the finished app and follow along

To check out the finished app and use Git, use the following command to clone the repository and check out the first step:

```
$ git clone https://github.com/ionic-in-action/chapter5.git
$ cd chapter5
$ git checkout -f step1
$ ionic serve
```

5.2   ionTabs: adding tabs and navigation

Your first task is to add in the base navigational elements: the ionNavBar and ionNavView components. ionNavBar will be useful to dynamically update the title bar depending on the tab you're using, and ionNavView will contain the tabs template. You saw these two working in the chapter 4 app, so refer back if you need a refresher on their purpose. If you're following along using Git, you can check out the code for this step:

```
$ git checkout -f step2
```

In this section you'll implement the basic tabs and navigation, as you can see in figure 5.2.

In the following listing, you'll update the www/index.html file with the navigation components.

> **Listing 5.1   Adding `ionNavBar` and `ionNavView` (www/index.html)**

Adds ionNavBar component and gives it a style

```
<body ng-app="App">                                          <-- body element has ngApp attached to it
  <ion-nav-bar class="bar-positive">
    <ion-nav-back-button class="button-clear">
      <i class="ion-chevron-left"></i> Back
    </ion-nav-back-button>
  </ion-nav-bar>
  <ion-nav-view></ion-nav-view>
</body>
```

Adds ionNavBackButton to show or hide during navigation

Adds ionNavView component

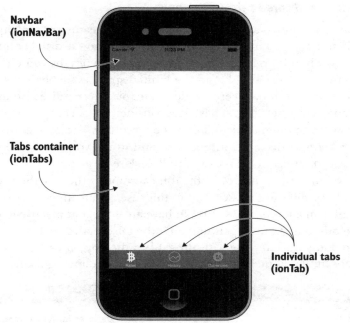

Navbar
(ionNavBar)

Tabs container
(ionTabs)

Individual tabs
(ionTab)

Figure 5.2   App with tabs, base navigation, and blank content

This places the components into your templates so they'll be able to render your routes. The `ionNavBackButton` component is in place for later when you have a view that can navigate into child views. Now you have to declare a route and a template before anything will appear.

Open the www/js/app.js file so you can declare your first route. Modify the existing contents to add the `config()` method as in the following listing.

Listing 5.2   Add first route to app `config()` method (www/js/app.js)

Declares App module and includes ionic module

Declares config() method and injects services

Sets default route

Declares a single state for tabs

```
angular.module('App', ['ionic'])
.config(function ($stateProvider, $urlRouterProvider) {
  $stateProvider
    .state('tabs', {
      url: '/tabs',
      templateUrl: 'views/tabs/tabs.html'
    });
  $urlRouterProvider.otherwise('/tabs');
})
```

Now you have your route declared and a default route set when no other matches are found. Before you can preview the app, you need to add the `tabs` template.

5.2.1   *Adding tabs container and three tabs to the app*

Tabs are very common in mobile apps, and Ionic provides a feature-rich component for you to create them quickly. Tabs are commonly used to show a visual connection between several views. There's no actual limit on the number of tabs you could use, but typically two to five tabs are used due to the limited space available. Tabs can be used nearly anywhere in your app, except inside of an ionContent directive due to a CSS collision that can occur when ionTabs is placed inside ionContent.

Ionic provides two components for building your own tabs: ionTabs and ionTab. Much like ionSlideBox, you declare ionTabs first, and inside you can have as many ionTab components as you need. In this case, you'll declare three tabs.

The tabs can have an icon, a title, or both. You can modify the way the titles and icons appear by applying different classes, and in this case, you'll apply a class to have the title show with an icon above it. Tabs also can have an active and inactive icon state for which you'll use different icons depending on if the tab is active or not.

Now it's time to add your template with the tabs to the app. Create a new file at www/views/tabs/tabs.html and include the content from the following listing.

Listing 5.3   tabs template (www/views/tabs/tabs.html)

> Declares ionTabs component to wrap all tabs and gives it a class to modify title and icon display

```
<ion-tabs class="tabs-icon-top tabs-positive">
  <ion-tab title="Rates" icon-on="ion-social-bitcoin" icon-off=
    "ion-social-bitcoin-outline">
  </ion-tab>
  <ion-tab title="History" icon-on="ion-ios-analytics" icon-off=
    "ion-ios-analytics-outline">
  </ion-tab>
  <ion-tab title="Currencies" icon-on="ion-ios-cog" icon-off=
    "ion-ios-cog-outline">
  </ion-tab>
</ion-tabs>
```

> Declares tabs with titles and icons for active and inactive states

---

Tabs are really pretty simple to declare, with title the only attribute you must declare for each tab. Right now your tabs are empty, but if you preview the app in the browser you'll see the tabs along the bottom like in figure 5.2. You can click on each tab and see the icon state change to indicate the active tab.

Before you start to add content into your tabs, you need to set up each tab with its own ionNavView.

5.3   *Adding ionNavView for each tab*

Your tabs are empty, and you want to use additional ionNavView components to load your components. This will allow each of the tabs to maintain its own navigational history. It allows you to use a back button that's only for a given tab instead of the whole app. In figure 5.3 you can see how the user experience would flow with each tab having its own navigational history. If you're following along using Git, you can check out the code for this step:

```
$ git checkout -f step3
```

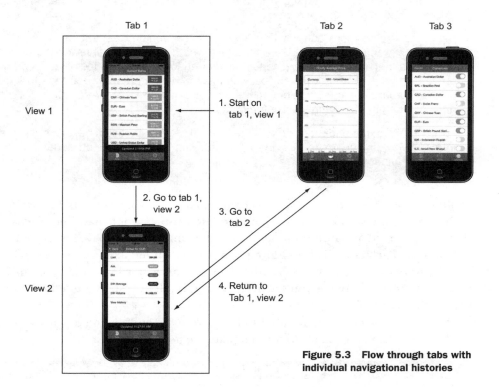

Figure 5.3 Flow through tabs with individual navigational histories

Tabs don't require individual views

Tabs can contain any content you wish to put inside. Essentially a tabbed interface is really just one large view that has only one tab displayed at once, with the other tabs in a hidden state. It would be similar to having several pages of paper stacked on top of one another, and at any time you can move a lower page to the top so it's visible.

The technique of using the `ionNavView` element inside of each tab gives you one major benefit. Each tab is able to have its own history. So instead of a stack of papers, it's now more like a stack of books where the topmost book is open to a particular page, and if you switched books you'd bookmark that page and return to the exact same spot later.

(continued)

Essentially it boils down to how you use the tabs. I'd classify two primary use cases: tabs for providing navigation, and tabs for fitting more content in a single view.

When using tabs for navigation, adding individual views is useful. This chapter example will demonstrate this use case.

Using tabs to fit more content into a single view wouldn't benefit from individual views. For example, you could use tabs in a weather app for displaying the current conditions. Because the current condition information is likely loaded all at once from an API, and the information is logically connected, you'd probably use tabs to separate the information into simpler chunks. Imagine there were three tabs: current conditions, weather map, and 10-day forecast.

My general recommendation is that if the content of the tabs could be logically placed into one view and controller, then you probably don't want to use individual `ionNav-View` components.

You'll start by adding the `ionNavView` components into your tabs. You'll have to give each one a name so they can be identified later. You can only have one `ionNavView` that's not named in your Ionic app, and the unnamed `ionNavView` is always the default view. Each tab will also be given a `ui-sref` attribute that will turn the tab icons into buttons to navigate between tabs. This section won't look drastically different when you preview it, but as you see in figure 5.4, it will now show a title in the header bar for the active tab.

Open the www/views/tabs/tabs.html template file and update to what you see in the following listing. Updates to this template are in bold.

Listing 5.4   `tabs` template with individual views (www/views/tabs/tabs.html)

```
<ion-tabs class="tabs-icon-top tabs-positive">
  <ion-tab title="Rates" icon-on="ion-social-bitcoin" icon-off=
    "ion-social-bitcoin-outline" ui-sref="tabs.rates">
    <ion-nav-view name="rates-tab"></ion-nav-view>
  </ion-tab>

  <ion-tab title="History" icon-on="ion-ios-analytics" icon-off=
    "ion-ios-analytics-outline" ui-sref="tabs.history">
    <ion-nav-view name="history-tab"></ion-nav-view>
  </ion-tab>
  <ion-tab title="Currencies" icon-on="ion-ios-cog" icon-off=
    "ion-ios-cog-outline" ui-sref="tabs.currencies">
    <ion-nav-view name="currencies-tab"></ion-nav-view>
  </ion-tab>
</ion-tabs>
```

Adds ui-sref to change view on tab selection

Defines and names ionNavView for each tab

This adds three new `ionNavView` components with a different name. The `ui-sref` attributes act like a normal `href` attribute to link to a particular state based on the

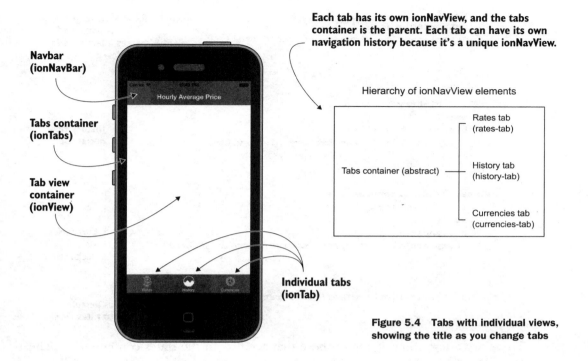

Figure 5.4 Tabs with individual views, showing the title as you change tabs

name, so instead of having a URL, you have a state name. Even though only one of these three views will be visible, all three will be part of the same parent tabs view.

Now you need to add routes to the config() that will support these new views. Ui-router has a feature called *nested states* that allows you to declare states with a hierarchy. In this case, the tabs route that displays the tabs is like the root state, and each tab is a child state underneath it. This is helpful when you need to logically organize states and helps the Ionic navigation components understand your app's navigational structure. You need to update the app config() with the new states and modify the tabs state as well. The following listing has the updated states configuration with updates bolded.

Listing 5.5 App `config()` with tab child states (www/js/app.js)

```
.config(function ($stateProvider, $urlRouterProvider) {
  $stateProvider
    .state('tabs', {
      url: '/tabs',
      abstract: true,
      templateUrl: 'views/tabs/tabs.html'
    })

    .state('tabs.rates', {
      url: '/rates',
```

❶ Updates tabs state to be abstract because you always want to use a child

❷ Declares tabs.rates state using dot notation for parent.child relationship

❸ Declares URL for route; it's a child route, so it appends this to URL of parent

```
      views: {
        'rates-tab': {
          templateUrl: 'views/rates/rates.html'
        }
      }
    })
    .state('tabs.history', {
      url: '/history',
      views: {
        'history-tab': {
          templateUrl: 'views/history/history.html'
        }
      }
    })
    .state('tabs.currencies', {
      url: '/currencies',
      views: {
        'currencies-tab': {
          templateUrl: 'views/currencies/currencies.html'
        }
      }
    });
  $urlRouterProvider.otherwise('/tabs/rates');
})
```

❹ Rates view targets view with this name and passes a template for that view

History view declaration

Currencies view declaration

❺ Updates default route to rates view

There are a few things going on here that are new in the states configuration. The tabs route ❶ now has the `abstract: true` property set, which makes it possible to declare it as a parent but doesn't allow it to be an active state.

The rates state has the name declared with `tabs.rates` ❷. This is to indicate the parent and child relationship they have. The URL is also declared here ❸, but take note that when you have a parent-child relationship, the URL is actually appended to the end of the parent URL. The rates view URL is actually found at /tabs/rates and not just /rates. Lastly, subviews of the state ❹ are declared. The view must be named the same as the name you gave to the `ionNavView` earlier, in this case `rates-tab`. The app now knows that when the rates tab is active, it should inject the specified template into that view. Later you'll declare other view properties such as controllers.

Lastly, the code updates the default route from /tabs to /tabs/rates ❺. This is because in the tabs you always want to be on one of the tabs, so the tabs container state is abstract. If you attempt to go to the tabs route (/tabs), it will now redirect you to the default rates view.

The last task in this section is to add the basic templates for each of the three tabs. You've already declared them in your states using the `templateUrl` property in the view. The next three listings contain simple templates with a view and title for each tab.

Listing 5.6   Rates tab basic template (www/views/rates/rates.html)

```
<ion-view view-title="Current Rates">
  <ion-content>
  </ion-content>
</ion-view>
```

> **Listing 5.7   History tab basic template (www/views/history/history.html)**

```
<ion-view view-title="Hourly Average Price">
  <ion-content>
  </ion-content>
</ion-view>
```

> **Listing 5.8   Currencies tab basic template (www/views/currencies/currencies.html)**

```
<ion-view view-title="Currencies">
  <ion-content>
  </ion-content>
</ion-view>
```

These templates are blank for the moment, but you'll update each one individually in the following sections. If you preview the app in your browser, you'll be able to see the title changing as you change tabs on the bottom. This finishes what you need to do with tabs, so let's get to work on creating the first tab and showing the current Bitcoin rates.

5.4   *Loading and displaying current Bitcoin rates*

Your app is all about showing information about Bitcoin, and the first tab is about showing the current market price for Bitcoin in different currencies. You'll use a free service from the BitcoinAverage API (https://bitcoinaverage.com) that provides near-real-time rates and histori-cal rates as well. It does this by averaging current market rates for Bitcoin across mul-tiple exchanges, and the exchanges vary by currency. If you're following along using Git, you can check out the code for this step:

```
$ git checkout -f step4
```

In this section you'll wire up the loading of the live data and display it in your tab. In figure 5.5 you can see the result of your work from this section. The date will appear with the last updated time for the results and the list of currencies will display the current prices and trend.

Figure 5.5   Rates tab with data loading for current Bitcoin prices shown in a `list` component

To help facilitate your list of currencies, you'll first create a `Currencies` service. It's very simple—just an array of the supported currencies for your app—but because it will be a service, you'll be able to reuse it in multiple parts of your app.

Open the www/js/app.js file and add the code from the following listing to the end of the file. Watch for syntax errors if the line before has a semicolon.

> **Listing 5.9 Currencies data service (www/js/app.js)**

Registers a service using Angular's factory method

Creates array of currencies and sets default selected state for each

```
.factory('Currencies', function () {
  return [
    { code: 'AUD', text: 'Australian Dollar', selected: true },
    { code: 'BRL', text: 'Brazilian Real', selected: false },
    { code: 'CAD', text: 'Canadian Dollar', selected: true },
    { code: 'CHF', text: 'Swiss Franc', selected: false },
    { code: 'CNY', text: 'Chinese Yuan', selected: true},
    { code: 'EUR', text: 'Euro', selected: true },
    { code: 'GBP', text: 'British Pound Sterling', selected: true },
    { code: 'IDR', text: 'Indonesian Rupiah', selected: false },
    { code: 'ILS', text: 'Israeli New Sheqel', selected: false },
    { code: 'MXN', text: 'Mexican Peso', selected: true },
    { code: 'NOK', text: 'Norwegian Krone', selected: false },
    { code: 'NZD', text: 'New Zealand Dollar', selected: false },
    { code: 'PLN', text: 'Polish Zloty', selected: false },
    { code: 'RON', text: 'Romanian Leu', selected: false },
    { code: 'RUB', text: 'Russian Ruble', selected: true },
    { code: 'SEK', text: 'Swedish Krona', selected: false },
    { code: 'SGD', text: 'Singapore Dollar', selected: false },
    { code: 'USD', text: 'United States Dollar', selected: true },
    { code: 'ZAR', text: 'South African Rand', selected: false }
  ];
});
```

This `Currencies` service is an array containing a list of objects containing information about the currency. The code is the standard code for the currency, the text is the name of the currency, and the selected property is used to determine if that currency should be shown or not in the list. You'll make that configurable later, but by default some are set to `false` to disable them. Now that you've created and registered this service, you'll be able to use it anywhere in your app.

The first place you'll use the `Currencies` service is in a controller for the rates view. This controller will take care of loading the current rates from the BitcoinAverage API. Once it's loaded, it will attach the data onto the `Currencies` service, and that data will be made available on the scope. The following listing has the rates tab controller for www/views/rates/rates.js.

Listing 5.10   Rates tab controller (www/views/rates/rates.js)

Declares RatesController and injects services used

Immediately sets data from Currencies service on scope

```
angular.module('App')
  .controller('RatesController', function ($scope, $http, Currencies) {

    $scope.currencies = Currencies;

    $scope.load = function () {
      $http.get('https://api.bitcoinaverage.com/ticker/all').success(
        function (tickers) {
          angular.forEach($scope.currencies, function (currency) {
            currency.ticker = tickers[currency.code];
            currency.ticker.timestamp = new Date(currency.ticker.timestamp);
          });
        });
    };

    $scope.load();
  });
```

scope method to load data that can be called on demand

Converts timestamp from response to valid JavaScript date object

Loops over list of currencies and stores ticker data on Currencies service

Makes HTTP request to BitcoinAverage for current rates

Triggers a load when controller is first loaded

This controller takes care of loading the data when the load() method is called, using the $http service. The Currencies service is injected and stored on the scope, which your view will use to display all of the data. You also store the current rates on the Currencies service, which will come in handy later. This is a single data object that you'll pass around and use multiple times in other places. While you could use other techniques for sharing data, this approach works well for this particular situation.

All right, so you have the ability to load your data, but now you'd like to display it on the screen. It's time to update your template to loop over the currencies and display the data loaded by the controller. Open the www/views/rates/rates.html file and update it as you see in the following listing.

Listing 5.11   Rates tab template with currency data (www/views/rates/rates.html)

```
<ion-view view-title="Current Rates">
  <ion-content>
    <ion-list>
      <ion-item ng-repeat="currency in currencies | filter:{selected:true}">
        {{currency.code}} - {{currency.text}}
        <span class="price" ng-if="currency.ticker.last ==
currency.ticker['24h_avg']">
          {{currency.ticker.last || '0.00'}}<br />0.00
        </span>
```

❶ **ngRepeat to loop over currencies and filter out any that aren't active**

❷ **Price box shown when current price equal to 24-hour average**

Price box shown when current price below 24-hour average ❸

Price box shown when current price above 24-hour average ❹

```
      <span class="price negative" ng-if="currency.ticker.last <
    currency.ticker['24h_avg']">
        {{currency.ticker.last}}<br /><span class="icon ion-arrow-down-
    b"></span> {{currency.ticker['24h_avg'] - currency.ticker.last |
    number:2}}
      </span>
      <span class="price positive" ng-if="currency.ticker.last >
    currency.ticker['24h_avg']">
        {{currency.ticker.last}}<br /><span class="icon ion-arrow-up-
    b"></span> {{currency.ticker.last - currency.ticker['24h_avg'] |
    number:2}}
      </span>
    </ion-item>
  </ion-list>
</ion-content>
<ion-footer-bar class="bar-dark">
  <h1 class="title">Updated {{currencies[0].ticker.timestamp |
    date:'mediumTime'}}</h1>
</ion-footer-bar>
</ion-view>
```

ionFooterBar to keep a ❺ footer bar with last time data was loaded

This template has quite a bit going on, so let's start from the top. The list compo-nent is used here, and then ngRepeat to create a list item for each currency ❶. But in the ngRepeat there's a filter, unfortunately named filter (don't blame me, it's part of Angular), which removes any of the currencies that have the selected property set to false. Later, you'll make a configuration view that allows you to toggle currencies on or off, so this property is already filtering by the default settings in the Currencies service.

Inside of each of the items you bind some text, and then there are three span ele-ments with ngIf on them ❷, ❸, ❹. These are for displaying the current price and the trend compared to the past 24-hour average. There are three possible situations: the price is equal, higher, or lower than the 24-hour average. Only one of the three span elements will display, based on the current price and average calculation.

After the list, you can see the ionFooterBar ❺ is placed after the end of ionContent. The two components are aware of one another and aware of the tabs, so the footer is positioned above the tabs automatically and the content area is also sized based on the footer and tab bars at the bottom. This is important so the scrolling area is the correct size, but it's automatically handled for you by Ionic when you use these directives together.

You have to add some CSS to make your price boxes look correct, because Ionic doesn't have a component built for this exact purpose. Add the CSS from the fol-lowing listing and place it in the www/css/styles.css file.

Listing 5.12   Price box styling (www/css/styles.css)

```
.item .price {
  font-weight: bold;
  font-size: 13px;
  color: #fff;
```

CSS rules for all price boxes

```
    position: absolute;
    background: #666;
    right: 15px;
    height: 42px;
    top: 5px;                                      CSS rules for
    width: 80px;                                   all price boxes
    text-align: center;
    padding: 6px;
    line-height: 1.2em;
}
.item .price.positive {
    background: #66cc33;                           CSS to change background
}                                                  color for positive change
.item .price.negative {
    background: #ef4e3a;                           CSS to change background
}                                                  color for negative change
```

This CSS is modeled somewhat on the badges from Ionic, but the badges aren't able to handle multiple lines. This is all of the custom CSS you'll use for this app, so I've left it in the general styles.css file.

Okay, you're almost done, you just need to add the controller to your state declaration and include the JavaScript file into the index.html file. Open the www/index.html file and add the `</script>` tag for your controller before closing the `</head>` tag after all other JavaScript files that are declared:

```
<script src="views/rates/rates.js"></script>
```

Lastly, you need to add the controller to your state, so open www/js/app.js and modify the state, as you see in bold, to add the controller for the rates tab view:

```
.state('tabs.rates', {
  url: '/rates',
  views: {
    'rates-tab': {
      templateUrl: 'views/rates/rates.html',
      controller: 'RatesController'
    }
  }
})
```

Now if you reload the app in your browser, you should see the current rates loading for the currencies in the list. We've covered a lot in this section, but you can still make this experience better for users of your app. In the next section you'll introduce a new view to view the full details for a given currency instead of just the current price and trend.

5.5 Display a currency's details in the same tab view

The current rates are great, but markets have more information than what's shown so far. You want your app users to be able to see all of the available data, which includes the current ask, bid, and trade volume values. You can do this by creating a new view that the rates tab can navigate to, and use the Back button on that tab only to go back

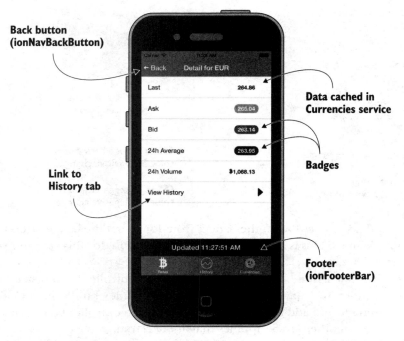

**Back button
(ionNavBackButton)**

**Data cached in
Currencies service**

Badges

**Link to
History tab**

**Footer
(ionFooterBar)**

**Figure 5.6   Detail view with Back button shows details about a currency while
still on rates tab**

to the main list. You can see the detail view in figure 5.6. If you're following along
using Git, you can check out the code for this step:

```
$ git checkout -f step5
```

You can see the rates tab is still active even though you'll introduce another view,
allowing this tab to have two levels of navigation with the Back button to take you back
to the main rates view. If you navigate to another tab and return, then the detail view
will still be active with the Back button to return to the rates. This allows users to
remember the current state of a tab, which provides a better user experience.

   You'll start by creating the controller for the detail view. It doesn't have to load any
data itself; it just uses the Currencies service to display data that was already loaded in
the rates view. The following listing has the controller that should go into
www/views/detail/detail.js.

Listing 5.13   Detail controller (www/views/detail/detail.js)

```
angular.module('App')
.controller('DetailController', function ($scope, $stateParams, $state,
    Currencies) {

  angular.forEach(Currencies, function (currency {
    if (currency.code === $stateParams.currency) {
      $scope.currency = currency;
```

**Registers
controller
and injects
services**

**Loops over each currency
to find requested currency
and stores it on scope**

```
    }
  });

  if (angular.isUndefined($scope.currency.ticker)) {
    $state.go('tabs.rates');
  }

});
```

▲ **Loops over each currency to find requested currency and stores it on scope**

If currency and ticker data isn't set, returns to rates view

When you declare this state, you'll add a parameter called currency, and the controller uses the $stateParams service to access the value of that parameter. You'll see how that's passed to the state shortly. Once you know the currency, you loop over each of the currencies until the code matches, and set the currency model on the $scope for the template. Lastly, you check if the currency model is valid, and if not, you go back to the rates view. Because this tab doesn't load data itself, if you refreshed the browser on the detail view it would have nothing to display, and this will redirect to the rates view instead of showing a blank detail view.

Now you need to get the template added for the detail view. The data needs to be displayed, and you'll use the list and badges to show the values. At the bottom there will be a link to the historical data for that currency, which will link to another tab. Create the new template and place it in www/views/detail/detail.html with the code from the following listing.

Listing 5.14   Detail template (www/views/detail/detail.html)

```
<ion-view view-title="Detail for {{currency.code}}">
  <ion-content>
    <ion-list>
      <ion-item>Last <span class="badge badge-
      stable">{{currency.ticker.last}}</span></ion-item>
      <ion-item>Ask <span class="badge badge-
      balanced">{{currency.ticker.ask}}</span></ion-item>
      <ion-item>Bid <span class="badge badge-
      assertive">{{currency.ticker.bid}}</span></ion-item>
      <ion-item>24h Average <span class="badge badge-
      dark">{{currency.ticker['24h_avg']}}</span></ion-item>
      <ion-item>24h Volume <span class="badge badge-stable icon ion-social-
      bitcoin"> {{currency.ticker.total_vol | number:2}}</span></ion-item>
      <ion-item ui-sref="tabs.history({currency: currency.code})"
      class="item-icon-right">View History <span class="icon ion-arrow-right-
      b"></span></ion-item>
    </ion-list>
  </ion-content>
  <ion-footer-bar class="bar-dark">
    <h1 class="title">Updated {{currency.ticker.timestamp |
    date:'mediumTime'}}</h1>
  </ion-footer-bar>
</ion-view>
```

◁ **Binds currency code into view title**

◁ **Displays each value in a badge, which is floated right in a list**

◁ **Adds link to view history, which links to tabs.history state and passes a currency code parameter**

This template has a list of the values you want to display, and uses the badges. Badges are used simply by adding an element with the badge class and a badge-[color] preset class. The same color name guidelines apply, such as badge-assertive. You bind the values and also add a small Bitcoin icon for the volume value.

The last list item has the `ui-sref` attribute, just like on your tabs. But here you use it like a function and pass an object, which is the way you can pass parameters to another state. We'll look at how the history tab uses this value in another section, but for the moment it will link to the history tab.

As usual, you need to include this new route in the state configuration and include the controller script in the index.html file. Add the following line to the index.html file after the other scripts:

```
<script src="views/detail/detail.js"></script>
```

Now open www/js/app.js and declare this new state. Add the following state definition into your `config()` method from the following listing.

Listing 5.15   Detail state definition (www/js/app.js)

```
.state('tabs.detail', {
  url: '/detail/:currency',          :currency indicates a parameter
  views: {                           that will be currency code
    'rates-tab': {
      templateUrl: 'views/detail/detail.html',    Reuses same rates tab
      controller: 'DetailController'              view because this
    }                                             state is designed to be
  }                                               displayed there
})
```

Declares template and controller (annotation pointing to templateUrl/controller lines)

The state declaration here is similar to the rates state, and reuses the same view. The `:currency` parameter will be set to a currency code, and passed to the state so it knows which currency to use. This value is made available to the `$stateParams` in the detail controller, which you already used in listing 5.13.

The last step is to make the list of items in the rates view link to the detail view for that currency. You need to update the rates template with two small changes, which are bold in the following listing.

Listing 5.16   Rates template update to link to detail view (www/views/rates/rates.html)

```
<ion-view view-title="Current Rates" hide-back-button="true">
  <ion-content>
    <ion-list>
      <ion-item ng-repeat="currency in currencies | filter:{selected:true}"
        ui-sref="tabs.detail({currency: currency.code})">
        {{currency.code}} - {{currency.text}}
```

Adds hide-back-button attribute so Back button doesn't appear on rates

Adds ui-sref and target tabs.detail state, passing currency code as a parameter

Here you tell the view it should never display the Back button. Because the current rates list is like the top-level page, you don't want users to be able to go back—they should select an item from the list to view instead.

Then you use the `ui-sref` attribute again and link to the `tabs.detail` state. You pass the currency code as a parameter so the detail view knows which currency was selected.

You can now preview your app, and when you click or tap on a currency, it will take you to the detail view. The Back button will be visible for you to go back to the rates view. You'll make one last improvement to the rates view, and then you'll build out the other two tabs.

5.6 Refresh the Bitcoin rates and display help

The rates are loading and you can view the detail, but currently there's no way to refresh the rates. Your app users will want to be able to get updated rates, and a common technique is to use the `ionRefresher` component that allows users to pull down on the screen and release to trigger a refresh of the data.

You also want to make sure that users have a quick help panel that explains the information they're looking at. You'll use the `ionPopoverView` component to display this help information. Figure 5.7 has both the `ionRefresher` and `ionPopoverView` components' active states for you to preview. If you're following along using Git, you can check out the code for this step:

```
$ git checkout -f step6
```

Figure 5.7 Popover and pull-to-refresh components in action

5.6.1 *ionRefresher: pull-to-refresh the rates*

Ionic's `ionRefresher` component allows any `ionContent` component to have a hidden panel that's displayed as a user pulls down on the content area, and if the user pulls far enough and releases, it will call a function to reload data. When the reload has finished, the component will hide again.

You have to update both the rates template and controller to support `ionRefresher`. First you need to add the `ionRefresher` component into your template, and in the following listing you can add the new line that's bold to the template in www/views/rates /rates.html.

Listing 5.17 Adding `ionRefresher` to rates template (www/views/rates/rates.html)

```
<ion-view view-title="Current Rates" hide-back-button="true">
  <ion-content>
    <ion-refresher on-refresh="load()" pulling-text="Pull to Refresh">
    </ion-refresher>
    <ion-list>
```

> **ionRefresher component must be first inside of ionContent and will call load method**

This may seem deceptively simple, but this is all you have to do to add the component to the template. It will inject the hidden `ionRefresher` component above the content, and when the user pulls, the component will appear. It also shows an icon; you can configure which icons are used, but here you use the default icon type. The `pulling-text` attribute lets you add a message to inform users what this component will do.

When the `ionRefresher` component is pulled far enough and released, the icon will change to a spinner and call the `load()` method declared using `on-refresh`. You already have a `load()` method in your controller that handles the loading of the data, so the only thing you have left to do is tell the `ionRefresher` component when the data has loaded. On its own, the component doesn't know when the data is done loading and will never hide, just like the infinite scroll component from chapter 4. You have to update the `load()` method and broadcast an event that will tell the `ionRefresher` component to complete.

Open the rates controller in www/views/rates/rates.js and update the load method with the bold portion in the following listing.

Listing 5.18 Updating load method to close `ionRefresher`

```
$scope.load = function () {
  $http.get('https://api.bitcoinaverage.com/ticker/all').success(function
    (tickers) {
    angular.forEach($scope.currencies, function (currency) {
      currency.ticker = tickers[currency.code];
      currency.ticker.timestamp = new Date(currency.ticker.timestamp);
    });
```

```
    }).finally(function () {
        $scope.$broadcast('scroll.refreshComplete');
    });
};
```

Chains a finally() method that fires after HTTP request
has completed, regardless of success or failure

Broadcasts the scroll.refreshComplete
event so ionRefresher knows to close

You use the `finally()` method, which is part of the Angular promises API (discussed in chapter 3), to broadcast the `scroll.refreshComplete` event regardless of success or failure of the HTTP request. You don't want the refresher to continue showing even if there was an error, so the `finally()` method is able to execute no matter what. That's all you need to do to support the pull-to-refresh feature in your view. Planning ahead to make sure that you can reload data easily makes this component easy to implement.

5.6.2 *$ionicPopover: showing help in a popover*

The `$ionicPopover` component is typically used by having a button in the header that opens the popover. You aren't limited to what you can put into an `$ionicPopover` component, but the popover does take up only a portion of the screen. If you need to use the full screen, then you'll need another component. In this case, you'll display some basic content about what's currently on the screen, and give credits to the source of the data.

Depending on what platform your app is running, the popover displays differently to mimic the style of the platform styling. You'll likely want to avoid trying to change the styling of a popover container because it will need to be verified on all platforms.

You'll start by adding a new template file with the contents of your popover. I like to think of the popover like a subview, where it loads a template into a container without creating a completely new view. I also suggest putting the template file inside of the view folder instead of in a new folder, so create a new file at www/views/rates /help-popover.html and insert the contents of the following listing.

Listing 5.19   Popover template (www/views/rates/help-popover.html)

Uses
ionHeaderBar
in popover

```
<ion-popover-view>
    <ion-header-bar>
        <h1 class="title">About Bitcoin</h1>
    </ion-header-bar>
    <ion-content>
        <div class="padding">This shows the last bitcoin transaction price for
        a currency and compares it to the 24 hour rolling average rate.</div>
        <div class="padding">Data is available up to once a minute.</div>
        <div class="padding">The data for this application is from the
        <a href="https://bitcoinaverage.com/api">Bitcoin Average</a> API.
        </div>
    </ion-content>
</ion-popover-view>
```

Uses ionPopoverView to
wrap template; acts like
ionView for popovers

Uses ionContent and adds
HTML content for popover

This template is wrapped in an `ionPopoverView` instead of an `ionView` because this is a specialized template just for popovers. Then you use the `ionHeaderBar` and `ionContent` components to wrap your content, which is simple HTML with text.

Now you need to register the popover so the view knows about it, and this is done in the controller. Much like you declare a state in the app `config()`, you need to declare the popover in your controller. Because a popover isn't meant to be a globally visible feature, you're able to isolate it in one view to reduce overhead and complexity. Open the rates controller in www/views/rates/rates.js again and update it with the following listing.

Listing 5.20   Registering popover with controller (www/views/rates/rates.js)

Declares a popover from template URL
and assigns parent scope as scope

Injects
$ionicPopover
service

```
angular.module('App')
.controller('RatesController', function ($scope, $http, $ionicPopover,
    Currencies) {

  $scope.currencies = Currencies;

  $ionicPopover.fromTemplateUrl('views/rates/help-popover.html', {
    scope: $scope,
  }).then(function (popover) {
    $scope.popover = popover;
  })

  $scope.openHelp = function($event) {
    $scope.popover.show($event);
  };

  $scope.$on('$destroy', function() {
    $scope.popover.remove();
  });
  ...
```

When template has loaded,
assigns popover to scope

Scope method to open popover;
requires $event to be passed

Rest of
controller
remains the
same

Listens for $destroy event,
which is when view is destroyed,
and cleans up popover

First you have to inject the `$ionicPopover` service. Then you use it to create a new popover from a template URL. The popover does create its own scope, but you connect the scopes by passing an object with `{scope: $scope}`. Often you'll need this so the popover can access the parent scope. The `then()` method executes when the template has loaded and assigns a new popover to the `$scope.popover` property.

Now the popover has been set up, and you're able to use the `$scope.popover` `.show($event)` method to show the popover. You'll need to add an `ngClick` to a button to trigger it, and pass the `$event` variable as a parameter. The `$event` value is the event object from the click event, which contains the information about which element was clicked. The popover uses that information to calculate where on the page to put the popover. There's also a `$scope.popover.hide()` method that can programmatically hide the popover, or the user can tap on the area outside of the popover to close it.

Lastly, you listen for the scope $destroy event, which fires when the current scope is unloaded from memory. To prevent memory leaks, you remove the popover from the application because you're no longer using it.

Why do some components need to be manually removed?

Most of the components in Ionic can be cleaned up automatically when they're no longer in use, which helps to free up memory and improve performance. Some components, namely modals and popovers, require the app to remove the component when the scope is destroyed.

The $destroy event fires when the current scope has been deleted from memory. Anything that exists in that scope is removed at the same time, but popovers and modals both create isolated scopes that persist. Because of this architecture, there isn't an automatic way to remove the modal or popover from memory.

If you forget to do this in your app, it probably won't cause your app to become very slow. How much of an impact it might have depends on the complexity and memory use of the popover or modal. It might not have a noticeable impact on most apps if it's forgotten, but it's best to remove them.

Now it's time to add the button that will trigger the popover. Open the rates template at www/views/rates/rates.html one last time and add the bold code from the following listing.

Listing 5.21 Adding button to trigger popover (www/views/rates/rates.html)

```
<ion-view view-title="Current Rates" hide-back-button="true">
  <ion-nav-buttons side="primary">
    <button class="button" ng-click="openHelp($event)">About</button>
  </ion-nav-buttons>
  <ion-content>
  ...
```

Rest of template remains the same

Adds a button and uses ngClick to call openHelp while passing $event

ionNavButtons allows you to declare buttons in top navbar area

Now your new button will call the function to open the popover, and the popover will position itself to be under the button. The $event value here is a special Angular feature available for ngClick and other event directives that passes the event object along. The ionNavButton will appear on the primary side, which may vary from platform to platform if that's the right or left.

That completes the rates view. You've added a popover for help information and a pull-to-refresh feature for updating the rates in your list. Next you'll tackle the history tab that will load data and chart the historical price for the past month.

5.7   Charting historical data

Your app users will want to be able to see how the Bitcoin price has been trending over the past month for a given currency. You'll use the popular Highcharts charting library, along with an Angular directive for Highcharts called highcharts-ng. This isn't meant to be a primer on how to use Highcharts, but you can view the documentation at http://highcharts.com. If you're following along using Git, you can check out the code for this step:

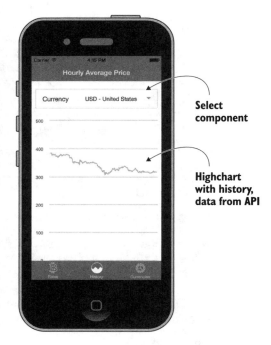

```
$ git checkout -f step7
```

You'll load data again from the Bitcoin-Average API, but this time the data will come not as JSON but as CSV (comma-separated value) data. This particular API doesn't send back JSON data (the CSV format is more concise, so it takes fewer bytes to send information), so you'll have to parse and format the data into a format that Highcharts can understand.

You can see the result of this section

Figure 5.8 History tab showing a chart of average prices over the past month, with a box to change currency in the chart

in figure 5.8. There's the chart as well as a box above that has the name of the currency. This is a select box that allows you to change the currency for the chart.

5.7.1   Setting up third-party libraries

Your app is going to use some third-party libraries, so you need to download a copy of them and set them up in your app. You'll use the ionic add feature, which uses Bower under the hood as a utility for downloading libraries into your project. If you don't have Bower installed, you can install it using npm:

```
$ npm install -g bower
```

Then you need to install two libraries: the Highcharts charting library and the Angular wrapper for Highcharts called highcharts-ng. You can have Ionic download and put the recent copy into your project using the following command:

```
$ ionic add highcharts-release#4.0.4 highcharts-ng#0.0.7
```

With this command you've chosen to install a specific version of each library, just so you can be sure the example in this book works as expected. They're downloaded and stored in the www/lib directory.

Now you need to include the necessary script tags in your index.html file. The first two are for Highcharts and the third is the Highcharts Angular wrapper:

```
<script src="lib/highcharts-release/adapters/standalone-
    framework.js"></script>
<script src="lib/highcharts-release/highcharts.js"></script>
<script src="lib/highcharts-ng/dist/highcharts-ng.js"></script>
```

The last step is to declare the `highcharts-ng` module as a project dependency so you can use it. Open www/js/app.js and add it as a new dependency:

```
angular.module('App', ['ionic', 'highcharts-ng'])
```

Now you're set up with the third-party scripts that you need, so let's move on to building up your template for the history tab.

5.7.2 History tab template using Highcharts and a select box to toggle currency

You created a blank template for the history tab before, so you need to update it to include the select box component for your currency selector, and set up the Highcharts component. You'll use an inset list with just one item to create the select box container, as shown in the following listing.

Listing 5.22 History template with chart (www/views/history/history.html)

```
<ion-view view-title="Hourly Average Price" hide-back-button="true">
  <ion-content>
    <div class="list list-inset">
      <label class="item item-input item-select">
        <div class="input-label">
          Currency
        </div>
        <select ng-change="changeCurrency()" ng-model="history.currency">
          <option ng-repeat="currency in currencies | filter:{selected:true}"
    value="{{currency.code}}" ng-selected="history.currency ==
    currency.code">{{currency.code}} - {{currency.text}}</option>
        </select>
      </label>
    </div>
    <highchart config="chart"></highchart>
  </ion-content>
</ion-view>
```

Annotations:
- Hides Back button on this view
- Uses inset list to contain select box
- highchart component that accepts a config attribute with a chart object
- Uses a normal HTML select box with ngChange and ngModel to track value changes
- Creates an option for each active currency

The select box component is based on the default HTML select box and is styled by Ionic to give it a mobile-friendly appearance. When a select box is used on a mobile device, the platform takes over and provides the experience. There's little control apps have over this, but in this case you're happy to let the platform display the select box in a way that feels most native for that platform.

You'll again use the `Currencies` service to display a list of the active currencies in the select box. `ngModel` allows you to track the value of the select box. When the value changes, `ngChange` triggers the `changeCurrency()` method, which will update the view to display the chart for that currency.

Lastly, the `highchart` directive used here takes a chart object, which you'll declare in your controller. Based on the values of your chart object, the directive will work with Highcharts to render a chart based on the data you'll load.

This is all you need in your template, but your controller has to do a bit of work to make everything behave properly.

5.7.3   *History tab controller loads data and sets up chart*

Your controller will need to handle setting up the chart, loading the chart data, and formatting it so the chart can use it. You'll again turn to the `$http` service to load the data, and format the chart object according to the rules that Highcharts will understand. Because the data you're getting isn't in the exact format Highcharts needs, you'll convert data before you display it. The controller also will handle changing the currency and will load the list of currencies to use in the template.

Create a new controller at www/views/history/history.js and add the code from the following listing into it. We'll break down the code carefully because there's a lot going on.

Listing 5.23   History controller (www/views/history/history.js)

Creates controller and injects services ❶

Stores list of currencies on scope ❸

Function to handle changing state after a new currency is selected ❹

```
angular.module('App')
.controller('HistoryController', function ($scope, $http, $state,
    $stateParams, Currencies) {

  $scope.history = {
    currency: $stateParams.currency || 'USD'
  };
  $scope.currencies = Currencies;

  $scope.changeCurrency = function () {
    $state.go('tabs.history', { currency: $scope.history.currency });
  };

  $scope.chart = {
    options: {
      chart: {
        type: 'line'
      },
      legend: {
        enabled: false
      }
    },
```

Defines history model set on select box, defaulting to US dollars ❷

Chart definition object that Highcharts directive turns into a chart ❺

```
        title: {
          text: null
        },
        yAxis: {
          title: null
        },
        xAxis: {
          type: 'datetime'
        },
        series: []
      };

      $http.get('https://api.bitcoinaverage.com/history/' +
        $scope.history.currency +
        '/per_hour_monthly_sliding_window.csv').success(function (prices) {

        prices = prices.split(/\n/);
        var series = {
          data: []
        };

        angular.forEach(prices, function (price, index) {
          price = price.split(',');
          var date = new Date(price[0].replace(' ', 'T')).getTime();
          var value = parseFloat(price[3]);
          if (date && value > 0) {
            series.data.push([date, value]);
          }
        });

        $scope.chart.series.push(series);
      });

      $scope.$on('$ionicView.enter', function() {
        $scope.history = {
          currency: $stateParams.currency || 'USD'
        };
      });
    });
```

5 Chart definition object that Highcharts directive turns into a chart

6 Loads history information based on selected currency

7 Splits prices string into an array of rows of prices

8 Creates a blank series to store all of the data in

9 Loops over each row of prices

10 Splits each row from a comma-separated string to an array

11 Parses and formats time and price values

12 If date and value are valid, adds point to series

13 Adds completed series of data to chart

14 Listens for $ionicView.enter event to reset currency model when cached incorrectly

There seems to be a lot going on, but most of it's just formatting data and setting up the chart. Let's start from the top. First you set the history model, and this contains the currency value from $stateParams **1**. If no currency was provided, you then default to US dollars **2**. Then you store the currencies onto the $scope for the template **3**.

The changeCurrencies() **4** method takes the value of the select box and updates the current state to use it. It calls the $state.go method, which is the programmatic equivalent to ui-sref in the template.

The rest of the controller is dedicated to the chart **5**. You start by making a chart object that's used by the highcharts-ng module and handles creating a chart for you. You can review the documentation for highcharts-ng to get a full understanding of the object at https://github.com/pablojim/highcharts-ng.

The last part is loading and formatting the data. The `$http` service loads the price data in a CSV format ❻ because that's all the API provides. This is problematic because JavaScript doesn't have a built-in way to handle CSV, but you can still parse it yourself. The chart needs a series, which is a single set of data, so you create a blank series. Using the split method, you break the CSV into JavaScript arrays that you can work with ❼, ❽. The data also comes with some metadata that you don't want, so you filter it out and use only the data points ❾, ❿, ⓫. You can inspect the response in the browser developer tools from the server to see how there may be extra lines in the response that you don't want. Then you add the data points to the series, and add the series to the chart ⓬, ⓭. At this point, the line will appear with the price data.

The last block is an event listener to listen for Ionic's built-in navigation events. Ionic has a nice feature that allows a state to be cached in memory, which makes it faster to return to it later. By default, it will cache 10 states, and after that it will drop the oldest state from memory based on a user's history.

In this case, you use the `<select>` element with an `ngChange` event to trigger the app to navigate to another view. When a user changes the value of the select, that value is stored on the model for that view and then the app navigates to another. Imagine you started on the history view for US dollars, and changed the select to Euros. The first state for US dollars would be cached with the select value pointing to Euros, and if you returned to the US dollars view later, it would remain on Euros. To solve this, you listen to the `$ionicView.beforeEnter` event ⓮, and always reset the value of the select to the correct value from the URL.

This can become a problem when you expect your controller to execute every time the state is loaded. When it becomes cached and later reused, it doesn't have to be reloaded. Any code in the controller that executes without being inside of a scope method doesn't rerun when the state is brought back from the cache. In this case, that's most of the code in your controller, and therefore you can't expect the code that sets the currency value for the select ❷ to run again. By using the Ionic navigational events, you can execute logic every time the state is loaded, regardless if it was cached or not.

You need to finish this tab by adding the controller script in your index.html file, and then updating the state definition to include the parameter and controller. In index.html, add the `</script>` tag for the `history` controller at the end of the existing scripts:

```
<script src="views/history/history.js"></script>
```

Then open the www/js/app.js file and modify the history state with the bold code shown in the following listing.

Listing 5.24   Updated state definition for history tab (www/js/app.js)

```
.state('tabs.history', {
  url: '/history?currency',                     ⟵———┐  Adds currency parameter
  views: {                                          │  for this state
    'history-tab': {
```

```
        templateUrl: 'views/history/history.html',
        controller: 'HistoryController'                ◁──────  Declares controller
      }                                                          for this view
    }
  }))
```

Now you can preview the app and view the history tab. The chart will load and you can change the selected currency to view another chart. You also already have support to link to the history tab in the detail view of the rates tab. If you go back to the rates tab and view the detail for a currency, choose the View History link and it will take you to the history tab for that currency.

Your final task is to set up the currencies tab, which will allow you to toggle and reorder the currencies in the other tabs.

5.8   *Currencies tab with list reordering and toggles*

The last tab will let you change the list order of the currencies and toggle currencies on or off for display. This is like a preferences screen so that users are able to decide which currencies they care about and ignore the rest, or move their favorite currencies up to the top. You can see the list of currencies with toggles and reordering in action in figure 5.9. If you're following along using Git, you can check out the code for this step:

```
$ git checkout -f step8
```

Figure 5.9   Currencies tab with list of currencies to toggle on or off, and ability to reorder the list

5.8.1 *ionReorderButton: adding reordering to a list*

You'll start by adding the template for the currencies tab, and add the reordering feature using the `ionReorderButton`. Reordering can only work with the `ionList` directive. It works by setting a reordering state to `true` or `false`, and based on that value the reordering handles appear or hide. When they're activated, you can drag the item using the handle to a new position, and then your controller will handle updating the model to reflect the new ordering. Open the currencies template at www/views/currencies/currencies.html and update it to reflect the following listing.

Listing 5.25   Currencies template (www/views/currencies/currencies.html)

Adds button that toggles state.reordering value

Uses show-reorder to declare list can be reordered, and what model to use to activate

```
<ion-view view-title="Currencies">
  <ion-nav-buttons side="primary">
    <button class="button" ng-click="state.reordering =
    !state.reordering">Reorder</button>
  </ion-nav-buttons>
  <ion-content>
    <ion-list show-reorder="state.reordering">
      <ion-item ng-repeat="currency in currencies">
        {{currency.code}} - {{currency.text}}
        <ion-reorder-button class="ion-navicon" on-reorder="move(currency,
    $fromIndex, $toIndex)"></ion-reorder-button>
      </ion-item>
    </ion-list>
  </ion-content>
</ion-view>
```

ionReorderButton must be included and calls a method after an item is moved

You've created a list of currencies that are able to be reordered. The `ionList` component uses the `show-reorder` attribute to evaluate if the `ionReorderButton` should be shown or not. These two work together to create the reorder functionality. The button in the navbar is used to toggle the `state.reordering` property, which will trigger the reordering to show or hide.

The `on-reorder` method allows you to write a method that handles what to do when the reordering is complete. It provides two special parameters, `$fromIndex` and `$toIndex`. This gives you the index values for the item in the array so you know the position to move it from and to. You'll add this method in your controller next. Create a new file at www/views/currencies/currencies.js and insert the contents of the following listing.

Listing 5.26   Currencies controller (www/views/currencies/currencies.js)

Declares controller and injects services

Attaches currencies to scope

```
angular.module('App')
.controller('CurrenciesController', function ($scope, Currencies) {
  $scope.currencies = Currencies;
  $scope.state = {
    reordering: false
  };
```

Declares default reordering state value

```
$scope.$on('$stateChangeStart', function () {
  $scope.state.reordering = false;
});
```
Listens for state changes and turns off reordering when leaving tab

```
$scope.move = function(currency, fromIndex, toIndex) {
  $scope.currencies.splice(fromIndex, 1);
  $scope.currencies.splice(toIndex, 0, currency);
};
});
```
Handles moving an item from one index value to another by splicing item in array

Your controller is fairly lean and starts by setting values on the scope. You listen for the `$stateChangeStart` event because you want to disable reordering any time the currencies tab loses focus, and this event will fire any time the tab changes. This is just a convenience for users; otherwise, if the reordering is active when they leave the tab, it will still be active when they return. The `move()` method takes the item that's being moved along with the two index values for where it was and where it needs to go. Using `splice`, you remove it first from the array and then re-insert it at the new location.

At this point your list of currencies can be reordered, and once the items are reordered, the other tabs will also reflect the new ordering. This is part of the power of using a shared service like the `Currencies` service. Changes made in one place are reflected across any state using the same service.

5.8.2 *ionToggle: adding toggles to list items*

You also want to be able to toggle currencies on or off so you only have to see the items you care about. There's an `ionToggle` component you can use, but here you'll use the CSS version of the toggle because the `ionToggle` component doesn't work well with the `ionReorderButton`. The `ionToggle` component is just a helpful abstraction of the CSS version that you'll be using, but it doesn't provide any extra features.

Open the currencies template once more, and you'll add the `ionToggle` component in for the final feature. In the following listing you'll see the additions to make inside the `ionItem` component to include the toggle.

Listing 5.27 Adding toggler to currencies list (www/views/currencies/currencies.html)

Declares a label with toggle class →

Adds item-toggle class to get toggle styling

```
<ion-item class="item-toggle" ng-repeat="currency in currencies">
  {{currency.code}} - {{currency.text}}
  <label class="toggle toggle-balanced">
  <input type="checkbox" ng-model="currency.selected">
    <div class="track">
      <div class="handle"></div>
    </div>
  </label>
  <ion-reorder-button class="ion-navicon" on-reorder="move(currency,
    $fromIndex, $toIndex)"></ion-reorder-button>
</ion-item>
```
Uses a checkbox input and gives it a model for currency.selected

Adds elements needed for CSS to style a toggle icon

This ionToggle component uses the checkbox input to keep track of the value for the toggle. Checkboxes and togglers are both Boolean values, so the CSS styling of a toggle overlays a traditional HTML checkbox. You use the model currency.selected for each currency to filter out items that aren't enabled in the other tabs. As you toggle any item on or off, the other tabs are updated immediately to show or hide the currency. The power of the shared Currencies service is at work again.

You can now preview the app and everything should be complete. The app allows you to view the current rates for a currency and details about that currency, view a chart of the rate's monthly history, configure which of the currencies you wish to view, and order them as you desire.

5.9   *Chapter challenges*

You now have a lot of components under your belt. To challenge yourself, further improving your understanding and familiarity with these components, you can attempt the following tasks:

- *Autorefresh the rates*—Work on a technique to automatically refresh the rates once a minute. Angular has a useful $interval service that you might consider using.
- *Persist the currency settings*—There are techniques such as using localStorage or indexedDB that you can use to persist the currencies ordering and toggle states. Work on adding logic to manage the loading of currency from a cache before resetting the values to a default.
- *Chart more data*—The BitcoinAverage API provides more types of historical data, such as prices since Bitcoin started. Add more configuration to the history tab that allows a user to change to different types of chart data. Review the API details on the BitcoinAverage API.
- *Improve the detail view*—The detail view is very basic and just lists information. Try to make a more compelling visual experience using more of Ionic's CSS components or by creating your own.

5.10   *Summary*

In this chapter we've covered a lot about Ionic components and leveraging the Highcharts charting library with data from the BitcoinAverage API. Let's review the major topics we covered:

- Tabs are a great way to provide a navigational structure in your app. Sometimes you need basic tabs, and sometimes you need tabs with individual navigational histories like in the example app.
- Including third-party scripts and Angular modules is easy to do, but each module has its own features that have to be learned individually.

- Lists have the ability to be reordered, have support for badges, and are able to include toggle components.
- Using a shared service like the `Currencies` service makes it possible to share data between views.

Next, in chapter 6 you'll learn about the remaining major components and features of Ionic, such as side menus, modals, and scrolling components.

Weather app, using side menus, modals, action sheets, and ionScroll

This chapter covers

- Using a side menu as the basis of your app for navigation
- Displaying options to users with action sheets and popups
- Using a modal to display related content over another view
- Building more-advanced scrolling interactions

In this chapter you'll build a weather app, and in the process you'll showcase more components that Ionic has to offer. The base of the application navigation will be the side menu component. It will allow you to find and view weather conditions, forecasts and favorite locations; display sunrise and sunset data inside of a modal window; and use a paginated scrolling pane to view the weather information.

Throughout the chapter we'll look at a number of Ionic's features and components. The side menu will be the basis for your app navigation, and you'll use just a single left menu that can appear to navigate around the app. You'll use the action sheet component to provide users a list of options, such as to note a favorite location. Using a modal, you'll display the next year's chart of sunrise and sunset values. To make this chart perform better, you'll use the collection repeat feature of the Ionic lists, which reduces memory for large lists by rendering only the necessary items.

You'll use two different services for loading data in this app. Forecast.io is a popular weather API service that provides current conditions and forecast data for a given geolocation based on latitude and longitude. To determine the locations, you'll use Google's geolocation service to search for locations and their coordinates. Both are free; however, you'll need to register for an API key to use Forecast.io.

In figure 6.1 you can see many of the different views of this app. You'll build them up piece by piece, but the bulk of the app will exist inside of the weather view.

You can view the completed project at https://ionic-in-action-chapter6.herokuapp .com and the source code at https://github.com/ionic-in-action/chapter6.

Side menu
- **Shows list of links**
- **List of favorites**
- **Shows and hides**
- **Access via button**

Search
- **Search for locations**
- **Use search box**
- **List component**

Weather
- **Custom scrolling experience**
- **Use vertical pages**
- **Modal to view sunrise chart**
- **Action sheet for options**

Settings
- **App settings**
- **Radio component**
- **List component**
- **Range component**
- **Delete list items**

Figure 6.1 The weather app example for this chapter. The side menu allows you to navigate between views.

6.1   *Setting up the chapter project*

You can follow along in this chapter either by creating a new Ionic app and adding the code from the listings in this chapter, or by cloning the finished app from the *Ionic in Action* GitHub repository and following along with each step. Once you've finished setting up the app, start to serve the project so you can preview the app in a browser with the `ionic serve` command.

CREATE A NEW APP AND ADD CODE MANUALLY

To create a new project for your app using the Ionic command-line interface (CLI) utility, open the command line and execute the following command (remember, you can refer to chapter 2 if you need a refresh on how projects are set up):

```
$ ionic start chapter6 https://github.com/ionic-in-action/starter
$ cd chapter6
$ ionic serve
```

CLONE THE FINISHED APP AND FOLLOW ALONG

To check out the finished app and use Git to follow along for each step, use the following command to clone the repository and check out the first step:

```
$ git clone https://github.com/ionic-in-action/chapter6.git
$ cd chapter6
$ git checkout -f step1
$ ionic serve
```

6.2   *Setting up the side menu and views*

You've seen how to build navigation yourself and how to use tabs, so now you'll use side menus for primary navigation. Side menus are used frequently because they slide in and out of view on demand, allowing you to provide quick access to primary links without cluttering the main content. A side menu can be opened on the right or left at once, and in this example you'll use just the left side. If you're following along using Git, you can check out the code for this step:

```
$ git checkout -f step2
```

A side menu can be opened in three ways, depending on the implementation. By default, Ionic supports opening side menus by swiping to the side to pull the side menu open. You can also disable this in case you need to be able to use swipes for another purpose. You can use a button to open the side menu, usually placed in the top left corner of the screen, which will be demonstrated in this example. Lastly, you're able to toggle the menu programmatically using the sidebar delegate service.

In the example for this chapter, you'll use just one side menu, but you're able to use multiple side menus in a single app. There are many configuration options and ways to make use of the side menu, but they all leverage the same basic structure you'll use here.

In this section you'll set up the base application and navigation using side menus. This is done using the ionSideMenus components, and you'll allow the side menu to appear from swiping to the right, or by using the button option with a toggle icon in the top left. You'll also set up two blank routes that you'll fill in later. You can see the side menu in action in figure 6.2, the result of your work in this section.

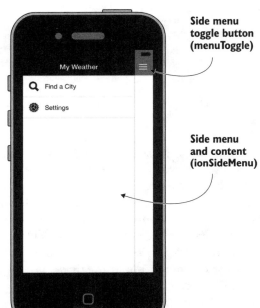

Side menu toggle button (menuToggle)

Side menu and content (ionSideMenu)

Figure 6.2 The side menu in action: the left is the closed state and the right is the opened state

To begin, you'll modify the www/index.html file from the generated project for your app to set up your side menu. The following listing contains the side menu and content area.

Listing 6.1 Side menu setup (www/index.html)

```
<body ng-app="App">
  <ion-side-menus>
    <ion-side-menu-content>
      <ion-nav-bar class="bar-positive">
        <ion-nav-buttons side="left">
          <button class="button button-clear" menu-toggle="left">
            <span class="icon ion-navicon"></span>
          </button>
        </ion-nav-buttons>
      </ion-nav-bar>
      <ion-nav-view></ion-nav-view>
    </ion-side-menu-content>
    <ion-side-menu side="left">
```

Declares ionSideMenus container to wrap side menu and content areas

Uses ionSideMenuContent to hold the main center content

Using navigation components inside of side menu content area with toggle icon

Declares a side menu, assigning it to left

```
  <ion-header-bar class="bar-dark">
    <h1 class="title">My Weather</h1>
  </ion-header-bar>
  <ion-content>
    <ion-list>
      <ion-item class="item-icon-left" ui-sref="search" menu-close>
<span class="icon ion-search">
</span> Find a City</ion-item>
      <ion-item class="item-icon-left" ui-sref="settings"
menu-close><span class="icon ion-ios-cog">
</span> Settings</ion-item>
    </ion-list>
  </ion-content>
  </ion-side-menu>
</ion-side-menus>
</body>
```

Using a new header for side menu

ionContent is used with list of links for navigation

Side menus are easy to declare, because they only require using the `ionSideMenus`, `ionSideMenuContent`, and `ionSideMenu` directives in the markup. No JavaScript is required to set up the side menu. You first wrap the entire content area with `ionSideMenus`, which takes care of setting up the functionality based on the other directives that are declared. Without it, the side menu wouldn't function. Inside of `ionSideMenus`, you add two child elements, `ionSideMenuContent` and `ionSideMenu`. You declare the side menu to be placed on the left by using the `side` attribute. You can only declare one `ionSideMenuContent` element for each side menu, but you can declare up to two `ionSideMenu` elements for the right and/or left.

Inside of the content area, you declare the same navigational directives you've used in the past. This way, your side menu acts like a global base that contains your navigation view container. I think this structure makes the most sense because your side menu typically is used for global navigation in your app.

If you look at the `ionNavButtons`, you'll see a single button with `menu-toggle="left"`. The `menuToggle` directive is used to take care of toggling the side menu open or closed when the button is activated. Likewise, in the side menu item list you see `menu-close` on the navigation links. The `menuClose` directive will close any open side menu when the item is activated. When you tap on "Find a City," it will close the left menu automatically; otherwise, the side menu would remain open even while the navigation area updated with the new content.

You should think of each `ionSideMenu` and `ionSideMenuContent` like their own views. In the side menu, you've used a header bar and content area to wrap the navigation list; otherwise, the content area wouldn't calculate the correct size and location of elements.

The side menu can contain any content you want, but a list of navigation links is the most common use case for the side menu. You might also use a right side menu to provide additional search filters or even secondary navigation.

Everything is done for the side menu in listing 6.1. You can review the side menu documentation to see some other features and get details about the features of the delegate service in case you need to have programmatic control over the side menu.

The links declared in the side menu currently won't work until you declare those routes, but you can toggle the side menu open and closed or swipe to pull it open. You'll start by setting up the search view, which will allow users to find locations and their coordinates.

6.3 Searching for locations

When the app first starts, users will need to be able to configure the locations that they would like to view. Using Google's Geolocation API, you can search for locations by any type of input text, such as a ZIP code, city name, and even more-specific locations such as a particular address. You'll create a new view that allows users to search and view a list of results from this API. You can see the search in action in figure 6.3. If you're following along using Git, you can check out the code for this step:

```
$ git checkout -f step3
```

To accomplish this, you'll need to register a new state with your state provider and define the template and controller. Your template will contain a search field and a button, while your controller will handle the API request to get the list of results. By

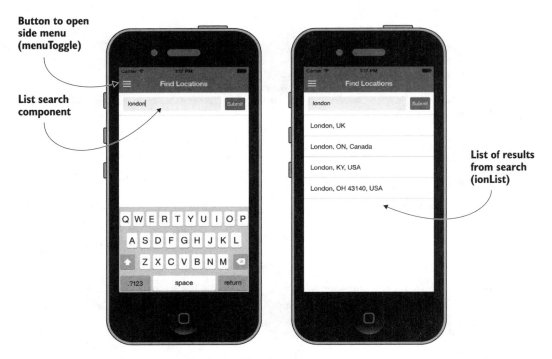

Figure 6.3 Search view in action, with keyboard and results

now you should be familiar with declaring a new state, so let's start with that inside of your www/js/app.js file, as in the following listing.

Listing 6.2   Declare the search state (www/js/app.js)

```
angular.module('App', ['ionic'])
.config(function ($stateProvider, $urlRouterProvider) {          Adds config()
                                                                 method for app
  $stateProvider
    .state('search', {
      url: '/search',
      controller: 'SearchController',                           Declares search state
      templateUrl: 'views/search/search.html'
    });
                                                                 Uses search as
  $urlRouterProvider.otherwise('/search');                      default view
})
```

Because this is the first state, you need to add the `config()` method and then inject the `$stateProvider` and `$urlRouterProvider` services. You declare the search state and set it to the default route. Now you need to add your template and controller.

The template for the search view is in listing 6.3, and contains a search box and a list component to display the list of results. Create a new file at www/views/search/search.html and add the contents of the following listing.

Listing 6.3   Template for search (www/views/search/search.html)

```
<ion-view view-title="Find Locations">
  <ion-content>
    <div class="list">
      <div class="item item-input-inset">
        <label class="item-input-wrapper">
          <input type="search" ng-model="model.term" placeholder=
"Search for a location">
        </label>
        <button class="button button-small button-positive"
ng-click="search()">Submit</button>
      </div>
      <div class="item" ng-repeat="result in results" ui-sref="weather({city:
      result.formatted_address, lat: result.geometry.location.lat, lng:
      result.geometry.location.lng})">{{result.formatted_address}}</div>
    </div>
  </ion-content>
</ion-view>
```

Searches list item with ngModel for search box and a button

Repeats over list of results when available to display address and link to weather view

Here you have a basic template with a list. The first list item is the search box, and then if any results exist, they'll be displayed below it. This box uses the inset input style to give it a little different visual appearance, where the box is slightly grayed. The input is also declared to be the search type, because it will modify the display of the keyboard for searching on a device.

You haven't declared the weather state yet, but you can see the link is added to the state using `ui-sref`. In this case, you'll pass the city, latitude, and longitude values from the result.

To power this template, you need the controller. Create a new file at www/views/search/search.js and add the code from the following listing. Also add a new `</script>` tag in your www/index.html file:

```
<script src="views/search/search.js"></script>
```

Listing 6.4   Search controller (www/views/search/search.js)

```
angular.module('App')
.controller('SearchController', function ($scope, $http) {          Defines search
  $scope.model = {term: ''};                                        term model

  $scope.search = function () {
    $http.get('https://maps.googleapis.com/maps/api/geocode/json',
      {params: {address: $scope.model.term}}).success(function (response) {
      $scope.results = response.results;
    });                                              Method to handle searching
  };                                                  from Geocoding API using
});                                                  term and storing on scope
```

In your controller you define the default model, which will be reset every time the view is loaded. Then the `search()` method is called when the button is tapped, and it makes the HTTP request to the Google Geocoding API. The response gets stored on `$scope.results`, which will update the view with the list when it's available.

Your search view is now complete. Next you'll build out the settings view and a few custom services that you'll use to store and share data.

6.4   Adding settings view and data services

Your app needs to have some configuration options, particularly to allow users to select what type of units they wish to see (such as temperatures in Fahrenheit or Celsius). It will then allow users to select how many days to view for the forecast. Lastly, it will allow users to manage their list of favorite locations by deleting items in the list. If you're following along using Git, you can check out the code for this step:

```
$ git checkout -f step4
```

You'll need to add a new state with a controller and template for your settings view. Then, to manage your app, you'll need two services that can be used to share data and methods between views. Lastly, you'll also update the side menu to include a list of the favorite locations for quick access.

6.4.1   Create services for locations and settings

Your first step is to create two services, one to keep track of the favorite locations and another for settings. You'll create two services using Angular's factory method that you

can then inject into any controller. The Settings service will be just a simple
JavaScript object with properties, and the Locations service will contain some methods to help you manage the list of locations.

You'll add these two services into the main app JavaScript file to keep your example more streamlined, but you could also add these as individual modules. Open
www/js/app.js and add the two new services from the following listing to your app.

Listing 6.5 Services for Locations and Settings (www/js/app.js)

```
.factory('Settings', function () {            Declares Settings
  var Settings = {                            service as a factory
    units: 'us',
    days: 8                                   Creates and returns a
  };                                          JavaScript object with
  return Settings;                            default settings
})
.factory('Locations', function () {          Declares Locations
  var Locations = {                          service as a factory
    data: [{
      city: 'Chicago, IL, USA',              Creates Locations
      lat: 41.8781136,                       object and stores a
      lng: -87.6297982                       default value for
    }],                                      Chicago in data array
    getIndex: function (item) {
      var index = -1;
      angular.forEach(Locations.data, function (location, i) {
        if (item.lat == location.lat && item.lng == location.lng) {
          index = i;
        }
      });                                     Method to
      return index;                           determine index
    },                                        value of a location
    toggle: function (item) {
      var index = Locations.getIndex(item);
      if (index >= 0) {
        Locations.data.splice(index, 1);      toggle method adds
      } else {                                or removes an item
        Locations.data.push(item);            from Locations
      }
    },
    primary: function (item) {
      var index = Locations.getIndex(item);
      if (index >= 0) {
        Locations.data.splice(index, 1);      primary method moves
        Locations.data.splice(0, 0, item);    item to top position or
      } else {                                adds it to top if new
        Locations.data.unshift(item);
      }
    }
  };
  return Locations;                           Returns Locations object
});                                           with data and methods
```

Here you use Angular services to help define a service that can be shared between different controllers. Later you'll add each of these to different views, but any changes made to these services will be immediately reflected in other views. If you recall from chapter 5, you used the same technique for the list of currencies, where each currency could be toggled on or off and the changes would be reflected instantly across the app. You'll use `Locations.data` as the array that stores the list of locations, which should contain the city name, latitude, and longitude values. To start, I've preset Chicago in the list because it's one of my favorite cities.

The `Locations` service has three methods. The `getIndex()` method gives you the index value of an item from the `Locations.data` array, if the item exists. The `toggle()` method will add or remove a location from the `Locations.data` array, after it checks if the location is already in the `Locations.data` array or not. The `primary()` method is used to either add a new item to the top of the list, or to move an existing item to the top of the list.

6.4.2 Show favorites in side menu list

Now that you have your `Locations` service, you can display the list of favorite locations in the side menu. To do this, you need to add a controller for your side menu so you can inject the `Locations` service into the scope, and then add a new item to the navigation list with `ngRepeat` to display all of the favorite locations.

First, you'll define the controller in your app JavaScript file where you just added your services. Because this controller belongs in the side menu instead of an isolated view, you can keep it together with the rest of the main app code. This very simple controller is found in the following listing.

> **Listing 6.6   Side menu controller (www/js/app.js)**

```
.controller('LeftMenuController', function ($scope, Locations) {
  $scope.locations = Locations.data;
})
```

Creates a controller and injects services

Assigns locations data array to scope

This very simple controller just assigns the array of locations to the scope. You don't need to do anything more complex in the controller, but you do need to add this controller to the side menu template. In the www/index.html file, update the `ionSideMenu` and add the `ngController` directive to attach this new controller to the side menu:

```
<ion-side-menu side="left" ng-controller="LeftMenuController">
```

You haven't used `ngController` in your Ionic apps, but you did use it in the chapter 3 primer on Angular. Normally, you declare the controllers for each view in your app `config()` using the `$stateProvider`. In this case, the side menu isn't its own state, so you have to attach the controller yourself. With this controller, the side menu now will have access to the list of locations, so you can update the list to loop over the favorites.

Keep www/index.html open, and add the two bold lines from the following listing to the list.

Listing 6.7 Adding location items to navigation list (www/index.html)

Adds a divider to display some text →

```
<ion-list>
  <ion-item class="item-icon-left" ui-sref="search" menu-close><span
    class="icon ion-search"></span> Find a City</ion-item>
  <ion-item class="item-icon-left" ui-sref="settings" menu-close><span
    class="icon ion-ios-cog"></span> Settings</ion-item>
  <ion-item class="item-divider">Favorites</ion-item>
  <ion-item class="item-icon-left" ui-sref="weather({city: location.city,
    lat: location.lat, lng: location.lng})" menu-close ng-repeat=
    "location in locations"><span class="icon ion-ios-location">
    </span> {{location.city}}</ion-item>
</ion-list>
```

Loops over list of locations, links them to weather state, applies menuClose, and displays city name

The ngRepeat now loops over the array of locations, and will link to the weather state (which you'll define later). Now, when you open the side menu, the default Chicago location should appear under favorites. Later, when more locations have been added by users, they'll also appear here. Now you need to build your settings view.

6.4.3 Adding the settings template

Your settings template will contain three primary areas: a radio list to choose between imperial or metric units, a range input to configure the number of days to show in the forecast, and a list of favorite locations with the ability to delete items. Let's take a look at the complete code in listing 6.8 and review the several components individually. Create a new file at www/views/settings/settings.html. The resulting user interface will look like figure 6.4.

Listing 6.8 Listing 6.8 Settings template (www/views/settings/settings.html)

Uses ionRadio component to toggle between unit types

Uses input range to set number of days to display

```
<ion-view view-title="Settings">
  <ion-content>
    <ion-list>
      <ion-item class="item-divider">Units</ion-item>
      <ion-radio ng-model="settings.units" ng-value="'us'">Imperial
      (Fahrenheit)</ion-radio>
      <ion-radio ng-model="settings.units" ng-value="'si'">Metric
      (Celsius)</ion-radio>
      <div class="item item-divider">Days in forecast <span class=
      "badge badge-dark">{{settings.days - 1}}</span></div>
      <div class="item range range-positive">
        2 <input type="range" name="days" ng-model="settings.days"
      min="2" max="8" value="8"> 8
      </div>
```

```
        <div class="item item-button-right">Favorites
        <button class="button button-small" ng-click="canDelete =
        !canDelete">{{canDelete ? 'Done' : 'Edit'}}</button></div>
      </ion-list>
      <ion-list show-delete="canDelete">
        <ion-item ng-repeat="location in locations">
          <ion-delete-button class="ion-minus-circled" ng-
      click="remove($index)"></ion-delete-button>
            {{location.city}}
          </ion-item>
      </ion-list>
      <p class="padding">Weather data powered by <a
      href="https://developer.forecast.io/docs/v2">Forecast.io</a> and
      geocoding powered by <a
      href="https://developers.google.com/maps/documentation/geocoding/">
      Google</a>.</p>
    </ion-content>
  </ion-view>
```

Creates a divider with a button that toggles canDelete state

Creates a list and shows Delete button based on value of canDelete

Loops over list of locations

Deletes button that displays only when delete state is active on list

Credits for API sources

Let's start with the radio options. The `ionRadio` component is a wrapped-up radio button designed for mobile devices. Instead of displaying the small circle like it would normally do on a web page, it's restyled as a list with a checkmark to indicate the

Radio list component (ionRadio)

Range component

List of favorites

Button to toggle delete state

List items can be deleted (ionDeleteButton)

Figure 6.4　Settings view with a list of radio options, a range input, and a list with entries that can be deleted

selected item. It also assumes it's used inside of a `list` component, so it adopts the same display as a list item. That's why you don't have to place it inside of a list item. You assign the same `ngModel` value to both `ionRadio` inputs, and when a user selects one, the other will disable, as you'd expect with a radio list.

The next component is an input range slider. This is a newer HTML element to which Ionic applies styling. You see it in figure 6.4 as the line with a circular handle, which can be moved back and forth to set a value. In this case the options are values 2–8, because in your forecast data you'll always show the first day, so the setting determines how many additional days to display. As you drag the range, the value automatically updates.

The last component is `ionList` with the option to delete items from the list. The visual experience of showing the Delete button is built into the `ionList` component, but the actual logic to handle the deletion of an item is left up to the developer to implement. To use the `delete` feature, you use the `show-delete="canDelete"` attribute. When the expression is `true`, the Delete button will appear; otherwise, it will hide. You also have to declare an `ionDeleteButton` inside of each item, and give it a class for the icon you want to use. The listing also uses `ngClick` to call a method on the controller, which will take care of removing the item. There's a button in the item divider that toggles the `canDelete` value from `true` to `false`. The button also uses a more complex expression, which is a ternary operator, and changes the text from `Edit` to `Done`, depending on the value of `canDelete`.

At the end, you credit the two sources of your data. Sometimes APIs allow you to use their services for free, but ask for credit. To comply with that term, the credit is shown in listing 6.8.

6.4.4   *Settings view controller*

To finish up your settings view, you need the controller. You'll access the `Locations` and `Settings` services you created earlier and add the logic to remove a location when the Delete button is pressed.

Create a new file at www/views/settings/settings.js and add the controller found in the following listing.

Listing 6.9   Settings controller

```
angular.module('App')
.controller('SettingsController', function ($scope, Settings, Locations) {
    $scope.settings = Settings;
    $scope.locations = Locations.data;
    $scope.canDelete = false;

    $scope.remove = function (index) {
      Locations.toggle(Locations.data[index]);
    };
});
```

Annotations:
- **Declares controller and injects services** → points to `.controller('SettingsController', function ($scope, Settings, Locations) {`
- **Sets settings and locations data on scope** → points to `$scope.settings = Settings;` and `$scope.locations = Locations.data;`
- **Sets default state for deletion** ← `$scope.canDelete = false;`
- **Method to handle removing an item from list of locations** → points to `$scope.remove` block

This controller is fairly simple because you essentially only do two things. First, you set some values on the $scope, some of which come from the services you defined. Remember, these are JavaScript objects you created earlier, and any changes made in the settings view to those values will be reflected elsewhere. Second, the remove() method takes the index value of the location, and then calls the Locations.toggle() method with the item to remove. Because you abstracted the adding and removing of locations into the Locations service, you don't have to rewrite the logic here.

Now you need to add a new state for settings and make sure you add the settings controller to your application. Start by opening www/index.html and adding a new </script> tag for your controller after the other </script> tags:

```
<script src="views/settings/settings.js"></script>
```

Then open www/js/app.js and declare the state for settings as you see in listing 6.10. This is the final step before you can see the settings view in action. Add this into the state provider declaration.

Listing 6.10   Settings view state declaration (www/js/app.js)

```
.state('settings', {
  url: '/settings',
  controller: 'SettingsController',
  templateUrl: 'views/settings/settings.html'
})
```

You've finished the settings view, which contained two Ionic form components—radio items and a range input—as well as a list with the ability to delete items. Now it's time to set up the weather view.

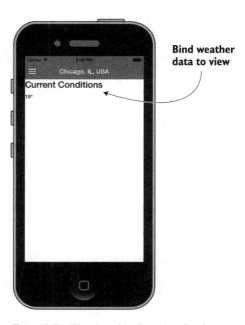

Bind weather data to view

6.5   *Setting up the weather view*

The last view you'll set up is the weather view, which is designed to display the current weather and forecast for a location. In this section you'll create the base for the weather view, and then add more complexity to it in the remaining sections of this chapter. If you're following along using Git, you can check out the code for this step:

```
$ git checkout -f step5
```

The result of this section can be seen in figure 6.5. The view will be fairly simple at this point, but you'll add more design and content as we go.

Figure 6.5   Weather view base loading from Forecast.io and showing current temperature

6.5.1   *Get a Forecast.io API key*

The Forecast.io service requires an API key to make requests. It only requires you to create an account with an email address and password, and—unless you want to use their paid service—it doesn't require a credit card or other personal information. Go to https://developer.forecast.io/ and sign up for your free account to get your token. You'll need this token in a few moments.

6.5.2   *Using Ionic CLI proxies*

Forecast.io doesn't support cross-origin resource sharing (CORS) as of this writing, which means that by default you can't load data from their API in a browser. This means that your requests for data from Forecast.io in your JavaScript will fail.

> ### CORS (cross-origin resource sharing)
> CORS is a set of security rules that browsers implement so that your web applications can load data from another domain. By default, browsers will block access to loading data from another domain because you can't trust what that external domain will send you. But if you trust the source of data and the API supports CORS, you're able to load that data. You can read more about CORS at http://enable-cors.org or in the book *CORS in Action* at http://manning.com/hossain.
>
> The other RESTful APIs used in this book have all supported CORS and therefore haven't required any additional work on your end.

The Ionic CLI utility provides a feature that allows you to bypass this limitation by using a proxy. Essentially it allows you to create something like a shortcut or alias URL that's attached to the server that the `ionic serve` command sets up, and the CLI can pass your original request through to the real API URL.

In a production application, you still need to properly address the Forecast.io API's CORS limitations, but in another way. When your app runs on a device, it doesn't have the ionic CLI utility to proxy the API requests. Therefore, you must implement another solution by either updating the API to support CORS or having a public CORS proxy service built for your app.

In your app, there's an ionic.project file that you should open. This file contains a JSON object for configuring the Ionic project, and here you can define a new property to map a list of URLs to proxy. Keeping the JSON valid, add the bold part from the following listing to your ionic.project file. It may contain information other than what is shown in this listing.

> **Listing 6.11   Declare proxy in ionic.project file (ionic.project)**

```
{
  "name": "chapter6",
  "app_id": "",
  "proxies": [
```

Adds a new proxies property, which is an array of objects

Adds a path, which will be new
proxy URL to call in your app

```
    {
      "path": "/api/forecast",
      "proxyUrl": "https://api.forecast.io/forecast/YOUR_KEY/"
    }
  ]
}
```

Adds a proxyUrl property, which
is endpoint that will be called

You've just declared a proxy, so in your app you can call /api/forecast and it will actually proxy through your local server and go to the proxyUrl defined in listing 6.11. Now you can replace YOUR_KEY with the API key from Forecast.io.

The next time the ionic serve command is run, the proxy will be set up. It will also work if you're using ionic emulate or ionic run with the live reload option turned on. This will allow you to develop locally with the Forecast.io service, and you can use the same technique for building apps locally with other services that don't support CORS.

6.5.3 *Add the weather view controller and template*

You'll now get the weather view added to your application. You'll just get the forecast to load and display the current temperature. Later you'll add a number of Ionic components and content to this view.

First, let's tackle the template. This is very vanilla—it will display the name of the location in the header bar and show the current temperature. In figure 6.5 you can see it's a chilly 18°F in Chicago. Create a new file at www/views/weather/weather.html and use the code from the following listing.

Listing 6.12   Base weather view template (www/views/weather/weather.html)

```
<ion-view view-title="{{params.city}}">
  <ion-content>
    <h3>Current Conditions</h3>
    <p>{{forecast.currently.temperature | number:0}}&deg;</p>
  </ion-content>
</ion-view>
```

There isn't too much going on here—you just bind some data into the title and the content areas. That data will be loaded in the controller next. You use the number filter on the temperature to round the value to a whole number because the value returned by the service is more accurate for your needs. You assume that users will expect the temperature value to be given in whole numbers.

Now let's add the controller. It also is fairly light at the moment, but you'll expand it slowly as you go along. The following listing contains the controller that you'll need to add into a new file at www/views/weather/weather.js.

Listing 6.13   Weather controller (www/views/weather/weather.js)

```
angular.module('App')
.controller('WeatherController', function ($scope, $http, $stateParams,
    Settings) {
  $scope.params = $stateParams;
  $scope.settings = Settings;

  $http.get('/api/forecast/' + $stateParams.lat + ',' + $stateParams.lng,
    {params: {units: Settings.units}}).success(function (forecast) {
      $scope.forecast = forecast;
  });
});
```

Defines controller and injects services

Attaches service data to scope

Makes HTTP request to load forecast

When this controller executes, it will first store some values on the $scope. The $stateParams are assigned to the $scope.params and used to get the location name for the header bar. The settings are also set on the scope, for future use. Then it makes an HTTP request to your proxy URL, adding the latitude, longitude, and units type for the request. When it returns, it stores the forecast on the scope for the template to use.

Lastly, you need to add the new state to your state provider list, and add the controller to the index.html file. Open the index.html file and add the following </script> tag to include the controller after the other </script> tags:

```
<script src="views/weather/weather.js"></script>
```

Then open www/js/app.js and add the last state for weather from the following listing. This will finish the weather view for the moment.

Listing 6.14   Weather view state declaration (www/js/app.js)

```
.state('weather', {
  url: '/weather/:city/:lat/:lng',
  controller: 'WeatherController',
  templateUrl: 'views/weather/weather.html'
});
```

In the next section, you'll build out a paginated scrolling view for your forecast information.

6.6   *ionScroll: building custom scrolling content*

This section focuses on providing a custom scrolling experience for the forecast data, and adding the necessary markup and styling to give it a nice appearance. Because there are so many weather apps available, it's important to craft a good user experience. If you're following along using Git, you can check out the code for this step:

```
$ git checkout -f step6
```

Scroll area fixed and shows first page of content

Content container with three pages stacked sits inside scroll area

Content container moved up to view second page

Figure 6.6 Using `ionScroll` with paging enabled for separated forecast content

You'll use `ionScroll` to create a pagination vertical scroller. This means that as a user swipes up or down, the scrolling will always continue until the next page. In some ways this is like the `ionSlideBox`, but vertically and with a slightly different experience. Then you'll add the content and styling for each of the pages in the scroller. Lastly, you'll add a few filters to help format your data in a more meaningful way.

At the end of the chapter, you'll be able to scroll through a weather forecast like you see in figure 6.6. The scrolling only stops when it reaches the next page.

6.6.1 Using ionScroll with paging

First you need to create the scrolling experience with `ionScroll`. Normally you would use `ionContent`, with its default vertical scrolling ability and automatic filling of the content. But `ionScroll` gives you a little more control over how the scrolling content area functions, and in this case it provides the paging feature you desire.

The `ionScroll` directive has to be given a width and height value. This is something `ionContent` does for you automatically, but `ionScroll` doesn't. Because your app can be loaded onto different devices with different screen sizes, you have to be able to calculate the size of `ionScroll` based on the size of the screen.

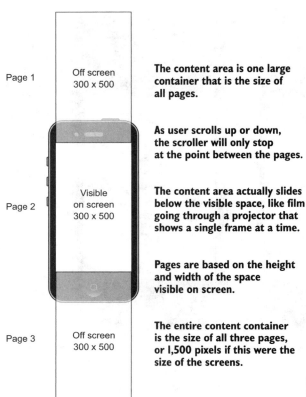

Page 1   Off screen   **The content area is one large**
          300 x 500   **container that is the size of**
                        all pages.

                        As user scrolls up or down,
                        the scroller will only stop
                        at the point between the pages.

          Visible   **The content area actually slides**
Page 2   on screen   **below the visible space, like film**
          300 x 500   **going through a projector that**
                        shows a single frame at a time.

                        Pages are based on the height
                        and width of the space
                        visible on screen.

Page 3   Off screen   **The entire content container**
          300 x 500   **is the size of all three pages,**
                        or 1,500 pixels if this were the
                        size of the screens.

Figure 6.7   How ionScroll with paging
will allow you to scroll by page

ionScroll will work by creating an area three times the height of the device that will scroll and stop at each page. With some calculations, you'll generate this content area and it will be able to scroll up or down between the pages. Look at figure 6.7 to see how these layers work to create the scrolling experience.

For your scrolling area, you'll make ionScroll the same size as the viewable area, and then create a div element inside of ionScroll with three times the height of ion-Scroll. This div element inside will be able to slide up or down to provide the scrolling effect you're after. You'll lock scrolling to vertical only, and with the paging feature enabled, it will also scroll until it hits the next page. Imagine the ionScroll was 500 pixels tall; the div inside would be 1,500 pixels tall and have three pages (500 × 3 = 1,500). Because it's 500 pixels tall, when paging is enabled scrolling will always stop on a boundary that's based on the ionScroll height, in this case 0 pixels (page 1), 500 pixels (page 2), or 1,000 pixels (page 3).

Let's start by looking at the template with ionScroll included. It uses some calculations that will be added to the controller soon, so it won't function until you've updated the controller.

Listing 6.15 Weather template with `ionScroll` (www/views/weather/weather.html)

Uses ionContent to position ionScroll properly

```
<ion-view view-title="{{params.city}}">
  <ion-content>
    <ion-scroll direction="y" paging="true" ng-style=
      "{width: getWidth(), height: getHeight()}">
      <div ng-style="{height: getTotalHeight()}">
        <div class="scroll-page page1" ng-style=
        "{width: getWidth(), height: getHeight()}">
          Page 1
        </div>
        <div class="scroll-page page2" ng-style=
        "{width: getWidth(), height: getHeight()}">
          Page 2
        </div>
        <div class="scroll-page page3" ng-style=
        "{width: getWidth(), height: getHeight()}">
          Page 3
        </div>
      </div>
    </ion-scroll>
  </ion-content>
</ion-view>
```

Uses ionScroll and locks direction to vertical only with paging; gives exact height and width styling

Creates inner div and gives it a height equal to all three pages stacked

Pages each declared with same width and height of the ionScroll area

Here you use `ionContent` and then put `ionScroll` inside of it. `ionContent` will give you a container that takes into account the size of the header bar. Inside of that, `ionScroll` exists, and it gets the height and width from the controller calculations. `ionContent` will not actually scroll, because `ionScroll` will be the exact size of the visible space.

You have one `div` element inside of `ionScroll`, and it has the total height of all three of the scroll pages. The scroll pages are inside, and are stacked on top of one another, like you see in figure 6.7.

Now you can add the controller methods used to calculate sizes so you can preview how it scrolls. Open the controller at www/views/weather/weather.js and add the code from the following listing inside the controller.

Listing 6.16 Controller methods to determine sizes (www/views/weather/weather.js)

```
var barHeight = document.getElementsByTagName
    ('ion-header-bar')[0].clientHeight;
$scope.getWidth = function () {
  return window.innerWidth + 'px';
};

$scope.getTotalHeight = function () {
  return parseInt(parseInt($scope.getHeight()) * 3) + 'px';
};

$scope.getHeight = function () {
  return parseInt(window.innerHeight - barHeight) + 'px';
};
```

Gets first header bar's height

Gives items width of app

Gets total height by multiplying height of space by number of pages

Gives items height of app without header bar

You start off by getting the height of the header bar, because this may vary from platform to platform. The `getWidth()`, `getHeight()`, and `getTotalHeight()` methods use the size of the window itself to determine the amount of space available, minus the bar height. This programmatic approach to determining the size is required only because different devices have different screen sizes, and you want the pages to be the same size as the screen. You can create a scrolling region with items of a fixed size to scroll through them using the same logic but providing an explicit size.

Now that you understand scrolling, you're ready to add the content for each page into the scrolling pages. The following listing has the updated template for www/views/weather/weather.html.

Listing 6.17 Content for weather template (www/views/weather/weather.html)

```
<ion-view view-title="{{params.city}}">
  <ion-content>
    <ion-scroll direction="y" paging="true" ng-style="{width: getWidth(),
      height: getHeight()}">
      <div ng-style="{height: getTotalHeight()}">
        <div class="scroll-page center" ng-style="{width: getWidth(), height:
      getHeight()}">
          <div class="bar bar-dark">
            <h1 class="title">Current Conditions</h1>
          </div>

          <div class="has-header">
            <h2 class="primary">{{
              forecast.currently.temperature | number:0}}&deg;</h2>
            <h2 class="secondary icon" ng-class=
      "forecast.currently.icon | icons"></h2>
            <p>{{forecast.currently.summary}}</p>
            <p>High: {{forecast.daily.data[0].temperatureMax |
      number:0}}&deg; Low: {{forecast.daily.data[0].temperatureMin |
      number:0}}&deg; Feels Like: {{forecast.currently.apparentTemperature |
      number:0}}&deg;</p>
            <p>Wind: {{forecast.currently.windSpeed | number:0}}
      <span class="icon wind-icon ion-ios7-arrow-thin-up" ng-style=
      "{transform: 'rotate(' + forecast.currently.windBearing +
      'deg)'}"></span></p>
          </div>
        </div>

        <div class="scroll-page" ng-style="{width: getWidth(), height:
      getHeight()}">
          <div class="bar bar-dark">
            <h1 class="title">Daily Forecast</h1>
          </div>
          <div class="has-header">
            <p class="padding">{{forecast.daily.summary}}</p>
            <div class="row" ng-repeat="day in forecast.daily.data |
      limitTo:settings.days">
              <div class="col col-50">{{day.time + '000' |
      date:'EEEE'}}</div>
```

Uses has-header class to position content of this page

Uses a header bar like a subheader

Uses icons filter to map to an icon based on conditions

Uses wind direction given in degrees to rotate an arrow to point in that direction

Uses limitTo filter to only show number of days from settings

Uses date filter to convert a Unix timestamp into day of the week

Uses chance filter to round percentage to a 10 value ⟶

```
                  <div class="col"><span class="icon" ng-class="day.icon |
          icons"></span><sup>{{day.precipProbability | chance}}</sup></div>
                  <div class="col">{{day.temperatureMax | number:0}}&deg;</div>
                  <div class="col">{{day.temperatureMin | number:0}}&deg;</div>
                </div>
              </div>
            </div>
            <div class="scroll-page" ng-style="{width: getWidth(), height:
          getHeight()}">
              <div class="bar bar-dark">
                <h1 class="title">Weather Stats</h1>
              </div>
              <div class="list has-header">
                <div class="item">
                  Sunrise: {{forecast.daily.data[0].sunriseTime |
                  timezone:forecast.timezone}}</div>
                <div class="item">
                  Sunset: {{forecast.daily.data[0].sunsetTime |
                  timezone:forecast.timezone}}</div>
                <div class="item">Visibility:
          {{forecast.currently.visibility}}</div>
                <div class="item">Humidity: {{forecast.currently.humidity *
          100}}%</div>
              </div>
            </div>
          </div>
        </ion-scroll>
      </ion-content>
    </ion-view>
```

Gets sunrise/sunset time, which is converted into location timezone (annotation at lines for sunrise/sunset)

The template has a lot of content, but it's mostly binding data into the view and elements used for styling and positioning. Each page has a bar element, which contains the title for that page. Inside of the following element, you have different content for each. Until you create the filters, the application won't be able to correctly load.

Inside of the second page, you use the Ionic grid features to help lay out your content. There's a div element with the row class, and then several divs inside with the col class. If you're familiar with CSS frameworks like Bootstrap, you'll recognize a CSS grid system being used. In other words, the CSS grid is like an auto-adjusting layout with rows and columns. It allows you to lay out your content visually like a table, but without having to use the table element (which is intended to be used with tabular data, not for layout purposes). In this case, you have four columns, and the first column is set to take 50% of the width. Ionic's CSS grid component uses the CSS flexbox feature to automatically adjust the layout of columns, so if you don't specify a specific column width, the columns are automatically equally sized with any remaining space.

Right now it will look a little disorganized when you preview this view. You need to add some CSS to get the design to look a little smoother. Open the www/css/styles.css file and add the CSS rules from the following listing.

Listing 6.18 Styling for weather view (www/css/styles.css)

```
.scroll-page .icon:before {
  padding-right: 5px;
}
.scroll-page .row + .row {
  margin-top: 0;
  padding-top: 5px;
}
.scroll-page .row:nth-of-type(odd) {
  background: #fafafa;
}
.scroll-page .row:nth-of-type(even) {
  background: #f3f3f3;
}
.scroll-page .wind-icon {
  display: inline-block;
}
.scroll-page.center {
  text-align: center;
}
.scroll-page .primary {
  margin: 0;
  font-size: 100px;
  font-weight: lighter;
  padding-left: 30px;
}
.scroll-page .secondary {
  margin: 0;
  font-size: 150px;
  font-weight: lighter;
}
.scroll-page .has-header {
  position: relative;
}
```

These CSS rules apply to the contents of the scrolling pages only, and are just used to give some cleaner display to the elements. In your apps, you'll likely write more CSS than in these examples, but your focus is always on Ionic's features.

6.6.2 *Creating filters for forecast data*

If you recall from chapter 3, filters are used to modify the display of data in the view. You could put the filter logic into the controller, but then they aren't very easy to reuse. You get a lot of data from Forecast.io, but it isn't always in the format you'd like. For example, you get a timestamp for the sunrise and sunset values, but a timestamp isn't very human-friendly. You can build a filter that will convert a timestamp into a more friendly value like "5:46 p.m."

First, you'd like to show an icon related to the weather forecast. For example, if it's raining, you'd like to use one of Ionic's rainy icons. Because you've already used the filters in your template, you now need to implement them. Then you'd like to modify the chance of rain values to always round them to the nearest tenth value. Normally the chance of rain is reported like 20%, not 17%.

Lastly, you need to fix the sunrise and sunset timestamps. They're currently shown based on the user's time zone. For example, if you lived in Chicago and viewed the weather in London you'd see the local version of the time from Chicago. This is confusing, because in that case the sunrise would be in the middle of the night. You'll use a JavaScript library called Moment.js to help you manage the time zones and display the times according to the weather location's time zone and not the user's time zone.

First, you'll install the Moment.js library files using the `ionic add` feature. You can install the files quickly using the following command from the root of your project. If you're following along using Git, this is already installed and you don't need to run this:

```
$ ionic add moment-timezone
```

It will take a moment to download and install Moment.js and Moment Timezone, both of which you need to use to correctly manage time zones. Moment Timezone declares Moment.js as a dependency, so you don't have to install it separately. When they're downloaded, add them to your index.html file after the Ionic `</script>` tag and before the `</script>` tags for your app files:

```
<script src="lib/moment/moment.js"></script>
<script src="lib/moment-timezone/builds/moment-timezone-with-
     data.js"></script>
```

Now that you have the Moment.js library set up, you can create a new filter that will handle converting the timestamp into the correct time zone of the weather location. You're lucky because the forecast data provides you with the time zone of the location, so you don't need to do anything special to find it.

The following listing has the code for all three filters that you want to create. Open www/js/app.js and add these three filters as part of your app.

Listing 6.19 Filters for weather view

```
.filter('timezone', function () {          ⟵  Creates timezone filter to convert
  return function (input, timezone) {           to weather location time zone
    if (input && timezone) {
      var time = moment.tz(input * 1000, timezone);     Only if timestamp and
      return time.format('LT');                          time zone are provided
    }                                                     will it convert timestamp
    return '';                                            based on time zone
  };
})
.filter('chance', function () {            ⟵  Creates chance filter to convert to a
  return function (chance) {                    percentage chance for precipitation
    if (chance) {
      var value = Math.round(chance * 10);      If a value is given, rounds
                                                percentage to a multiple of 10
```

```
        return value * 10;
      }
      return 0;
    };
  })
  .filter('icons', function () {
    var map = {
      'clear-day': 'ion-ios-sunny',
      'clear-night': 'ion-ios-moon',
      rain: 'ion-ios-rainy',
      snow: 'ion-ios-snowy',
      sleet: 'ion-ios-rainy',
      wind: 'ion-ios-flag',
      fog: 'ion-ios-cloud',
      cloudy: 'ion-ios-cloudy',
      'partly-cloudy-day': 'ion-ios-partlysunny',
      'partly-cloudy-night': 'ion-ios-cloudy-night'
    };
    return function (icon) {
      return map[icon] || '';
    }
  })
```

> **If a value is given, rounds percentage to a multiple of 10**

> **Creates icons filter to convert a condition type into an icon**

> **Based on a map of conditions to icons, returns icon if found**

The filters here are fairly straightforward. The `timezone` filter will convert a time-stamp to display based on a specific time zone. The `chance` filter will take a percentage value and round it to the nearest tens value. The `icons` filter will take the icon value from the forecast data and map it to an icon.

Now your app will be able to run and display the full weather forecast. With the `ionScroll` component, you're able to scroll up and down, but it will always stop at the next page. This section may have been a bit complex, but looking at each individual component should help clarify what it's doing. Your next step is to create a new option button that will open up an action sheet with a list of options for your users.

6.7   *Action sheet: displaying a list of options*

The action sheet component is another useful tool when you wish to display a list of options to users. In this situation you'd like to display a list of options for users so they can toggle the location as a favorite or they can set the location as the primary location. If you're following along using Git, you can check out the code for this step:

```
$ git checkout -f step7
```

To show a list of options, the action sheet is a list of buttons that slides up from the bottom of the screen. Usually there's a Cancel button, and sometimes there's a special button that indicates a destructive action such as deleting. Tapping on the area out-side of the buttons will close the sheet, much like a modal or popover. You can see the action sheet in figure 6.8.

The action sheet component is something iOS users will find familiar, but Android doesn't have an equivalent native component. You should consider the implications of using this feature when you plan to also support Android and, while there's no

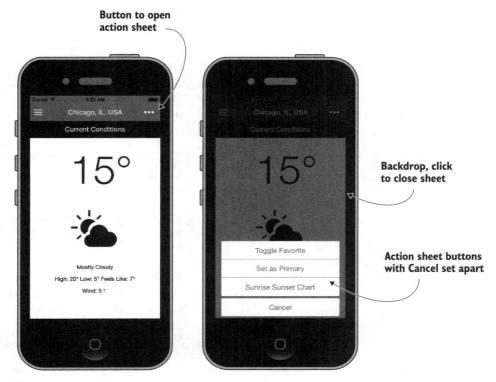

Figure 6.8   Button that opens the action sheet with options

technical reason it won't work on Android, it might not be the most intuitive for Android users.

There's no template for the action sheet because it's run entirely from the $ionicActionSheet service. You'll need to declare the list of buttons, and what should happen when each button is selected. Start by adding a more button to your view that will be able to trigger the action sheet, found in the following listing.

Listing 6.20   Action sheet more button (www/views/weather/weather.html)

```
<ion-view view-title="{{params.city}}">
  <ion-nav-buttons side="left">
    <button class="button button-clear" menu-toggle=
    "left"><span class="icon ion-navicon"></span></button>
  </ion-nav-buttons>
  <ion-nav-buttons side="right">
    <button class="button button-icon" ng-click="showOptions()"><span
    class="icon ion-more"></span></button>
  </ion-nav-buttons>
  <ion-content>
```

Redeclares sidebar toggle left button

Adds new nav button to right side

Adds a nav button to call showOptions

Continues with rest of template

This will add a new button to the right side of the title in the header bar that has the more icon, which is three dots. It will call a method in the controller that you'll write next, and that method will handle the logic to open the action sheet. You also added the same left button again; otherwise, it would be replaced because you declared a new button for this view.

You'll need to update the controller in www/views/weather/weather.js. You'll need to also inject the $ionicActionSheet service into the controller, which isn't shown here. See the code for this method in the following listing.

```
$scope.showOptions = function () {
  var sheet = $ionicActionSheet.show({
    buttons: [
      {text: 'Toggle Favorite'},
      {text: 'Set as Primary'},
      {text: 'Sunrise Sunset Chart'}
    ],
    cancelText: 'Cancel',
    buttonClicked: function (index) {
      if (index === 0) {
        Locations.toggle($stateParams);
      }
      if (index === 1) {
        Locations.primary($stateParams);
      }
      if (index === 2) {
        $scope.showModal();
      }
      return true;
    }
  });
};
```

Uses show method to set up and show an action sheet; must have injected $ionicActionSheet

An array of objects for buttons; object must have a text property

Shows optional Cancel button and gives it text

Method to handle button clicks; index of selected button is provided

Uses Locations service to toggle current location as favorite

Uses Locations service to set current location as primary

You'll add something here in next section to open a modal

Returning true will close action sheet; otherwise, it will remain open

This controller method is called by your button, and the action sheet is immediately told to show itself. You assign the value of $ionicActionSheet.show() to the sheet variable, which returns a function that can close the sheet. At any point you could call sheet() to close it. The show() method takes an object with various properties, and here you've chosen to create three buttons in the buttons array, plus the Cancel button, which is defined separately. The Cancel button is a separate property because it's a special button. By default, the Cancel button will just close the sheet, which is the behavior you've adopted here. You can optionally handle the Cancel (and destructive) button click events yourself with custom functions.

The last property is the buttonClicked function. This is called when a button is selected, and provides the index of the button from the first list. If the Cancel or destructive buttons are selected, this function doesn't execute because they have their own versions, not shown here. Because you have three buttons, you have three conditionals to check the value of the index and execute logic based on the button. The first two buttons use the `Locations` service you created earlier, but the third won't do anything just yet. You'll add that button in the next section.

That's all you need to have the action sheet component in your app. Now to address that last button; you want it to open up a modal that will slide up from the bottom to display more information.

6.8 *ionModal: displaying the sunrise and sunset chart*

Modals are used heavily in user interfaces today. A modal is a temporary view that's layered above the current view. On websites, modals are often used to prompt a user to sign up for a newsletter or to force focus on a subset of content that darkens the rest of the content. If you're following along using Git, you can check out the code for this step:

```
$ git checkout -f step8
```

On a mobile device, a modal may be used in slightly different contexts, but the principles remain the same. The main draw of the modal is the fact that it can open above the current content, but be closed to return. Some example modal uses include showing a preview of a search result item without leaving the search result page, opening a modal with a list of additional search filters, or displaying an alert or notice for a weather event. You can see a modal in action in figure 6.9.

Modal sliding up into view from bottom

Close button

Collection repeat with sunrise and sunset times

Figure 6.9 The modal opens by sliding up from the bottom and overlaying the entire app.

Modals are designed to overlay the entire app when the app is running on a smaller phone device. If the app runs on a larger tablet device, the modal will not actually fill the entire app, but will float in the middle. You can modify the exact size with CSS, but by default the size of the modal is a percentage of the size of the screen on tablets. This is important because it means that without some custom styling, the modal window size will vary from device to device.

6.8.1 Setting up a modal

In the example here, the modal will show the sunrise and sunset chart for the location. You'll start by using the $ionicModal service to create a new modal instance, and then update the third button in the action sheet to trigger opening the modal. Much like the popover, you also have to clean up the modal when the scope is destroyed to prevent memory leaks.

To begin, open the controller in www/views/weather/weather.js and inject the $ionicModal service into the controller, shown in the following listing.

Listing 6.22 Modal in weather view (www/views/weather/weather.js)

```
$scope.showModal = function () {                          Method to open a modal
    if ($scope.modal) {
      $scope.modal.show();                                If modal already exists,
    } else {                                              shows it again
      $ionicModal.fromTemplateUrl('views/weather/modal-chart.html', {
        scope: $scope
      }).then(function (modal) {                          When template loads, stores
        $scope.modal = modal;                             modal instance on scope
        $scope.modal.show();
      });                                                 Then shows modal
    }
};

$scope.hideModal = function () {
    $scope.modal.hide();                                  Method to hide modal
};

$scope.$on('$destroy', function() {
    $scope.modal.remove();                                When current view is
});                                                       destroyed, also removes
                                                          modal from memory
```

(left margin annotation: **If doesn't exist, loads modal template and assigns scope to use**)

This syntax is nearly identical to the ionPopover syntax you saw in chapter 5. Modals are isolated views, meaning they need a new template. In this case, you load that template from a URL, but you can also provide that template inline. I recommend using this method to avoid writing HTML inside of JavaScript.

You start by creating the showModal() method, which will immediately check if the modal is already created or not. If it is, it will just show it again. Otherwise, it will create the modal.

For modal creation the `fromTemplateUrl()` method takes two arguments: a string for the template URL and an object. You can specify additional options, such as the type of animation or if the hardware back button can close the modal (for some Android devices). Modals create an isolated child scope, and the scope parameter tells the modal which scope should be the parent for the modal. By default it's the root scope, and you want this modal to have access to your weather scope so you assign it as the parent instead.

Because loading a template is asynchronous, it returns a promise that you resolve with `then()`. It gives you an instance of a modal controller object, which has properties like show and hide to control the modal.

Listening for the scope `$destroy` event is something you must do with each modal you create, or else it will always remain in memory. Most of the Ionic components are able to clean up after themselves, but due to the way the modal is designed, this isn't possible.

Potential memory leaks and performance

Ionic and Angular are both focused on performance and preventing situations where the app can become sluggish. A memory leak is a problem in JavaScript where something that was loaded into the browser memory allocation isn't properly handled and removed when it's no longer needed. JavaScript engines today have very good garbage collection, which is the task of reclaiming memory that's no longer needed.

Most of Ionic's features can be easily reclaimed when they're no longer in use. For example, when a user navigates to another view, the memory allocated for the old view can be destroyed. Ionic's navigation also provides the ability to cache and keep things in memory, which makes it faster to return to that view later.

Modals and popovers are two types of components that you must manually clean up when you're finished with them. They're services that you use in the controller to create a new view, and because you create them you must also remove them. Ionic doesn't know when they're no longer in use, unlike the views that you declare in your `$stateProvider`.

If you forget to clean up a modal or popover, it isn't likely to crash your app. But if you use a lot of modals or popovers without clearing them, every time you use one it would remain in memory until the user closed the app. The best thing to do is always clean up, as shown in listing 6.22.

To get the modal to actually appear, you need to create the template file for it. Create a new file at www/views/weather/modal-chart.html and add the contents from the following listing.

Listing 6.23   Modal contents template (www/views/weather/modal-chart.html)

**ionModalView
must wrap
contents of
modal
template**

```
<ion-modal-view>
  <ion-header-bar class="bar-dark">
    <h1 class="title">Sunrise, Sunset Chart</h1>
    <button class="button button-clear" ng-click="hideModal()">
    Close</button>
  </ion-header-bar>
  <ion-content>
  </ion-content>
</ion-modal-view>
```

**Adds a header
bar with a
Close button**

**Empties content
area for moment**

ionModalView is a specialized version of ionView that you'll use elsewhere, and is required when making a modal template. Just make sure to wrap your modal template in ionModalView to properly get the design and positioning for a modal window.

Because it's a blank view, you add a header bar and content area. The header bar has a Close button that calls the hideModal() method, which is from the parent scope (the weather scope). You want to have some content, so you can now add the content for the sunrise and sunset times.

6.8.2   *Collection repeat: making the sunrise and sunset list fast*

You want to show the sunrise and sunset times for the entire year, which you can calculate using the aid of a helpful library called SunCalc. Because the sunrise and sunset cycle repeats yearly, you only need to show the chart for one year.

You can use a normal list with ngRepeat to create the long list of items, but that means you'd create 365 items when only a small number can actually appear on the screen at once. If you create all 365 items in a list, they all still render and take up memory regardless if they're on- or offscreen. This will impact the performance of your list, mostly from having to render too many Document Object Model (DOM) elements, and can cause it to be slow to display or have poor scrolling smoothness.

To address this, you'll use the collection repeat feature. Instead of creating 365 items, it will create just enough to display on the screen, as shown in figure 6.10. When the user scrolls, it will destroy items that go out of view and create new items and add them to the list. This will give you much better memory management, and most importantly provide a smoother scrolling experience. Any large set of data that you want to scroll through can benefit from using collection repeat.

There are some caveats to using collection repeat, which may not always suit your needs. For instance:

- It only works with arrays of items, which means you can't have an object and use collection repeat.
- Unless you define the exact height and width of each item in the list, it will assume they're all the same size as the first item. If all items are the same size, then you shouldn't declare the height and width, but if they vary you should.
- It will take up the entire size of its container.

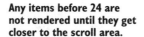

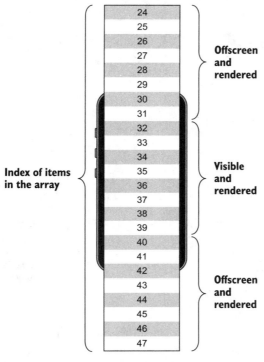

Any items before 24 are not rendered until they get closer to the scroll area.

Index of items in the array

Offscreen and rendered

Visible and rendered

Offscreen and rendered

Any items with index over 47 are not rendered until they get closer to the scroll area.

Figure 6.10 How the collection repeat feature renders only the items visible onscreen, plus several items on the boundaries offscreen, to increase performance

- Angular's one-time binding shouldn't be used. The way that items are created and destroyed conflicts with the one-time binding feature.
- To make the styling work well, you should avoid doing anything that will show or hide items in the list or change an item's dimensions.
- Images with a collection repeat can cause performance issues, so when possible, cache the images ahead of time or avoid using them.

Before you can use collection repeat, you need to create an array with the year's sunrise and sunset times. First, you need to install the SunCalc library:

```
$ ionic add suncalc
```

Then you can include the library in your index.html file by adding the `</script>` tag after the other library scripts:

```
<script src="lib/suncalc/suncalc.js"></script>
```

Lastly, you'll create the chart when the modal is requested. You'll update `showModal()` in the weather controller to generate the list of times for the next year before the modal appears. Open www/views/weather/weather.js and update the `showModal()` method as shown in the following listing.

Listing 6.24   Generating chart (www/views/weather/weather.js)

```
$scope.showModal = function () {
  if ($scope.modal) {
    $scope.modal.show();
  } else {
    $ionicModal.fromTemplateUrl('views/weather/modal-chart.html', {
      scope: $scope
    }).then(function (modal) {
      $scope.modal = modal;
      var days = [];
      var day = Date.now();
      for (var i = 0; i < 365; i++) {
        day += 1000 * 60 * 60 * 24;
        days.push(SunCalc.getTimes(day, $scope.params.lat,
$scope.params.lng));
      }
      $scope.chart = days;
      $scope.modal.show();
    });
  }
};
```

Annotations:
- **Creates variables for your calculations** → `var days = []; var day = Date.now();`
- **For each day, adds another day to timestamp** → `day += 1000 * 60 * 60 * 24;`
- **Uses SunCalc to get times based on latitude, longitude, and day** → `days.push(SunCalc.getTimes(...))`
- **Assigns list of days to scope** → `$scope.chart = days;`

Here you create an array with the times for each day of the year, starting from tomorrow for a whole year. SunCalc requires timestamp, latitude, and longitude values to be able to calculate the sunrise and sunset values. Those values are pushed into the array, and then stored on the scope, because the modal will need to access the chart array for collection repeat.

To implement collection repeat, you need to open your modal template again. Edit the www/views/weather/modal-chart.html file and update the content with the code shown in the following listing.

Listing 6.25   Collection repeat in action (www/views/weather/modal-chart.html)

```
<ion-content>
  <div class="list">
    <div class="item" collection-repeat="day in chart">
      {{day.sunrise | date:'MMM d'}}: {{day.sunrise | date:'shortTime'}},
      {{day.sunset | date:'shortTime'}}
    </div>
  </div>
</ion-content>
```

Annotations:
- **Uses a list to contain items** → `<div class="list">`
- **Uses collection repeat, like ngRepeat** → `collection-repeat="day in chart"`
- **Binds date, sunrise, and sunset times to list item** → `{{day.sunset | date:'shortTime'}}`

Collection repeat is implemented with the same syntax as `ngRepeat`—that is, `item in array`—though it does support some other more complex expressions listed in the documentation. You've used the `list` component to style your items, though this doesn't matter to collection repeat. It only cares that each item is the same size, unless you explicitly declare the size of each item. Then you bind the data into the view using the date filters.

Collection repeat has far better performance on large data sets. It will only render a few items that are off the screen in either direction instead of the entire list, which saves memory and processing requirements to scroll. You could try `ngRepeat` in place of collection repeat in listing 6.25, and you may see some of the performance differences when on a device. When your set of data is large enough to see some lag on many devices, collection repeat can bring much-needed performance improvements.

You'll add one last feature: a popup to confirm or alert users when they change their favorite locations.

6.9   *Popup: alert and confirm changes to favorites*

Right now when you select the Toggle Favorites button in the action sheet, it silently updates the choice for you without telling you what happened. Users appreciate getting visual feedback about their changes, and one way to do this is to use a popup. If you're following along using Git, you can check out the code for this step:

```
$ git checkout -f step9
```

Popups are familiar to web users because they appear with a message and a button or two asking you questions like "Are you sure?" or alerting you saying "We are sorry an error occurred." Ionic provides three types of popup defaults—alert, confirm, and prompt—or the choice to design your own. You can see the alert and confirm options in figure 6.11. Each of the three defaults has a unique use case:

- Alerts are meant to simply convey information, such as a message about success or failure to complete an action.
- Confirms ask you to verify you meant to do something, such as confirm that you meant to delete an item.
- Prompts are designed to ask you for some information, such as a title for an item you're about to save.

There are many ways to design an interface to provide feedback to users, and popups are best used when you want to be completely sure a user has read the message or when you need to prompt for feedback before continuing. Popups should be used with caution, however, because they're interruptive to the user experience.

To add the popup, you'll add it into the `Locations` service toggle method. You'll confirm the user intends to remove the favorite, and alert the user when the favorite is added. Right now, when the user toggles a favorite location, it's done in the background and the user doesn't get any feedback or confirmation that it was completed.

Figure 6.11   Popups with an alert (left) and a confirm (right) as used in the app

Open the www/js/app.js file and locate the Locations service. First you need to inject the $ionicPopup service into the Locations service as follows:

```
.factory('Locations', function ($ionicPopup) {
```

Now replace the existing toggle() method with the code from the following listing, which will add both an alert and a confirm popup during toggling.

Listing 6.26   Using $ionicPopup to alert and confirm (www/js/app.js)

```
toggle: function (item) {
  var index = Locations.getIndex(item);
  if (index >= 0) {
    $ionicPopup.confirm({
      title: 'Are you sure?',
      template: 'This will remove ' + Locations.data[index].city
    }).then(function (res) {
      if (res) {
        Locations.data.splice(index, 1);
      }
    });
  } else {
    Locations.data.push(item);
    $ionicPopup.alert({
      title: 'Location saved'
    });
  }
},
```

Creates a confirm popup and passes object to define; by default will have OK and Cancel buttons

Gives title and content of popup

When a button is selected, function is called and res will be true when OK is selected to delete item

Creates an alert popup with a title; by default will have just OK button

The confirm popup is used to verify that the user wishes to delete the item, and unless you override the settings in the configuration object, it will have two buttons: OK and Cancel. When a button is selected, the promise will resolve the function and pass the value of res as Boolean. If the user chooses OK, res will be true and will then proceed to handle deleting the item.

The alert popup is fired after the item is already added, and just informs the user the location was saved. The button will close the popup automatically.

Popups have a lot of configuration options that aren't used here, but you may find it useful to read about them in the documentation. For example, you can change the OK or Cancel button text, change the button color style, or even create a more complex popup where you define all of the buttons and properties yourself.

This concludes the features you'll build into this app. Before we conclude, I'd like to challenge you to improve this app with some of the knowledge you've gained from earlier chapters.

6.10 *Chapter challenges*

This chapter covered the major remaining Ionic components. Now that you've seen them in action, I challenge you to extend this weather app with additional features from earlier chapters:

- *Add a way to reload the forecast*—The current conditions are only loaded when the view is loaded. You can implement reloading of the forecast without leaving the view using the ionRefresh component or another method of your own design.
- *Implement the loading component*—The weather view and search views load data from an API, and while this is happening the user can still interact with the screen. Implement a loading component to provide feedback that the user interface is waiting for the data.
- *Allow reordering of locations*—You can delete locations in the settings view, but you can also implement a way to handle reordering of the locations using the ionList reordering feature.
- *Use tabs instead of* ionScroll—You could replace the ionScroll feature with tabs for the three different views. Tip: Just try to use the tabs without declaring each tab as a new state.
- *Set default view to primary location*—Right now, the default view is the search view, but if there's already a location stored, it might be nice to view it instead.
- *Persist the favorites and settings*—So far, every load of the app will reset the settings and favorites. Look at how to implement persistence in chapter 7 and improve the experience by remembering settings and favorites.

6.11 *Summary*

Through the last three chapters, we've covered most of the Ionic components and features available to you. In this chapter specifically, you learned how to do the following things:

- Set up and use a side menu as a base for your navigation
- Create a custom scrolling page experience using `ionScroll`
- Use an action sheet to display options for the user contextual to the current view
- Create a modal for showing related information without clearing the current view
- Performance improvements and use for collection repeat over `ngRepeat`
- Add popups for giving your users feedback and confirming their actions

In the next chapter, you'll learn about many advanced topics when building Ionic apps, such as how to work with offline mode, storing data, and customizing Ionic default settings and styles.

Advanced techniques
for professional apps

7

This chapter focuses on some advanced techniques that you could incorporate into most apps. As Ionic developers dig deeper into the platform, they'll likely discover that the core components, while useful, can't provide everything well-designed apps need. There should be an element of uniqueness for every app. Just using Ionic's components out of the box without any customization or creativity isn't the best approach for quality apps.

Using these various techniques, you'll be able to design apps that take the strengths of Ionic and extend it for a unique experience. You'll be able to mold an app to adapt its design and behavior for different platforms and improve the user experience through events and using storage.

7.1   *Set up chapter project*

This chapter is a bit different from the previous chapters where you built a full-scale app. Here the examples are minimized to focus on just the features we're discussing at the time. You can either download the chapter examples or use Git to check out a copy for yourself.

The examples are organized into folders for each section. I'll let you know which folder to look at when you're working with it. For each folder, you should only have to use `ionic serve` from that folder to preview the app in the browser. For some folders, you might consider running it in an emulator or on a device.

7.1.1   *Get the code*

To get the latest copy of the chapter example, you can download the completed files or check out the repository using GitHub. The following link will download the chapter example as a zip file, which you can extract and then view: https://github .com/ionic-in-action/chapter7/archive/master.zip. To check out the chapter examples, use the following command to clone the repository (this chapter uses the master branch, and doesn't have tags to check out each step):

```
$ git clone https://github.com/ionic-in-action/chapter7.git
$ cd chapter7
```

7.2   *Custom Ionic styling using Sass*

Ionic comes with a beautiful set of default colors and styles for every component. The examples so far have used very little custom styling and have relied heavily on Ionic's defaults. This is great for learning and shows the power of Ionic, but typically you'll want to customize the design for your needs in some way.

It's best practice to customize the display of your app for your own needs. This is particularly true regarding colors, because you want to give your app its own design and branding. It usually takes some time to consider what works best for your app, and boils down to your vision for the app branding and styling.

I want to reiterate that you shouldn't try to modify the default Ionic CSS file. This is bad practice, and will cause problems when you want to update Ionic. Also, if you try to add new rules to change Ionic styling, it might cause you stress in the long term to maintain the list, especially if you're trying to change the default colors on every component.

In this section you'll use the example inside of the sass directory of your code project. You can refer to it for a working example of how Sass is configured. Let's use Sass to customize Ionic's styling for your own purposes.

7.2.1   *Setting up Sass*

Sass (Syntactically Awesome Stylesheets) is a CSS preprocessor. Sass is a superset of CSS, which means you can write regular CSS, and Sass understands it. Sass compiles down to CSS, so there's nothing special that the browser needs. But Sass provides a number of features that CSS doesn't (such as variables, nesting, and inheritance) that are very useful for customizing styling. You can learn more about Sass at http://sass-lang.com/.

Ionic has written its styling using Sass, and has used variables extensively. These variables can be declared once and used in multiple places. This makes it possible to change the variable for a color once, and have the color update anywhere it was used. There are hundreds of variables that control the primary color styles, fonts, padding, borders, and more. You can override any of the variables, and then regenerate the CSS with your new values.

First you need to set up your app to be ready for Sass. You need to make sure you've installed your Node dependencies for the project, and then run the `ionic setup` command, which will update a few parts of your app:

```
$ npm install -g gulp
$ ionic setup sass
```

The first command will install Gulp, which is a build tool. Ionic uses Gulp to run tasks, such as converting Sass files into CSS. Gulp uses the gulpfile.js file that Ionic created in your project when you first began. The file is used to manage the Gulp tasks. You can modify (or may have already) the Gulp file with additional tasks that you wish to run, but by default Ionic only creates tasks related to building Sass.

The second command handles setting up a few things required by Sass. It will install any dependencies required to run using the Node package manager (npm), and then check that your Gulp file has a Sass task. Assuming it finds one (it should unless you deleted it sometime), it will run the task and build the CSS for the first time. It will also add a few notes to the ionic.project file. Lastly, it updates the index .html file with a reference to the new customized compiled CSS file (www/css/ionic .app.css). You should verify the new file is correctly linked in the www/index.html file.

It's easiest to do this right away when you start a new project, instead of waiting to do it later. Now let's take a look at how to modify the default variables to customize Ionic.

7.2.2 *Customize Ionic with Sass variables*

Ionic has hundreds of default variables for different parts of the Ionic styling. The most obvious and useful to change are the nine default color options. The exact number of variables may change as Ionic updates, but you can find the complete list in the www/lib/ionic/scss/_variables.scss file. But don't change them in that file! Just use it as a reference to find the variables you need to customize, and you'll override them in another location.

To customize these variables, you'll modify the sass/scss/ionic.app.scss file. Inside there are some comments, but really there are two commands:

```
// The path to ionicons font files, relative to the built CSS in www/css
$ionicons-font-path: "../lib/ionic/fonts" !default;

// Include all of Ionic
@import "www/lib/ionic/scss/ionic";
```

The first is a variable that correctly links to the font icon directory because this file is in a different place than the default files. The second is an @import command, which will import the file found at www/lib/ionic/scss/ionic.scss, which then imports the rest of the Sass files. Any variables that you set before the @import command will override the default variables, and this is where you'll assign the new values. Any time you add variables, you'll need to rebuild the Sass files.

Imagine you want to change the default Ionic color to be colors set forth by Google's material design standard. Add the variables before the @import command with values to set a new default, as shown in the following listing.

Listing 7.1   Sass variables (sass/scss/ionic.app.scss)

```
$light: #FAFAFA;
$stable: #EEE;
$positive: #3F51B5;
$calm: #2196F3;
$balanced: #4CAF50;
$energized: #FFC107;
$assertive: #F44336;
$royal: #9C27B0;
$dark: #333;

// Include all of Ionic
@import "www/lib/ionic/scss/ionic";

@import "www/scss/app";
```

Sets default variables according to your requirements

Imports Ionic library Sass files; your variables will override existing Ionic ones

Imports a Sass file from app

Anywhere you have used Ionic color classes will now default to the new color, such as the bar-positive or tabs-positive color presets. You must regenerate the CSS first, and you can do so by running the Gulp task:

```
$ gulp sass
```

The file should rebuild in less than a second, and update the www/css/ionic.app.css file with the new color preset. This is pretty awesome, but it can get annoying to remember to always rerun the Gulp task every time you change some styling. There's also a watch task that will automatically rebuild any time you save changes. It has to run in its own command-line window, so it can be running continuously in the background. Open a new command-line window or tab, and run the gulp watch command:

```
$ gulp watch
```

Alternatively, when you use ionic serve and you set up Sass, the serve command will automatically rebuild the CSS when you change the files and then refresh the CSS in the browser without reloading, so you'll get to see your changes instantly.

Sometimes the gulp watch or ionic serve commands will hit an error and stop running. Depending on your command line, the serve command might alert you, but if you notice that changes don't seem to be appearing as you make them, verify that the serve command is still running correctly. Occasionally syntax errors in your code can cause the serve command to fail.

7.2.3 *Using Sass for your own styling*

You can use Sass for your customizations beyond just changing Ionic variables. It's a good idea to write all of your custom styling using Sass as well. There are many features you can use to help, but you can write CSS if that's what you prefer. I personally recommend it, even if you aren't sure that you'll need the extra features of Sass. At a minimum, it will tell you about syntax errors as soon as you try to save the file.

The easiest way to start is to create new files inside of the scss directory and write your styles there. You'll need to add import statements in the ionic.app.scss file to load your scss files, just like it imports the Ionic styles. Note that you'll want to do this after importing the Ionic library. Here's an example of the syntax to import:

```
@import "customizations"
```

You can leave off the file extension if the files are named with .scss. By default, the Gulp task watches any Sass file in the scss directory, so it will start to automatically rebuild when you make changes to any of your styling as long as the watcher is running.

I like to keep my styles in the www directory. I've described before how I have my JavaScript, CSS, and HTML for the same view located in the same folder. This isn't a problem, because you can still use the ionic.app.scss file as the main app file, and then import the files from the www directory. By default, Ionic's Gulp task assumes you'll put all of your Sass files in the scss directory, so the watcher task doesn't look at the www directory for changes. You can change this easily by updating gulpfile.js, where you see the `paths.sass` property defined. This property takes an array of paths (which can include wildcards or glob patterns to match), and this example will add support to watch the www directory as well:

```
var paths = {
  sass: ['./scss/**/*.scss', './www/**/*.scss']
};
```

That's a simple little improvement that allows you to keep your styles together with the HTML and JavaScript for the view. You can organize your code however you like, but it's best to keep it consistent.

7.3 *How to support online and offline mode*

In all three examples from chapters 4 through 6, you assumed the device is online with an internet connection so you could load data into the app. But in the mobile world, internet connections can be spotty, or users might manually disable it (such as airplane mode for flying). You can do some things to check for the online status of a device and handle the situation when the device is offline:

- Use a Cordova plugin that can ask the device for the current connection status.
- Listen for online and offline events.

Let's demonstrate the second option. The Cordova plugin shouldn't be necessary to detect online or offline status. This section is only concerned about dealing with the presence or absence of a connection. You can investigate the Cordova Network Connection Plugin API to get more details about the type of connection (Wi-Fi verses cellular data, for example) if your use case requires it.

Browsers have support for determining if a browser has a connection or not to a server. The basic code to determine if you're online or offline is fairly simple. The challenge is in designing the application to properly handle both situations in the best way possible.

The following listing adds two event listeners to the application and checks the default status of the network connection to offline/www/js/app.js.

Listing 7.2 Listening for online and offline events (offline/www/js/app.js)

```
angular.module('App', ['ionic'])
.run(function($rootScope, $window) {

  alert($window.navigator.onLine);                     ❶ Shows alert with
                                                          online status on load

  $window.addEventListener('offline', function() {
    alert('offline');                                  ❷ Listens for offline
    $rootScope.$digest();                                 event and shows alert
  });

  $window.addEventListener('online', function() {
    alert('online');                                   ❸ Listens for online
    $rootScope.$digest();                                 event and shows alert
  });

})
```

The application example here is only to demonstrate how to create the event listener and check the online status on load. The `$window.navigator.onLine` value ❶ returns either `true` or `false`, depending on if the browser has a network connection. Then you add two event listeners to the window ❷, ❸ that listen for online or offline state changes. These will only fire when the status changes, but not on load. There's a `$digest()` call because changes that happen inside of a native event listener don't get registered with the Angular digest loop. If you changed something with your Angular application in the event callback, you'd have to end it with a call to `$digest()` to propagate those changes through the app.

To test this, you also need to realize this only tells you if you have a network connection, which may not always be what you want to check. For example, if you use `ionic serve` with live reload, the browser recognizes the Ionic live reload server as a network connection and therefore will not appear offline, even if you disconnect from the primary computer's network connection. The best way to test this is to emulate this without the live reload option, and then disable your computer's network connection to trigger the state change:

```
$ ionic platform add ios
$ ionic emulate ios
```

Once the app has launched in the emulator, you can toggle the connection and you should get an alert with the changed state. While this example is simplistic, it serves to introduce the means to detect changes.

7.4 Handling gesture events in Ionic

Sometimes you'll need to build your own component or interface and you'll want to handle user gestures and events such as swipes and drags. Ionic has several options for you to use to build this support.

Very few apps can be built without creating customized interface elements. Some apps require very unique touch experiences to interact with the elements. I advise against creating complex gestures or relying on users learning specific gestures, because most users have a low threshold for learning an app. If your custom interface doesn't make sense or provide enough contextual information about how to use it, then users are likely to abandon your app. Nobody likes to feel dumb or confused, so be considerate in how you build these interactions by favoring simplicity.

The two main ways Ionic provides support for gestures are with a set of directives to listen for events, or by adding event listeners programmatically into your controllers.

7.4.1 Listen for events with Ionic event directives

The Ionic event directives are a collection that will listen for a particular event and call an expression or function when the event fires. These events include hold, tap, drag, and swipe. The exact timings for these events to fire are listed in the documentation. This section uses the events directory of the project, and figure 7.1 shows the output.

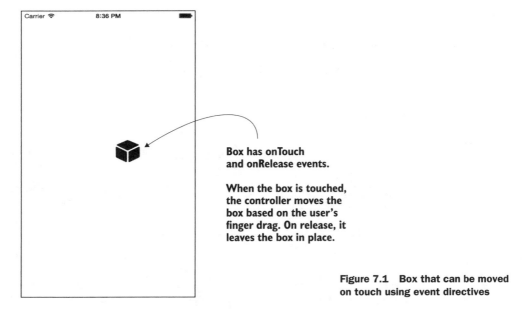

Box has onTouch
and onRelease events.

When the box is touched,
the controller moves the
box based on the user's
finger drag. On release, it
leaves the box in place.

**Figure 7.1   Box that can be moved
on touch using event directives**

These event directives are the easiest way to listen for events. Let's take a look at an example of how to use them. Listing 7.3 shows a directive that has a combination of events that lets users drag an icon around the screen, and it will also log to the console the number of milliseconds from the time a user touched the item until it's released. The code in the following listing has the directive, which for simplicity is added into the app.js file.

Listing 7.3 Box directive (events/www/js/app.js)

```
angular.module('App', ['ionic'])
.directive('box', function () {
  return {
    restrict: 'E',                                    ◁─┐ Links function for
    link: function (scope, element) {                   │ box directive to
      var time = 0, boxX = 0, boxY = 0;                 │ add listeners
      var leftBound = window.innerWidth - 50;
      var bottomBound = window.innerHeight - 50;          Sets up some variables
      scope.top = 0;                                      to track positions
      scope.left = 0;

      scope.startTouch = function (event) {               Touch event handler;
        time = event.timeStamp;                           tracks start time of drag
      };

      scope.endTouch = function (event) {                 Release event handler;
        console.log('You held the box for ' +             tracks total time of
(event.timeStamp - time) + 'ms');                         drag and logs to
        boxX = scope.left;                                console
        boxY = scope.top;
      };

      scope.drag = function (event) {
        var left = boxX + Math.round(event.gesture.deltaX);
        var top = boxY + Math.round(event.gesture.deltaY);

        if (left > leftBound) {
          scope.left = leftBound;
        } else if (left < 0) {
          scope.left = 0;
        } else {
          scope.left = left;
        }
        if (top > bottomBound) {                          Drag event
          scope.top = bottomBound;                         handler; moves
        } else if (top < 0) {                              position of box
          scope.top = 0;                                   based on drag and
        } else {                                           limits boundaries
          scope.top = top;                                 to edge
        }
      };
    },
    template: '<div id="box" class="icon ion-cube" on-
    touch="startTouch($event)" on-release="endTouch($event)" on-
```

```
        drag="drag($event)" ng-style="{top: top + \'px\', left: left +
        \'px\'}"></div>'
    }
})
```
◁── Inline template; box is an icon with events and styles updated by drag

This example creates an icon that can be moved around the screen. It checks that the icon doesn't go outside of the window space; otherwise, it will go anywhere the user drags it. The `onTouch` and `onRelease` event handlers are used to track the total time the user touches the icon, and the `onDrag` event handler does the work to move it around by changing scope variables for the top and left positions that `ngStyle` updates.

To use this, just add a box element to the app. Here you'll add the single box to the app and it will allow the user to begin dragging:

```
<body ng-app="App">
  <box></box>
</body>
```

There's also some CSS required for the positioning to work. CSS rules allow you to position an element absolutely by giving it top and left position values, which come from the drag event:

```
#box {
  position: absolute;
  width: 50px;
  height: 50px;
  font-size: 50px;
  text-align: center;
}
```

There are many different ways you could accomplish similar tasks, but this example highlights how event directives can be used to react to user gestures. I placed this example into a directive because best practice is to use a directive when you need to manipulate the DOM. But you could also have used the directives in a more standard template and put the event handler methods on the controller.

7.4.2 Listen for events with $ionicGesture service

Another way to listen for events is to use the `$ionicGesture` service. This allows you to listen for a wider range of events, but requires a more programmatic approach. The example for this section is found in the gestures directory of the project.

The `$ionicGesture` service needs to be injected into the controller, and then you can declare which events to listen to. You also have to declare the element to which the listener will attach itself. This makes it even more important to use the `$ionicGesture` service inside of a directive when possible, so you have easy access to the element.

You'll use the service to build a simple card that can be swiped off the screen, like you see in figure 7.2. While the user swipes the card to the right or left, it will animate in that direction, and once the user releases, if the card is far enough it will be

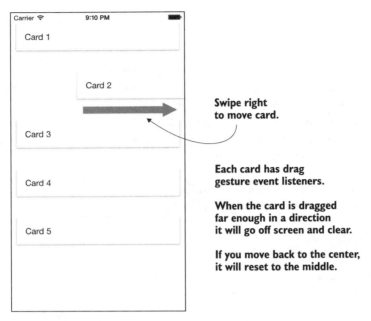

Figure 7.2   Gesture event listeners to swipe cards off the screen

removed from the screen, or it will reset to the center. This is shown in the following listing and found in the chapter 7 project inside of the gestures directory.

Listing 7.4   `$ionicGesture` service (gestures/www/js/app.js)

```
angular.module('App', ['ionic'])                              Injects $ionicGesture
.directive('card', function () {                              service into controller
  return {
    scope: true,
    controller: function ($scope, $element, $ionicGesture, $interval) {   ◁
      $scope.left = 0;

      $ionicGesture.on('drag', function (event) {                Listens for
        $scope.left = event.gesture.deltaX;                      dragend event
        $scope.$digest();                                        and determines
      }, $element);                                              if card should be
                                                                 removed or reset
      $ionicGesture.on('dragend', function (event) {      ◁
        if (Math.abs($scope.left) > (window.innerWidth / 3)) {
          $scope.left = ($scope.left < 0) ? -window.innerWidth :    If card is over 33%
            window.innerWidth;                                      offscreen, removes it
          $element.remove();
        } else {
          var interval = $interval(function () {
            if ($scope.left < 5 && $scope.left > -5) {
              $scope.left = 0;
              $interval.cancel(interval);
```

Annotations in left margin:

Listens for drag event and moves card horizontally while card is dragging

If card is still near middle, animates it back to center by moving five pixels every five milliseconds ▽

```
      } else {
        $scope.left = ($scope.left < 0) ? $scope.left + 5 :
         $scope.left - 5;
      }
    }, 5);
  }
  $scope.$digest();
}, $element);
},
transclude: true,
template: '<div class="list card" ng-style="{left: left + \'px\'}"><div
 class="item" ng-transclude>Swipe Me</div></div>'
  }
})
```

This card directive attaches two event listeners for drag and dragend. Technically you're listening for the drag events here, because swipe events don't fire until the swipe has occurred. If you listened for the swipe event, the cards wouldn't move until after the user had already completed the swipe, so it would have a visual delay that might confuse the user. The directive uses the controller to inject the service. When you attach an event listener using the on method, you have to pass it at least three things: one of the predefined event names, a callback function to fire when the event is triggered, and the element it should attach to. Because you use a directive here, it has access to the special $element service; otherwise, in a controller you'd have to use angular.element() to locate the proper element to attach the listener.

For this example to work, you just need to add one line of CSS to www/css/styles.css:

```
.card { position: relative; left: 0; }
```

Then you can add any number of these card directives to your app, and each can be individually swiped off the screen:

```
<body ng-app="App">
  <card>Card 1</card>
    <card>Card 2</card>
  <card>Card 3</card>
  <card>Card 4</card>
  <card>Card 5</card>
</body>
```

The contents of the card element are transcluded inside of the card, which is an Angular feature available to directives. Transclude essentially copies all of the HTML content inside of the directive tag, and places it into the directive template where ngTransclude is declared.

This approach is more flexible and is able to support more gesture events than the event directives you looked at earlier. But gesture events require a little more work to set up. In the end, both of them accomplish the same task, so the choice ultimately is preference over style.

7.4.3 *Available gesture events*

There are a lot of gesture events that you can listen for. Table 7.1 gives a list of the possible gestures, the event name, the directive (if available), and notes about what triggers the gesture event.

Table 7.1 Supported gestures, JavaScript event names, use notes, and possible directives (if available)

Gesture	Event	Directive	Notes
Hold	hold	on-hold	Touch an element for at least 500 ms
Tap	tap	on-tap	Touch an element for less than 250 ms
Double tap	doubletap		Two touches on same place, within 300 ms
Touch	touch	on-touch	Fires when a touch is detected
Release	release	on-release	Fires when a touch is released
Drag	drag	on-drag	Long touch while moving in any direction, generic
Drag start	dragstart		Fires when drag is first detected
Drag end	dragend		Fires when drag is released
Drag up	dragup	on-drag-up	Drag up on *y* axis
Drag down	dragdown	on-drag-down	Drag down on *y* axis
Drag left	dragleft	on-drag-left	Drag left on *x* axis
Drag right	dragright	on-drag-right	Drag right on *x* axis
Swipe	swipe	on-swipe	Quick touch and flick in any direction, generic
Swipe up	swipeup	on-swipe-up	Swipe up on *y* axis
Swipe down	swipedown	on-swipe-down	Swipe down on *y* axis
Swipe left	swipeleft	on-swipe-left	Swipe left on *x* axis
Swipe right	swiperight	on-swipe-right	Swipe right on *x* axis
Transform	transform		Two fingers touch and move, generic
Transform start	transformstart		Fires when a transform is first detected
Transform end	transformend		Fires when a transform is released

Table 7.1 Supported gestures, JavaScript event names, use notes, and possible directives (if available) *(continued)*

Gesture	Event	Directive	Notes
Rotate	`rotate`		Two fingers rotating
Pinch	`pinch`		Two fingers pinch and slide together or apart
Pinch in	`pinchin`		Two fingers pinch and slide together
Pinch out	`pinchout`		Two fingers pinch and slide apart

7.5 *Storing data for persistence*

In the examples from chapters 4 through 6, every time you loaded the app it would reset any changes you had made and start as if it were the first time the app was used. This is obviously annoying and a bad experience for users. For example, users expect that if they mark an item as a favorite, it will stay a favorite. Wouldn't it be great if the app could remember things and pick up where a user left off? The good news is that there are several ways to do this, and I'll show you the primary way that doesn't require any additional plugins.

Because Ionic apps are web applications, apps have the ability to use some of the built-in storage features of the web platform. They have support for `localStorage` for key-value pairs and either Web SQL, IndexedDB, or SQLite for a more robust database.

The general approach for either option is that you'll need to store data, and when the app resumes, the first task will be to load the data from storage. Any app that has the ability to log in will retain some kind of session and user information in storage to properly communicate with a back-end service.

Apps with persistent data should also be designed to handle the situation where data is cleared from the cache. Never assume that stored data will remain indefinitely.

When you store data on a device, you should take precautions against storing anything that users shouldn't be able to see. Anything on a device is potentially viewable by the device owner using debugging tools, but it's reasonable to store private data for that user (such as an OAuth token). Anything that should never be shown to the user should be stored in a server environment (such as a private API key for a web service).

7.5.1 *Using localStorage*

`localStorage` is a very simple storage option for your app that stores values in the browser cache directory. It's essentially a key-value-pair storage system, or you can think of it like a JavaScript object with the ability to create only one level of properties, which must always be strings. I turn to `localStorage` any time I can because it's the easiest way to store data. In a browser, users can clear the data from `localStorage` any time, but in a hybrid app they aren't able to clear the data unless they're using debugging tools.

localStorage is very easy to use but has two major limitations. First, values are stored as a string, regardless of what data type they were before. This means an integer will be turned into a string during storage. This can cause problems if you try to compare a string to a number using strict comparators (such as "1" === 1, which is false). Second, there are size limits on the total data you can store, which isn't standardized between browsers. You should consult the documentation for the platforms to see what the current capacity is (Android Browser 4.3 has 2 MB, Safari has 5 MB, and Chrome has 10 MB at time of writing), or visit http://mng.bz/7J3R for a good summary of many storage type limitations. This is a lot of space, but if you exceed it you'll get errors. It can become difficult to manage over time if you're working with a lot of data.

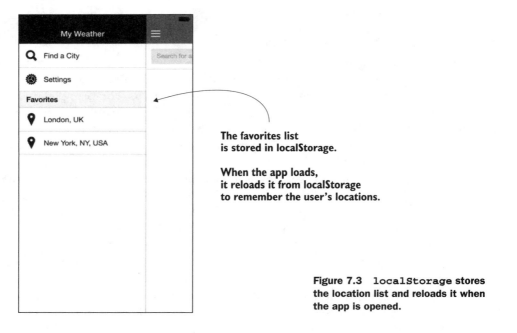

The favorites list
is stored in localStorage.

When the app loads,
it reloads it from localStorage
to remember the user's locations.

Figure 7.3   localStorage stores the location list and reloads it when the app is opened.

But if your storage needs are simple, localStorage is often the best solution. Figure 7.3 shows the updated weather app example from chapter 6 to store the locations list in localStorage and load it back into the app when it's reloaded. For this section you'll use the code inside of the storage directory. The only change from the chapter 6 example is in the Locations service in the storage/www/js/app.js file, shown in the following listing with changes in bold.

Listing 7.5   Save and load from localStorage (storage/www/js/app.js)

Creates store()
method to
handle saving
JSON string data
into localStorage

```
.factory('Locations', function ($ionicPopup) {
  function store () {
    localStorage.setItem('locations', angular.toJson(Locations.data));
  }
```

```
var Locations = {
  data: [],
  getIndex: function (item) {
    var index = -1;
    angular.forEach(Locations.data, function (location, i) {
      if (item.lat == location.lat && item.lng == location.lng) {
        index = i;
      }
    });
    return index;
  },
  toggle: function (item) {
    var index = Locations.getIndex(item);
    if (index >= 0) {
      $ionicPopup.confirm({
        title: 'Are you sure?',
        template: 'This will remove ' + Locations.data[index].city
      }).then(function (res) {
        if (res) {
          Locations.data.splice(index, 1);
        }
      });
    } else {
      Locations.data.push(item);
      $ionicPopup.alert({
        title: 'Location saved'
      });
    }
    store();                              ◁────────  Calls store() method after
  },                                                 toggling a location from list
  primary: function (item) {
    var index = Locations.getIndex(item);
    if (index >= 0) {
      Locations.data.splice(index, 1);
      Locations.data.splice(0, 0, item);             Calls store() method
    } else {                                         after setting a new
      Locations.data.unshift(item);                  primary location
    }
    store();                              ◁────────
  }                                                  When app starts, tries to
};                                                   load data from localStorage
                                                     or else sets a blank array
try {                                     ◁────────
  var items = angular.fromJson(localStorage.getItem('locations')) || [];
  Locations.data = items;
} catch (e) {
  Locations.data = [];
}

return Locations;
})
```

You can see localStorage is available globally in JavaScript because it's part of the primary JavaScript APIs. You create a store() function to abstract the logic because there are multiple places you want to store the data into localStorage. When store() is called, it takes the array of locations and stores them in localStorage, but first converts the array into a JSON string (because localStorage only handles strings). Then when the list of locations changes, the app calls the store() method to update the cached data.

In the try-catch statement, the app attempts to load the data from localStorage, and then parse the JSON if it was set. If nothing is set in localStorage or if there's an error loading data from localStorage, then the location list is set to an empty array.

Now the app will always try to load the list of stored locations and use that instead of starting with a blank list. This is obviously a very good improvement for users, and localStorage is very easy to implement.

You can inspect the localStorage values inside of the browser developer tools and should see an item with the list there. localStorage is app-specific, so the data you store is safe from other apps. But localStorage can be inspected by developers, meaning you can't safely store anything that you absolutely cannot allow others to see.

7.5.2 *Using Web SQL, IndexedDB, and SQLite*

Web SQL, IndexedDB, and SQLite are different types of browser-based databases. Like localStorage, the data is stored in the browser's cache system. These options are best for larger amounts of data, or data that you want to be able to directly query. But they're all more difficult to use, and support for them varies across platforms.

Web SQL is similar to a full-featured database with the ability to use SQL to query tables. It allows you to use SQL statements like SELECT, UPDATE, and so forth. The challenge is that the specification for Web SQL was abandoned back in 2010 when browser vendors couldn't come to agreement on the standard. At the time of writing, iOS and Android both support Web SQL, but it's possible that over time this support may be removed.

IndexedDB is an object store that's somewhere between Web SQL and localStorage. It uses a key-value storage like localStorage, but items have fields with specific data types and the ability to limit results by requesting certain fields with a given value. At the time of writing, IndexedDB isn't supported by iOS and Android.

SQLite is similar to Web SQL with a SQL-like syntax for loading data in and out of a local database. It also suffers from being abandoned by browsers and standardization bodies for first-class support in browsers. Now most support for SQLite comes through Cordova plugins.

Like localStorage, the data from these databases can't be viewed by other apps, but can still be viewed by developers when they debug using their device.

At the time of writing, Web SQL is the option that both iOS and Android support fully with the help of Cordova, and IndexedDB isn't properly supported. But Web SQL has been deprecated since 2010 and likely will be removed in the future, so in time support will likely shift to IndexedDB. But to be doubly sure of what's supported or not, you can check the Cordova storage documentation at http://mng.bz/1UYx.

Check that you're looking at the same version of the documentation that fits the project's Cordova version—you can run `cordova info` to find the version. You can also do a quick test yourself by running one of the following commands to tell you if it's supported or not on a given platform:

```
alert('WebSQL: ' + ((window.openDatabase) ? 'yes' : 'no'));
alert('IndexedDB: ' + ((window.indexedDB) ? 'yes' : 'no'));
```

You need to run these commands on an emulator or device to get the proper message. Just add these lines at the start of your JavaScript to alert you of support for the two options.

7.5.3 Other options from Cordova plugins

Cordova provides plugins to allow you to access additional features on a device. We'll look at some plugins in chapter 8 in depth, but you should know there are many options in the Cordova plugin repository for storage.

The options are varied and ever-changing. Some are able to bring IndexedDB or Web SQL support to all devices, others support different storage systems like SQLite, and others are designed to allow you to store entire files. You can discover storage plugins at http://plugins.cordova.io/npm/index.html.

7.6 Building one app for multiple platforms

One of the best features of building apps with Ionic is the ability to target multiple devices and platforms with one app. But sometimes you need to tweak behavior or design for a particular device or platform.

There are different situations where you need to think about different experiences for different platforms. Ionic provides some of this built into its core. For example, tabs on Android appear differently than they do on iOS. The reason is the Ionic developers wanted to be able to provide the same behavior (tabs) but make it look and feel native to that platform (styling). The tabs do the same thing, just the appearance varies slightly.

There are two main ways to target a platform: change the appearance or change the behavior. Before we look at them, let's dig a bit more into why you should bother building apps that adapt to different platforms.

7.6.1 One size doesn't always fit all

As an app developer, you should consider what makes the app best for your users, not what makes the app the easiest for you to build. Building apps with the exact same behavior on Android and iOS may not always work out for your users, and you should consider this carefully. This is especially true in cases where users are accustomed to certain interactions.

Android and iOS have many differences in their appearance and interaction behaviors. Even different versions of iOS and Android can differ greatly, and over time you can only assume that will continue. Ionic is committed to supporting the modern versions of these platforms, and as the mobile platforms continue to evolve, Ionic will adapt.

You must remember that Ionic is only able to do so much for app developers. Ultimately you're responsible for ensuring that the apps you build work and make sense on different platforms. It's worth spending time with the official native style guides for iOS and Android to familiarize yourself with the differences. Then when you're designing your app, you'll be able to consider the best design for each platform and if you need to design anything specific to a platform. Here's where you can find the official style guides:

- Android style guide: http://developer.android.com/design/style/index.html
- iOS style guide: https://developer.apple.com/library/ios/documentation/UserExperience/Conceptual/MobileHIG/

7.6.2   Adapt styling for a platform or device type

Ionic provides you a simple way to determine which platform or device you're using so you can adapt your app styling as necessary. Ionic determines what platform you're using, and adds a number of classes to the body element:

- `platform-ios` for iOS
- `platform-android` for Android
- `platform-browser` for browsers

These classes give you insight into what type of platform is used. You can also find other classes based on the version number of the platform, for example, `platform-ios-ios7`. In some cases you might need to target a specific version; the version class can provide you that information.

The two major reasons you'll need to use this technique are for providing platform-specific styling, and to address possible display bugs present only on a particular platform. In general, you probably will want to limit the amount of platform-specific design because it will add to the amount of testing you need to do.

You'll use the code from the adaptive-style directory for this section. This is a simple app that just shows the Ionic logo on a background, but depending on the platform, a different background color will display, as shown in figure 7.4. The template for the app is shown in the following listing and the CSS is shown in listing 7.7.

Listing 7.6   Adaptive styling template (adaptive-style/www/index.html)

```
<body ng-app="App">
  <ion-pane>
    <ion-content>
      <span class="icon ion-ionic"></span>
    </ion-content>
  </ion-pane>
</body>
```

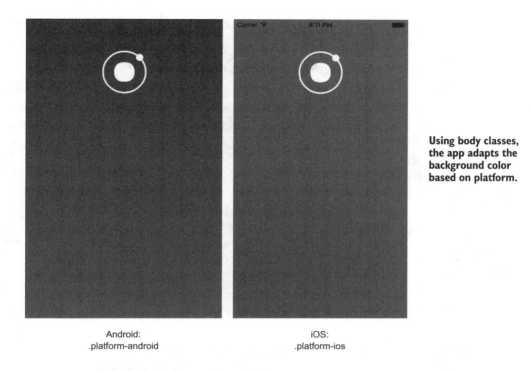

Using body classes, the app adapts the background color based on platform.

Android:
.platform-android

iOS:
.platform-ios

Figure 7.4 Platform-specific styling for Android (left) and iOS (right)

Listing 7.7 Adaptive styling CSS (adaptive-style/www/css/style.css)

```css
.scroll {
  text-align: center;
  padding-top: 50px;
}
.ion-ionic {
  font-size: 100px;
  color: #fff;
}
.pane {
  background: #333;
}
.platform-ios .pane {                                              ←── CSS selector to target iOS only
  background: #C644FC;
  background: -webkit-linear-gradient(top, #C644FC 0%,#5856D6 100%);
  background: linear-gradient(to bottom, #C644FC 0%,#5856D6 100%);  ─── CSS selector to target Android only
}
.platform-android .pane {                                         ←──
  background: #C62828;
  background: -webkit-linear-gradient(top, #C62828 0%,#F44336 100%);
  background: linear-gradient(to bottom, #C62828 0%,#F44336 100%);
}
```

By prefixing your CSS rules with the platform `body` class, you can see the different colors in the background by platform.

7.6.3 *Adapt behavior for a platform or device type*

You can also adapt the behaviors of the app for a particular platform. For example, you may want to use an action sheet component on iOS but a popover on Android to better fit in with the platform. Ionic can detect which platform is in use, and then modify behaviors accordingly.

The `ionic.Platform` service is available to provide you this information. It provides a list of methods such as `isIOS()` and `isAndroid()` to return a Boolean value if the platform is active, and you can also use the `platform()` method to return the name of the current platform.

In a fairly simple example shown in figure 7.5, pressing the more button (the icon with three dots) will behave differently depending on the platform. You'll check if it's iOS, and show the action sheet; otherwise, show the popover for Android, as in listing 7.8.

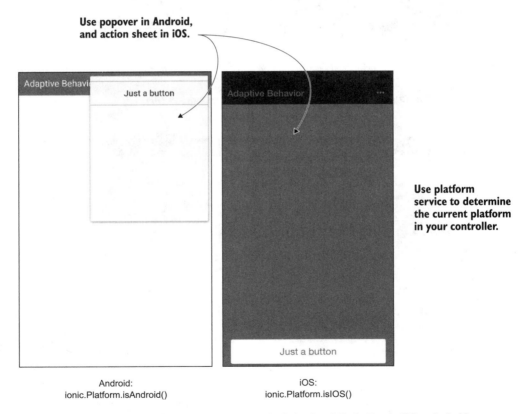

Use popover in Android, and action sheet in iOS.

Use platform service to determine the current platform in your controller.

Android:
ionic.Platform.isAndroid()

iOS:
ionic.Platform.isIOS()

Figure 7.5   Based on the platform, you can change the behavior of the button in iOS or Android.

```
angular.module('App', ['ionic'])                                    Creates
.controller('Controller', function ($scope, $ionicActionSheet,      controller and
    $ionicPopover) {                                                injects services
  $scope.more = function (event) {                                 ◁
                                                                    more() method
                                                                    to be called by
    if (ionic.Platform.isIOS()) {                                   ngClick
      $ionicActionSheet.show({
        buttons: [
          {text: 'Just a button'}
        ],                                          If iOS, shows action
        buttonClicked: function (index) {           sheet with dummy
          return true;                              button
        }
      });

    } else {
      var popover = $ionicPopover.fromTemplate('<ion-popover-view>  Otherwise,
      <button class="button button-full">Just a button</button>     shows popover
      </ion-popover-view>');                                        with dummy
      popover.show(event);                                          button
    }
  }
})
```

Uses ionic
.Platform
to
determine
if iOS

Here you create a controller with a single method that checks if the device is running
iOS or not. The `ionic.Platform` service isn't an Angular service, so you don't need to
inject it. There's an `$ionicPlatform` service, but it's intended for use with Cordova
plugins and doesn't provide information about the current platform.

Once the platform is determined, you choose to show the action sheet or popover.
The markup for this example is shown in the following listing.

```
<body ng-app="App">
  <ion-header-bar align-title="left" class="bar-positive" ng-
      controller="Controller">
    <h1 class="title">Adaptive Behavior</h1>
    <div class="buttons">
      <button class="button" ng-click="more($event)"><span class="icon
      ion-more"></span></button>                              ◁
    </div>                                            Uses ngClick to call
  </ion-header-bar>                                   more() method, and
</body>                                               passes event for popover
```

The `ionic.Platform` service is able to provide current information about the platform. It also has a few methods to modify the app behavior, such as the ability to set
the app to full screen or exit the app programmatically.

7.7   *Modify default behaviors with $ionicConfigProvider*

Ionic has a way to modify a number of default behaviors. You were able to modify the default styling using custom Sass variables, and this is the same idea, except you can modify behaviors such as transition types or default navbar title alignment.

The defaults for Ionic are designed to be focused on the correct platform. For example, in a navbar the title will align to the left on Android and will center on iOS to match the style guidelines. But you can force Ionic to render the titles the same regardless of the platform.

The complete list of configurable items is provided in the documentation. You'll build one example to modify the default tabs styling so that it's always striped, and you want the tabs on top. All of the configuration options can be modified in the same manner as you see in this example. In figure 7.6 you can see the result of updated defaults for the tabs.

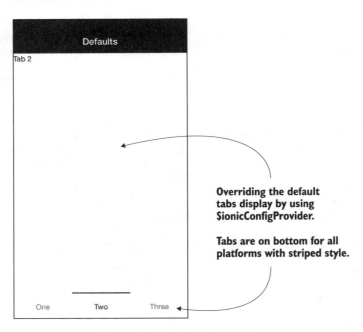

Figure 7.6   Overriding Ionic default values for tabs

The configuration defaults are set in the module `config()` method, in the same method that the states are declared. The following listing has the default configuration changes set for tabs.

Listing 7.10 Updating default configuration (config/www/js/app.js)

```
angular.module('App', ['ionic'])                              Injects
.config(function($ionicConfigProvider) {                      $ionicConfigProvider
                                                              into configuration
  $ionicConfigProvider.tabs.style('striped').position('bottom');
})
```

Injects
$ionicConfigProvider
into configuration

Calls tabs settings, and they can
be chained in some cases

The `$ionicConfigProvider` is the special service provider for Ionic's configuration, and you're able to update values by calling its methods and passing arguments. In this example you also can chain the two tabs methods together, but if you were changing the default for another aspect unrelated to tabs, chaining wouldn't work. This code will set tabs to be striped and on the bottom, which isn't the default behavior for tabs.

The configurations can still be overridden in the tabs implementation using classes. It might not be necessary to change the default for some things like the tabs display because you can still set the CSS classes on the tabs instance to modify its display. But some of the configurations can't be changed elsewhere, particularly the caching views information.

7.8   Summary

This chapter has given you additional tools and insights into how to build Ionic apps. Let's review the major topics we covered:

- How to build a custom version of the Ionic styles for your app using Sass, and the build processes that Ionic uses with Gulp
- Support for events and gestures, using both event directives and the `$ionic-Gesture` service
- `localStorage` for persisting data in the app, and other options such as Web SQL and IndexedDB
- Modifying app behavior and display based on the current platform of the device running the app to provide specialized experiences per platform
- Changing the default Ionic configuration to set global parameters for different parts of Ionic

In the next chapter we'll dig deeper into Cordova, and you'll learn how to use the ecosystem of plugins with your Ionic apps.

Using Cordova plugins 8

This chapter covers

- Managing native features of a device with Cordova plugins
- Using Cordova to more easily integrate with a device
- Improving the resort app with a camera and photo book
- Improving the weather app with geolocation

The apps you've built so far in this book have been able to do quite a wide range of interesting things, but you haven't been able to take full advantage of a device's features. In this chapter we'll focus on how you can use Cordova's community of plugins to enrich your apps through deeper integration with the device.

You've been using Cordova for your apps the entire time, because Cordova is the platform you use to wrap your web applications into a native web app. Cordova comes with a core set of features and uses a plugin system to extend the feature set. Plugins provide a way to use JavaScript to implement native features, such as the camera, instead of using the native platform language.

We'll look at ngCordova, which is an Ionic community–driven project that makes it easier to integrate many common Cordova plugins with Angular applications like Ionic. When possible, you'll want to use ngCordova instead of just the plugin itself.

Then we'll look at several examples of using Cordova plugins to extend the apps you built earlier in the book with native features. Regardless if you did the examples in the earlier chapters, you'll need to set up the completed project before you begin.

Cordova is a powerful platform with far more features than can be covered here. I recommend also looking at *Apache Cordova in Action* (Raymond K. Camden, Manning Publications, 2015) to dig deeper into Cordova.

> **Cordova is always evolving**
>
> All of the examples and code in this chapter are subject to regular updates. The Cordova plugin ecosystem often evolves quickly as it tries to keep up with devices and platforms, and the plugins in this chapter are written using the Cordova CLI 4.2.0 and the plugin versions specified in the examples.

8.1 Cordova plugins

For the most part, anything that works on a modern web browser will work in your hybrid apps. But your apps often need to do more than what's supported natively in browsers.

Devices come with a large variety of sensors and features, such as a camera or accelerometer. Because these aren't typically part of the browser; these are implemented as Cordova plugins.

Cordova comes with a pluggable architecture, where plugins can add new features that aren't in the core of Cordova. Some plugins are officially part of the Cordova project, and others are submitted and maintained by the community. For example, the Ionic team has submitted a keyboard plugin for Cordova. The searchable registry with hundreds of Cordova plugins can be found at http://plugins.cordova.io/npm/index.html.

The officially supported plugins are likely to be well maintained to handle any changes in Cordova itself, whereas the community plugins may be behind in support. It's always good to review the plugins before using them so you can verify they'll work with your version of Cordova.

Plugins may not be carefully maintained, so while a plugin might work for you initially, you should keep an eye on its development to ensure it's maintained. If you find bugs, often the best solution is to open a ticket or issue in the source code project (typically hosted on GitHub). Alternatively, if the owner of the plugin hasn't maintained it in awhile, you could consider making your own fork of the codebase; but in general it's best to try and solve the problems at the source.

You can even create your own Cordova plugins, but that would require you to know how to work with the native platforms your plugins will support. So while you're not limited to the plugins that already exist, you do need to the know the native platform language, such as Java or Swift, to create a Cordova plugin.

8.1.1   Considerations when using plugins

In many cases you'll want to use plugins, but there are a number of considerations you should review before including a plugin.

PLUGINS AREN'T ALWAYS NECESSARY

Before selecting and using a plugin, you should consider if a plugin is even necessary. Sometimes features are available in the browser without a plugin, such as basic network connection details, so it's unnecessary to add the connection plugin for Cordova. Many plugins were created in the past to add features that were missing at the time from browsers, but as platforms advance, more features may be native to a browser.

PLUGINS MAY REQUIRE PERMISSIONS

Plugins may require permissions from a user to work; for example, geolocation requires permission before the app can access the device location. Different platforms implement permissions differently, so be sure to review how that particular feature is implemented and what impact that has on users.

PLUGINS CAN HAVE LIMITATIONS

The best plugins are well documented, and outline how the plugins may have limitations on different platforms. There are often good reasons. For example, iOS and Android have slightly different ways of storing contact lists, so a plugin may not return the same data for both platforms, depending on what's actually available.

PLATFORM UPDATES MAY REQUIRE PLUGIN UPDATES

Inevitably, platforms will continue to evolve and change their underlying APIs. Because Cordova plugins use these platform APIs, if Android or iOS updates there's a chance that the plugins may need to be updated to support the newest features. It's also possible they may break due to using APIs that have been removed or changed, though platforms tend to do well with backward compatibility.

PLUGINS CAN BE BUGGY

I mentioned some plugins are part of the Cordova project, and these are likely to be the best-supported plugins. But anyone is able to submit a plugin, and there are no clear restrictions on minimum quality.

8.1.2   Installing plugins

Plugins are installed through the command line. You can search on the plugins site at http://plugins.cordova.io or search for plugins from the command line. You can use the command-line search to find notification plugins like this:

```
$ cordova plugin search notification
```

This will return a list of any plugins that are related to notifications. It will provide the plugin identifier and a short description, and you'll use the plugin identifier when you wish to install the plugin. Ionic includes several by default, such as `org.apache.cordova.device` and `com.ionic.keyboard`. Here's how you'd install the official Cordova notification plugin:

```
$ cordova plugin add org.apache.cordova.dialogs
```

It will fetch the latest plugin and add it to your plugins folder. You only need to do this once per plugin, per project. When you build the project (which happens before you emulate or run it on any device), it will automatically pull in the installed plugins. You can review the installed plugins by looking at your plugins folder.

8.1.3 Using plugins

Each plugin works a little bit differently, but they all expose a JavaScript service that you can use to interact with the plugin. For example, the API to use the camera is exposed through the `navigator.camera` object. Installing the plugin and running the app on an emulator or device will automatically expose the API.

You can't use the plugin until the app and plugin are both ready. During the loading of the app, a lot of things happen asynchronously, so Cordova provides the `deviceready` event to listen for when plugins are ready to be used. Unlike normal events that fire once and are done, when you add an event listener for the `deviceready` event, even after the event fires it will still handle the callback. This allows you to avoid the situation where you try to use a plugin feature before it's ready, causing some kind of error in the process. You should always wrap calls to Cordova features inside of an event listener for `deviceready`. In the next two listings, the two calls are identical, except one uses the native JavaScript `addEventListener` method and the other uses the `$ionicPlatform.ready` method. This is an example you see in the default Ionic projects to set up the keyboard plugin, implemented in both ways.

The following two listings each add an event listener for the `deviceready` event.

Listing 8.1   Using a plugin in native JavaScript

```
                                                          Adds event listener for
                                                          deviceready event

window.addEventListener('deviceready', function () {        ◁─┘
  if(window.cordova && window.cordova.plugins.Keyboard) {   ◁─
    cordova.plugins.Keyboard.hideKeyboardAccessoryBar(true); ◁─┐
  }
});                                    Calls Keyboard plugin method

                                           Checks that Cordova and
                                           plugin are available
```

Listing 8.2   Using a plugin using Ionic

When Angular is ready but before rest of app executes, runs some logic

Uses $ionicPlatform.ready method to add an event listener

```
angular.module('App')
.run(function($ionicPlatform) {
  $ionicPlatform.ready(function() {
    if(window.cordova && window.cordova.plugins.Keyboard) {
      cordova.plugins.Keyboard.hideKeyboardAccessoryBar(true);
    }
  });
});
```

Checks Cordova is ready and calls Keyboard plugin method

Assuming Cordova and the keyboard plugin are set up, the app will execute a call to the `hideKeyboardAccessoryBar` method. When building with Ionic, it's recommended to use the `$ionicPlatform` approach, which is used in the rest of the examples in this chapter.

8.1.4   *Using plugins with emulators*

We discussed in chapter 2 that emulators don't provide the same experience as a real device. When it comes to working with Cordova plugins, it's especially important to test your apps on a real device, but you can usually test them on an emulator as well.

Most plugins will work just fine with an emulator. Depending on the feature, the emulator might also allow you to simulate or modify the expected values. For example, you can modify the geographic coordinates for the emulator to simulate different locations without actually going there.

Some features aren't available in the emulator, or may behave slightly differently. Because emulators are only virtual devices, some of the physical device abilities aren't easily reproduced virtually. For example, on iOS there's no way to use the camera plugin in the emulator.

Some plugins won't work in an emulator due to missing features. If a plugin keeps failing, you should review the documentation to see if it works in an emulator. Error reporting about this problem can be poor, so it's one of the things to check when troubleshooting. Using a connected device can help you avoid this problem, so I recommend using a real device when possible.

8.1.5   *Plugins and platform limitations*

Some plugins are only designed to work with one type of device, and others may change behaviors for different platforms. This is a side effect of abstracting a similar feature in multiple platforms into a single plugin.

For example, the local notifications plugin had to change for iOS 8 due to changes in the way local notifications were implemented. In version 8, iOS began to require permission from a user before notifications could be added, and so the plugin had to adapt to this new requirement.

If you want to use the Cordova plugin for the action sheet, it's implemented using the action sheet for iOS and an alert dialog for Android. These two are the closest way to implement the ability to display a set of options, and so the plugin has to be flexible.

The Touch ID plugin is for iOS only, because there's no similar feature in Android. Touch ID is for fingerprint verification that recent iPhone and iPad devices have on the home button, but Android doesn't have the same support.

8.1.6 Angular and Cordova gotchas

There are a few issues that newer Angular developers might run into when working with Cordova plugins. In the next section we'll talk about ngCordova, which addresses these problems, but doesn't support every plugin.

Angular has what's called a *digest loop*, as shown in figure 8.1. Angular is able to track changes to values (which powers two-way data binding, for example) when events happen inside of this digest loop. It's a closed system, and JavaScript can execute independently of the digest loop, but then Angular isn't aware of anything changing. Anything that happens outside of Angular continues to work just fine, but you might expect Angular to execute things that don't get triggered. The digest cycle has to be notified when things occur, or else Angular has no idea that there was a change and doesn't run a digest cycle.

The most common challenge is getting Angular to know about code that executes outside of Angular's digest loop. Angular provides the ability to notify that changes have occurred, and trigger a new digest loop to update Angular. For example, you could request the device geolocation and expect it to update the position of the map as the user moves. By default, the Cordova geolocation plugin will update the location, but it won't change until the next digest cycle, which would be up to you to trigger, or the user may wait for something else to trigger it.

When you're using Cordova plugins, it's also important to note that there aren't Angular services that you can inject into your controllers. This isn't necessary because the plugin services are made available globally and can just be used (this may vary by plugin—the official plugins tend to use the global navigator object to add services).

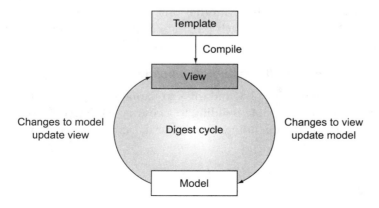

Figure 8.1 Angular digest loop (reprinted from *AngularJS in Action*)

Let's look at an example that uses the geolocation plugin to get the device location. To update Angular after Cordova is finished with some task, use the $scope.$apply() method as you see in the following listing.

Listing 8.3   Using $apply to update Angular

Creates a controller, but doesn't inject navigator object because it's global

Wraps call in $ionicPlatform.ready to ensure plugin is ready

```
angular.module('App')
.controller('Controller', function ($scope, $ionicPlatform) {
    $ionicPlatform.ready(function () {
        navigator.geolocation.getCurrentPosition(function (location) {
            $scope.location = location;
            $scope.$apply();
        });
    });
});
```

Calls $scope.$apply() to inform Angular to trigger digest

Assigns location to $scope, but won't automatically trigger digest

Calls Cordova geolocation plugin, which accepts a callback

Here's a simple controller that will get the geolocation for the device. You don't need to inject the navigator service because this is a global object outside of Angular's DI system. When the getCurrentPosition() method is called, the app passes a callback that handles what to do when the location is returned. When the location is returned, you assign it to the scope. But because the geolocation method isn't an Angular service, Angular doesn't know when it's completed and will not update the scope even though you've updated the location. This is why you call the $scope.$apply() method, which informs Angular the scope has changed and needs to be updated.

In this example, if the geolocation request fails (perhaps due to the user disabling location services for the app), it will continue to execute without setting the $scope.location value. The app needs the ability to handle the situation where the location isn't returned.

Lastly, Cordova plugins may implement different JavaScript APIs. There may be multiple plugins for the same feature, but each can function differently. For example, one plugin might use a callback, where another might use a promise to handle asynchronous calls. You'll need to review each plugin and understand its architecture to properly interact with it.

8.1.7   *Solutions to common issues with devices or emulators*

Once in a while things seem to go awry, and this can happen from accidentally changing the wrong setting or from trouble building to a connected device. Here are a few tips to try when you get stuck. Depending on your device and platform, different solutions might have better success.

DISCONNECT AND RECONNECT THE DEVICE

The device connection may not be communicating correctly, and sometimes just reconnecting the device can sort it out.

RESTART THE DEVICE AND COMPUTER

An oldie but goodie, the reboot trick can do wonders. I suggest rebooting both the device and the computer, and making sure the device isn't connected until the computer is ready again.

BUILD FROM XCODE/ANDROID STUDIO

If you're working with iOS, try to build the project from Xcode, or use Android Studio for Android. The command-line actions to run on a device may behave differently, so running directly from Xcode/Android Studio often works even when the command line fails.

RESET OR REBUILD THE EMULATOR

Emulators can be reset or rebuilt to be like new. This will make the emulator act like it's brand new, and any existing modifications will be gone. This is helpful to do when you really want to be sure nothing is retained from before.

UNINSTALL THE APP FROM THE DEVICE AND REBUILD

Disconnect and delete the app from the device. Even if the app is already installed, and running it normally doesn't cause problems, it can help to rebuild and deploy a fresh version.

REMOVE AND ADD THE PLUGINS

Just like with platforms, sometimes the plugins give errors. You can remove them with the command `cordova plugin remove [plugin]` or by deleting the plugins folder. You'll need to add all of the plugins back in if you delete the folder.

REMOVE AND ADD THE PLATFORMS

When I get obscure errors about not being able to build to the device, I'll typically remove the platform and set it up again. This can be done with the command `cordova platform remove ios` or by manually deleting the platforms folder in the project.

CREATE A NEW PROJECT

Typically a last resort, you can also just create a new project and copy over your changes. You'll want to copy over the files from the www directory, and then go about adding in the plugins and platforms again.

CHECK THE VERSIONS OF CORDOVA AND IONIC

You may need to update Cordova and Ionic. Also, on iOS you'll want to check that `ios-sim` and `ios-deploy` are up to date. These are all Node packages, so run `npm update -g [program]` to update them. If you update Cordova, you should update the project as well by running `cordova platform update [platform]`. It's good to back up your project in case trying to update causes more problems to arise due to changes in features.

8.2   *ngCordova*

Cordova plugins provide a lot of great features, but you can't use their features like you've used Angular's services. The ngCordova project was started by the Ionic community to create Angular-ized versions of Cordova's services. While ngCordova isn't only for Ionic, it was created with Ionic in mind. You can find the ngCordova site at http://ngcordova.com.

ngCordova supports dozens of Cordova plugins. The site can provide the most up-to-date list because more plugins are added as the community needs them. The ngCordova community welcomes contributions as well, if you're able to add support for another plugin not listed.

The primary benefits of using ngCordova instead of the default Cordova API are as follows:

- It implements each call to Cordova features as a promise to ensure a consistent programming experience with Angular.
- It handles calling the digest loop when necessary automatically so you focus on just writing your code.
- The Ionic community has already selected a good set of plugins for you to avoid having to research them yourself.
- It has good documentation for each plugin, at least one example for each, and links to the source documentation for any additional details.
- Every plugin comes with a mock service to use during unit testing.

8.2.1   *Installing ngCordova*

ngCordova is easily installed using the Ionic CLI and then needs to be included in the index.html file as well. Use the `ionic add` command to add ngCordova:

```
$ ionic add ngCordova
```

This will add ngCordova to the www/lib directory. Then add a `</script>` tag to your index.html file that will include the library:

```
<script src="lib/ngCordova/dist/ng-cordova.js"></script>
```

Now the last step is to include this new module into your application. Open the www/js/app.js file and update the list of dependencies to include ngCordova:

```
angular.module('App', ['ionic', 'ngCordova'])
```

That's all you need to do to install ngCordova into your app. Let's move on to an example so you can see it in action!

8.3   *Using a camera and photos in the resort app*

In the resort app from chapter 4, it might be a nice feature to allow users to create a photo book from their trip, as shown in figure 8.2. To do this, you have to request

1. Selecting Capture New opens the camera app.

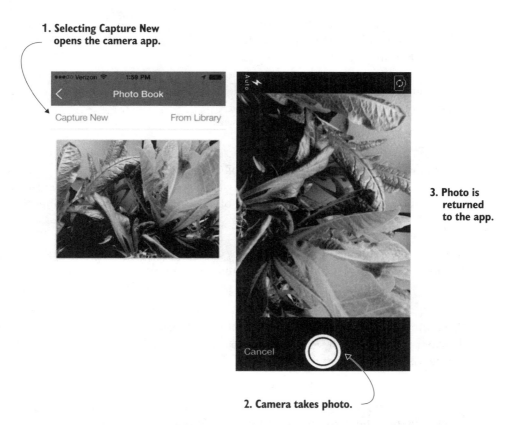

3. Photo is returned to the app.

2. Camera takes photo.

Figure 8.2 Photo book view with photos displayed and ability to capture new photos from camera app or add from library

access to a user's camera and photo library to display their photos. You'll keep the interface pretty simple so you can focus on the interesting parts of using a plugin.

8.3.1 Setting up the camera project

Start by setting up a new project based on the finished app from chapter 4. Use Git to check out the app; instead of using `ionic start`, you'll set up an existing project. Check out the last step from the chapter 4 example, and build on it with the following:

```
git clone https://github.com/ionic-in-action/chapter4.git chapter8-camera
cd chapter8-camera
git checkout step7
ionic plugin add org.apache.cordova.console
ionic plugin add org.apache.cordova.device
ionic plugin add com.ionic.keyboard
ionic platform add [ios/android]
```

Choose if you want to use iOS, Android, or both when you add the platform. Because you're using Git to clone the project, you need to manually add the plugins. Normally when you use the `ionic start` command to set up a project, the plugins are set up for you automatically. This ensures they get downloaded and set up in your project because they aren't stored in the repository.

You must have a device for the camera, so make sure you have it connected to your computer. Then you can build to the device by running the following command to deploy from the CLI, selecting `ios` or `android`:

```
$ ionic run [ios|android]
```

Please note you can't use the `livereload` command for this example, due to the way images are loaded using the file protocol. If you use `livereload`, Ionic actually loads over the HTTP protocol, and then images are blocked due to browser security settings.

The app should run and any console output will display in the terminal.

8.3.2 Adding the camera plugin

You need to first add the `camera` plugin, and you'll also use ngCordova again. Here are the commands to install the plugin and ngCordova:

```
ionic plugin add org.apache.cordova.camera
ionic add ngCordova
```

Once the `camera` plugin and ngCordova have finished installing, add ngCordova to the Angular application. Add the `</script>` tag to the index.html file after the Ionic bundle file:

```
<script src="lib/ngCordova/dist/ng-cordova.js"></script>
```

Then add the `ngCordova` dependency to your app. Open the www/js/app.js file and update the module definition with the new dependency:

```
angular.module('App', ['ionic', 'ngCordova'])
```

Now you can start to add the new view that will hold the photo book.

8.3.3 Creating the photo book view

First you need to create a new view for the photos. For this example you'll use the `cards` component to display photos. The view will have two buttons that allow users to either capture a new photo using the camera, or include an existing photo from the library. Add the new view template first; create a new file at www/views/photos/photos.html and use the code from the following listing.

Listing 8.4 Photo book template (www/views/photos/photos.html)

Creates a new view with Photo Book title →

Uses a subheader with two buttons for adding photos from camera or library

```
<ion-view view-title="Photo Book">
  <ion-header-bar class="bar-subheader">
    <button class="button button-positive button-clear"
      ng-click="getPhoto('camera')">Capture New</button>
    <button class="button button-positive button-clear"
      ng-click="getPhoto('photolibrary')">From Library</button>
  </ion-header-bar>
```

```
<ion-content>
  <div class="card list" ng-repeat="photo in photos">
    <div class="item item-image">
      <img ng-src="{{photo}}" />
    </div>
  </div>
</ion-content>
</ion-view>
```

Repeats over list of photos using a card component

Uses data URI scheme for adding photo to card

This template adds two buttons into a subheader for capturing a new photo or adding one from the library. These both will call a method in the controller, which you'll add next. The content area has ngRepeat on the card component, so each image will be displayed inside of the card.

The img element has ngSrc, which will be set to the file URI for the image. The camera plugin can also provide the Base64-encoded image data, but that can be memory-intensive to maintain. You do this because your camera plugin will give you the image content in this format, though there are other options that aren't implemented in this example.

Now you need to add the controller. Create another file at www/views/photos/photos.js and add the code from the following listing. This includes code for the camera, which we'll review in detail.

Listing 8.5 Photo book controller with camera plugin (www/views/photos/photos.js)

```
angular.module('App')
.controller('PhotosController', function ($scope,
    $ionicPlatform, $cordovaCamera) {

  $scope.photos = [];

  $scope.getPhoto = function (type) {
    $ionicPlatform.ready(function () {
      $cordovaCamera.getPicture({
        destinationType: navigator.camera.DestinationType.FILE_URL,
        sourceType: navigator.camera.PictureSourceType[type.toUpperCase()]
      }).then(function(photo) {
        $scope.photos.unshift(photo);
      }, function (err) {
        console.log(err);
      });
    });
  };
});
```

Creates controller and injects services needed

Method that handles calling camera plugin and photo library takes a type value

Creates model to hold photos

Checks if device is ready before calling camera plugin

Requests to get a picture

Parameter to request data URI version of image

Parameter to request either camera or photo library

Pushes returned photo data into model

Handles errors, currently just logging them

This controller now has the ability to request images from the camera or existing images from the library. First, create the controller and inject the $ionicPlatform and $cordovaCamera services so the app can use the camera. $cordovaCamera is provided by ngCordova to access the camera. After setting up an empty model for the photos, the getPhoto() method takes care of calling the camera plugin. It first checks if the device is ready, and then calls the camera getPicture() method.

The getPicture() method takes a few options, which are listed in the camera plugin documentation, such as declaring if the app should open the camera or photo library. When the photo is returned in the then() method, you receive the image URI and add it to the front of the photos array. If errors occur, they're logged to the console.

The last step is to finish wiring up this new view. Add the controller to the index.html file:

```
<script src="views/photos/photos.js"></script>
```

Then open the www/js/app.js file and add one more state for the photo book:

```
.state('photos', {
  url: '/photos',
  controller: 'PhotosController',
  templateUrl: 'views/photos/photos.html'
})
```

Lastly, you want to make a link to the photo book from the home view. Add one more list item to the home view in www/views/home/home.html:

```
<a href="#/photos" class="item item-icon-left">
  <i class="icon ion-images"></i> Photo book
</a>
```

Now you can run your app again on your device. You should see the new Photo Book link on the home screen, and when you tap it you'll see the new view. Choosing the Capture New button will open the camera to take a new photo, and the From Library button will open your existing photo library to select one.

It's important to note that you haven't implemented any kind of persistent storage for the images. If you leave the photos view and return later, any photos you stored will be missing. In a real-world situation you'd likely upload the images to a server or store a copy of the images using the file system of the device.

This example shows how to use the camera plugin and photo library to access a device's hardware features. It's relatively simple to do and pretty fast. Right now if a user denies the app permission to the camera or photos, the app won't crash but simply does nothing. It would be best to handle the error by showing the user a popup informing the user the app doesn't have permission to the camera, which can be changed in the device's settings.

8.4   *Using geolocation in the weather app*

In chapter 6, you built a weather app. It allows you to search for a location and get the current forecast for it, as shown in figure 8.3. But it would be helpful to know a user's location instead of searching for it. With the Cordova geolocation plugin, you can use the user's location to get the latitude and longitude and display the forecast for that location.

Figure 8.3   The app requests permission before being able to access the location on iOS.

8.4.1   Setting up the geolocation example

Let's start by setting up a new project based on the completed chapter 6 example. You'll then add the geolocation plugin and ngCordova to your project, implement the request to load the user's location, and update the app to accommodate the new features:

```
git clone https://github.com/ionic-in-action/chapter6.git chapter8-geolocation
cd chapter8-geolocation
ionic plugin add org.apache.cordova.console
ionic plugin add org.apache.cordova.device
ionic plugin add com.ionic.keyboard
ionic platform add [ios/android]
```

This will set up and emulate the finished version of the chapter 6 weather app, with the default plugins already set up. Because you're cloning the repository, you need to reinstall the core plugins (`console`, `device`, and `keyboard`). Normally the `ionic start` command will handle that, but you skip that step here when you clone the repository. For the platform and command, you'll need to select iOS or Android. Now you can run the app, so you should connect your device and then run the project on it:

```
ionic run [ios/android] -l -c -s
```

It should appear to be running the same app as you saw in the browser. Take a moment to use the app in a touch environment instead of just using it in the browser.

8.4.2   *Adding the geolocation plugin and ngCordova*

Start by getting the plugin and ngCordova set up. This should be familiar by now, but here are the steps again:

```
ionic plugin add org.apache.cordova.geolocation
ionic add ngCordova
```

This will download and install the geolocation plugin and then add ngCordova to the project. The last thing you need to do is add ngCordova to your Angular application. Add the </script> tag to the index.html file after the Ionic bundle file:

```
<script src="lib/ngCordova/dist/ng-cordova.js"></script>
```

Then add the ngCordova dependency to your app:

```
angular.module('App', ['ionic', 'ngCordova'])
```

This should set up everything to start using the plugin.

8.4.3   *Requesting a user's location*

You're interested in a user's location, particularly the latitude and longitude values. You may recall your weather API uses latitude and longitude, so this is perfect for this case. Request the user's location immediately upon first use, and then show the user the weather for the current location, as shown in figure 8.4.

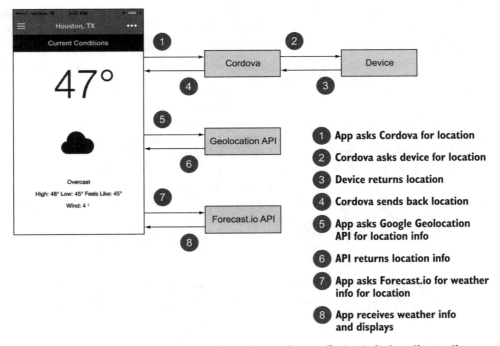

1 App asks Cordova for location
2 Cordova asks device for location
3 Device returns location
4 Cordova sends back location
5 App asks Google Geolocation API for location info
6 API returns location info
7 App asks Forecast.io for weather info for location
8 App receives weather info and displays

Figure 8.4   How the app requests for location and uses the coordinates to look up the weather

You'll need to update the `run()` method inside of www/js/app.js with the geolocation plugin request. If necessary, it will prompt the user to allow access to location information. Assuming the user agrees, it will then return to you the geolocation of the user. You'll use Google's Geolocation API to look up the address for that location, so you have a friendly name for reference, and then send the user to the forecast that's loaded from Forecast.io's API. The following listing has the code that you'll add to the app.js file, noted in bold.

Listing 8.6 Updated module `run()` method to access location (www/js/app.js)

Injects geolocation and other services

Wraps call inside of $ionicPlatform.ready to ensure plugins are ready to respond

```
.run(function($ionicPlatform, $cordovaGeolocation, $http, $state, Locations) {
  $ionicPlatform.ready(function() {
    if(window.cordova && window.cordova.plugins.Keyboard) {
      cordova.plugins.Keyboard.hideKeyboardAccessoryBar(true);
    }
    if(window.StatusBar) {
      StatusBar.styleDefault();
    }

    $cordovaGeolocation.getCurrentPosition().then(function (data) {
      $http.get('https://maps.googleapis.com/maps/api/geocode/json',
      {params: {latlng: data.coords.latitude + ',' +
      data.coords.longitude}}).success(function (response) {
        var location = {
          lat: data.coords.latitude,
          lng: data.coords.longitude,
          city: response.results[0].formatted_address,
          current: true
        };
        Locations.data.unshift(location);
        $state.go('weather', location);
      });
    });
  });
})
```

Existing code for other plugins

Calls geolocation plugin to get current position; if successful, gets data back

Uses reverse-location lookup to get address

Creates a new location and adds it to locations service

Uses $state.go to navigate to location

Calling `getCurrentPosition()` returns a promise, so you use `then()` to handle the response. Here you provide only a `success()` function, but you could provide a second function to handle the situation where permission is denied or another error occurs. But in this situation you just ignore the error and don't expose the current location feature.

Assuming you get the location data, use it to look up the address using Google's Geocoding API. This is the same service you used in the search view, except here you provide latitude and longitude coordinates. Then use the first result's address for the user's location. Note this might provide a very specific address or a general area, depending on how the Google Geolocation API responds, so there's room to improve this.

Lastly, add a new object to the Locations service, which contains a list of all of the locations for a user. This is kind of a unique location, so mark it with a current flag so you can distinguish it later on. Once the location is stored in the service, go to it because you assume the user would like to view the weather for the current location by default.

8.4.4   *Improving the weather app*

Because you've added the current location feature, there are a few additional tweaks you need to make for the app to work a little more smoothly. For example, you'd like to show the current location with a different icon, remove the default Chicago location, and not allow the current location to be deleted.

Open the www/js/app.js file again, and you'll modify it in two places. I've added ellipses to indicate areas where nothing has changed, so scroll to the two spots in the file shown in the following listing and modify the bold sections.

Listing 8.7   Weather app improvements (www/js/app.js)

```
...                                                        Code before LeftMenuCtrl
.controller('LeftMenuController', function ($scope, Locations) {
  $scope.locations = Locations.data;

  $scope.getIcon = function (current) {              Adds new scope
    if (current) {                                   method to get
      return 'ion-ios-navigate';                     proper icon for
    }                                                location
    return 'ion-ios-location';
  };
})
...                                                        More of file
  .factory('Locations', function ($ionicPopup) {
  var Locations = {                                  Removes default
    data: [],                                        location stored in
...                              Rest of file        Locations service
```

Here you add a new method for the left menu controller that can return the proper class for the icon. If the location is the current location, use the navigate icon; if not, use the location icon. This is just a simple visual improvement to help distinguish the current location. Lastly, remove the default Chicago location, because now that the app is using the current location, you don't need it anymore.

Now update the list of locations in the side menu located in the index.html file. The list item will use ngClass to call the getIcon() method you just added to show the correct icon. The bold line is all that you need to change from the following listing.

Listing 8.8 Side menu location icons (www/index.html)

```
...                                            <──── Template before side
<ion-list>
  <ion-item class="item-icon-left" ui-sref="search" menu-close><span
    class="icon ion-search"></span> Find a City</ion-item>
  <ion-item class="item-icon-left" ui-sref="settings" menu-close><span
    class="icon ion-ios-cog"></span> Settings</ion-item>
  <ion-item class="item-divider">Favorites</ion-item>
  <ion-item class="item-icon-left" ui-sref="weather({city: location.city,
    lat: location.lat, lng: location.lng})" menu-close ng-repeat="location
    in locations"><span class="icon" ng-class=
    "getIcon(location.current)"></span> {{location.city}}</ion-item>  <──┐
</ion-list>                                                 Adds ngClass
...                         <──── Rest of file               to call getIcon
```

Now when you run the app, you can see the current icon changes from any other stored locations. These kinds of small, user interface features are important to help provide context for users.

The last thing you want to do is prevent the current location from being deleted. You want the current location to be protected because it's a special location, and not one the user has favorited. Deleting the current location would disable the current location feature for the user, so you want to avoid this edge case.

There are many ways to approach this, but you'll just exclude the current location from the settings page. Open the settings template at www/views/settings/settings .html and add the bold line from the following listing.

Listing 8.9 Prevent current location deletion (www/views/settings/settings.html)

```
                                          Template code until location
                                          list remains unchanged
...                                        <──┘
<ion-list show-delete="canDelete">
  <ion-item ng-repeat="location in locations" ng-if="!location.current">  <──┐
    <ion-delete-button class="ion-minus-circled" ng-click=
    "remove($index)"></ion-delete-button>
    {{location.city}}                                   Adds ng-if to exclude
  </ion-item>                                              current location
</ion-list>
...                  <──── Continue with remainder of code
```

This change will prevent the current location from being displayed in the location list, and therefore prevent it from being deleted. You've now completed the example, and the ability to get the user's location is fairly simple, but powerful. Merging the user's location data with other information is a very useful way to create some interested apps.

What happens if the user denies permission for location? Well, the good news is your app will still work without the location information. It's important to consider this in your app design and ensure that it can still be used without geolocation when possible. The ability to access the location of a user can be disabled at any time, so don't assume it's working. The same is true of other types of plugins that have permissions, because any time permission is denied, your app still has to function in some manner. It might not be possible to run without location permissions, in which case you'd likely need to prompt the user with a friendly message. You can determine if the app is able to access geolocation by trying to use it, and in the error handler check if the response is a permission issue.

8.5   *Chapter challenges*

There are so many plugins and features that you could implement in your resort and weather apps, but here are a few specific ones that would be good practice when using Cordova plugins:

- *Handle cases where a user is offline*—We talked about how to handle offline situations in chapter 7, but see if you can apply that here. The app will fail now without a connection, so it's important to check how it works without a connection. Consider also using Angular's $http interceptors to handle errors.
- *Use the* file *plugin to save photos*—Right now, the photos in the resort app are only available until the app has been closed, because you're not saving the images anywhere. In reality, you'd want to keep those, but photos quickly become larger than the available localStorage space. Use the file plugin to store the photos and retrieve them each time the app is loaded.
- *Use the* calendar *plugin to add events*—In the resort app, the events could optionally be added to a user's calendar. Add a button that users can select to add the upcoming events to their calendar.
- *Prompt for app rating*—In any of the examples, you could prompt users to rate your app in the app store. This is best done when a user has been using the app for a little while and can provide a quality review.
- *Replace action sheet with plugin*—In the weather app, you use the action sheet component in Ionic. Try to replace the Ionic component with the action sheet plugin.

8.6   *Summary*

We looked deeper at Cordova and plugins in this chapter. I hope you're surprised at how easy it was to get photos and a user's location and use them in your app. This shows the power of using Cordova plugins, especially with ngCordova. You have the ability to access just about everything a mobile device can provide. Let's review the major topics covered in this chapter:

- Installing Cordova plugins provides additional native features for your Ionic apps.
- Common plugin problems and troubleshooting techniques.
- ngCordova makes it easier to work with Cordova plugins in your apps.
- Using the geolocation plugin to improve the weather app from chapter 6.
- Using the camera plugin to create a photo book for the resort app from chapter 4.

In the next chapter, you'll learn about writing tests for your app and about additional debugging tools and techniques.

Previewing, debugging, and automated testing

> **This chapter covers**
> - Previewing your app using Ionic View and Ionic Lab
> - Debugging from a device or emulator on iOS and Android
> - Setting up and writing automated tests for your app

Get ready: we're going to cover a lot of ground in this chapter about how to preview, debug, and properly test your app. The purpose of this chapter is to help you better manage quality in your app over time. You may recognize in projects you've worked on in the past that code maintainability tends to suffer and applications become more complex over time. It takes work and discipline by developers to counteract these trends, and this chapter identifies some tools that will help you do exactly that.

9.1   The differences among previewing, debugging, and testing

Let's dissect these three terms—previewing, debugging, and testing—a little bit before we jump into the chapter. The differences are highlighted in figure 9.1.

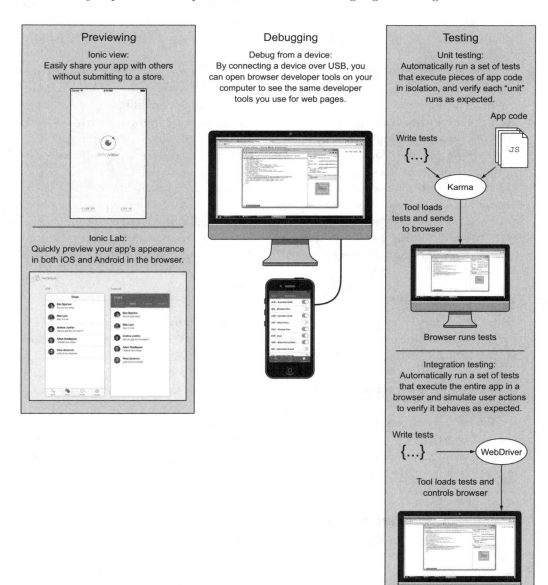

Figure 9.1   Key aspects of previewing, debugging, and testing apps

Previewing means viewing and interacting with the app on your device or emulator. Previewing is usually the first technique developers use to visually verify how the app looks and that it behaves as expected. Depending on previewing alone can cause a lot of headaches, because the process relies on the developer to manually run and interact with the entire app. As the app becomes larger and the number of platforms increases, manually previewing becomes exponentially more difficult to rely on for quality assurance. You'll look at a few additional ways to preview your app that are built into Ionic.

Debugging is the art of dissecting and discovering the source of a bug. Recall from chapter 1 the technologies and utilities that make up the Ionic stack. Debugging is the act of determining where the error is occurring. It's also possible that some bugs aren't related to your code, but rather something like a corrupt file. Many bugs are resolved today by doing a search online for the error message and finding blog or forum posts that address it. We'll discuss a few techniques and tools that will assist you in tracing your bugs back to their source.

Automated testing is the practice of writing code that can verify the intended behavior of other code. Computers are great at doing repetitive tasks, and testing tools can load your app and execute code to verify it works as expected. Automated tests require that you write a test, which is a way for the test tool to load some code and assert that it does a particular task. Manual testing has a place as well, but automating tests is significantly more practical for production apps.

9.1.1 Why testing is important

Imagine you have a medium-size app (whatever that means to you) that's for sale on the app stores. You're getting a lot of feedback about a particular problem many people are facing, which you thought you fixed in the past. You need to be able to quickly verify that this bug is fixed before you release a new version of the app. Writing a test is the best way to verify a bug is fixed, because you can run that test repeatedly without having to manually check for the bug in every release.

For web developers who haven't built larger applications, testing may seem like overkill or too much work to implement. Writing a professional, quality app should include testing abilities to maintain quality. But all apps benefit from testing, and you should strive to make this a high priority in your development. Testing has an initial cost to set up, but in the long run it always pays off.

9.2   Setting up the chapter example

This chapter example is based on the chapter 6 weather app, and this version includes the additional features for setting up and running automated tests. You can get this chapter example using the following `git clone` command or by downloading it from GitHub at https://github.com/ionic-in-action/chapter9/archive/master.zip:

```
git clone https://github.com/ionic-in-action/chapter9
```

Once you've cloned or downloaded it (and unzipped it if using a download link), navigate to the directory for the project and add the plugins and at least one platform. Because you checked out the example instead of using the `ionic start` command-line task, you have to manually add the plugins that are usually set up by `ionic start`:

```
ionic plugin add org.apache.cordova.console
ionic plugin add org.apache.cordova.device
ionic plugin add com.ionic.keyboard
ionic platform add [ios/android]
```

Now your project should be the same as the final version of chapter 6, plus the additional testing files that you'll need through this chapter.

9.3   Additional ways to preview apps

There are some useful ways to preview your app that we haven't covered yet, and each is helpful for different types of situations. Ionic is continually creating features for its developers, which is one of the biggest reasons they love it.

You'll look at two additional ways to preview your app besides using `ionic serve`, `ionic emulate`, or `ionic run`. First, with Ionic Lab you can preview your app with both Android and iOS side by side. Second, with Ionic View you can upload an app to the Ionic platform, and others can download and preview your app using the Ionic View app without going through an app store.

9.3.1   Ionic Lab

When you need to preview the display of your app on iOS and Android at the same time, you can use the Ionic CLI's Lab feature. This technique doesn't require a Mac to preview iOS; however, it's not a real emulator and only provides a visual preview and comparison. It's part of the `ionic serve` command you already know, but when it opens in the browser, you'll see two versions of the app running. In figure 9.2 you can see how one of the views from the chapter 5 example appears with Ionic Lab. This can help you catch bugs related to how the interface appears on different devices.

In figure 9.2 you can see how on the left, the iOS version, the tabs are displayed on the bottom, and on the right the tabs are displayed at the top. This quickly shows how the appearance of the app differs by platform. To use Ionic Lab, run the `serve` command with the `--lab` flag:

```
$ ionic serve --lab
```

This will automatically open a new browser window with the two versions side by side. In chapter 7 we talked about how it's important to design your app to consider the platform's style guides, and this is a great way to quickly preview how your app appears. The same limitations of viewing your app in the browser still apply, so some Cordova features may not work without being in an emulator or on a device.

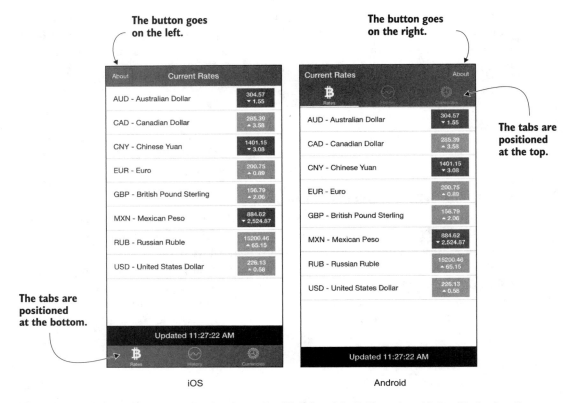

The button goes on the left.

The button goes on the right.

The tabs are positioned at the top.

The tabs are positioned at the bottom.

iOS   Android

Figure 9.2   Ionic Lab allows you to preview your app with iOS and Android running side by side to view the differences between the visual displays of each platform.

9.3.2   *Ionic View*

Ionic has a platform of additional features that Ionic developers can use to make their lives easier. Ionic View (http://view.ionic.io/) is a mobile app that anyone can install from the app stores to preview apps made with Ionic. That means you can have clients or beta testers preview your app without actually publishing it to the app stores. For example, you might use it to show your boss the app during your regular progress meetings. Figure 9.3 shows two chapter examples uploaded to my Ionic View app. This doesn't provide you any direct help in developing your app, but it's primarily a way to show the app to others without having to submit it through a store first.

   To use Ionic View, you need to have an account with Ionic. You can get a free account at https://apps.ionic.io/signup. Then log in from your command line:

```
$ ionic login
```

Fill in your login details there. Once you're authenticated, you'll be able to upload any of your apps to the Ionic platform and share it over Ionic View.

In the command line, navigate to the project directory that you'd like to upload. From there, you can run the command to upload the app, and Ionic will register and upload it to your account:

```
$ ionic upload
```

This command will take any valid Ionic project and send it to the Ionic platform servers. It creates a unique ID for the app and attaches it to your account so you can share it. You can view and manage your uploaded apps at https://apps.ionic.io/apps.

After uploading, you can open the Ionic View app on your device, and you should see a list of the apps that you've uploaded. When you tap any app, Ionic View will download and run the app on your device without having to connect the device and deploy it directly.

Figure 9.3 Ionic View app with two uploaded chapter example apps

Choose an app and tap it to download and view it. You'll notice that it runs full-screen, so to exit the app, use three fingers and swipe down.

IONIC VIEW LIMITATIONS

There are a few limitations to Ionic View. Due to the architecture of the platform, Ionic View can only support a certain set of Cordova plugins. You can view the list of supported plugins in the documentation at http://docs.ionic.io/docs/view-usage. Some plugins may not be supported because of security concerns.

Ionic View also doesn't provide debugging information. Production apps are more limited in their abilities to debug for security reasons. Debugging abilities require communication between the app and a computer, which is why you don't want an app you didn't create being able to access your computer directly. You'll need to review the Ionic View documentation to learn about any debugging abilities that might exist should they add features.

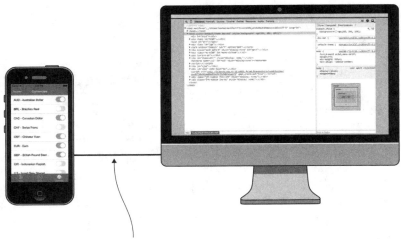

The browser recognizes a connected device over USB. This allows you to open developer tools for WebView on the device.

Figure 9.4   How browser developer tools can help debug a web view on a connected device

9.4   *Debugging from a device*

So far you've been using the browser on your computer to do development and debugging. But things may happen when you load the app on your device that you need to be able to debug. Because you aren't writing a native app, it would be great to just use the same browser debugging tools that you've been using. The good news is you can!

Both Android and iOS allow you to use the browser developer tools to debug from an emulator or a connected device. Essentially, Chrome or Safari (depending on the platform) allows you to connect to the device and treats the WebView inside of the app as a browser window where you can use developer tools, as you see in figure 9.4.

In chapter 2 we talked about how you can emulate the app or run the app on a device using the Ionic command-line interface (CLI) utility, which has an option to output the console messages into the command line. The following command is for iOS, or substitute ios with android to emulate Android:

```
$ ionic emulate ios -l -c
```

The problem with this is that you only get the JavaScript errors logged into the browser console. This is fine if you need to check for JavaScript errors that you normally see in the browser console, but it provides no ability to inspect the DOM and look at element styles. With the ability to have the complete set of developer tools, you can inspect virtually any aspect of your app.

Debugging is only available for apps that you've built and deployed onto a device yourself. Apps aren't designed to be debugged when they're installed from the store.

9.4.1 Debugging from an Android device

Android remote debugging is fairly easy to work with, but requires enabling the debugging options on your device first. If you haven't already done this, you can review the steps in section 2.2. Then you can set up the best browser for debugging and get the debugging tools started.

SETTING UP GOOGLE CHROME CANARY BROWSER

It's suggested that you get the Google Chrome Canary browser for Android development. Chrome Canary is the bleeding-edge version of Chrome, and it's intended to allow developers to test new features and changes in Chrome before they go into the primary version most people use. Android development documentation says that for best results when connecting and debugging your app, the browser on your computer should be more advanced than the one installed on the device. Chrome Canary will ensure that's the case because it's like a continuously updated beta version. You can download it from https://www.google.com/intl/en/chrome/browser/canary.html.

Once you have a connected device, open Chrome Canary and go to the `chrome://inspect` address. You have to type this into the address bar, and then you'll see the screen in figure 9.5 shown on page 214. If no devices are found, the list will be blank. Because your device is running, you can click the Inspect link to open the Chrome developer tools for the app. You can modify the styles, see the JavaScript console logs, look at network calls such as your API requests, and anything else you can normally do with the developer tools.

Android emulators don't allow you to debug with this technique. But there's another tool called Genymotion that runs like an emulator, but actually appears to the computer as if it's a connected device. You can download and use it for free on personal projects from https://www.genymotion.com, and it also requires VirtualBox: https://www.virtualbox.org. When you want to deploy your app to Genymotion, you just need to have Genymotion open and then use the `ionic run android` command. If you try to emulate, it will not use Genymotion.

That's all you need to do to get access to the debugging tools for Android devices.

9.4.2 Debugging from an iOS device or emulator

Debugging on iOS is pretty similar to Android, except it uses Safari. Start by enabling debugging through Safari on your device. This should be enabled by default for the iOS emulators, but you can still check the settings to verify. On your device, go to the Settings app. Open the settings for Safari, and then choose the Advanced option at the bottom. Make sure the Web Inspector option is toggled on, which is used by Safari to allow debugging of a web view. These steps are shown in figure 9.6, page 215.

Open chrome://inspect to see
connected devices. Devices must
already be on and connected.

Click on the Inspect link
by the device to open the
developer tools for the device.

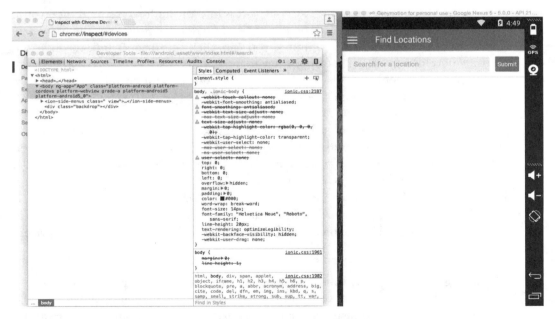

Figure 9.5   How to open the developer tools for a connected Android device

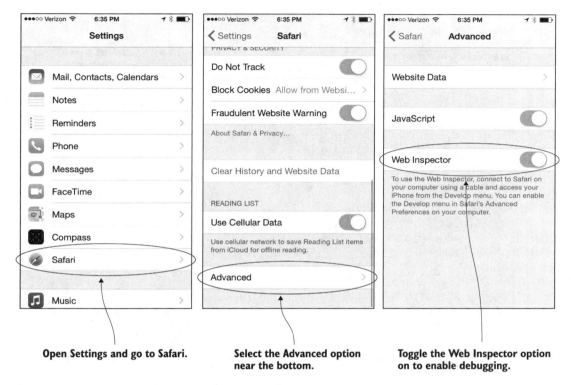

Open Settings and go to Safari. **Select the Advanced option near the bottom.** **Toggle the Web Inspector option on to enable debugging.**

Figure 9.6 Enabling the Web Inspector option on mobile Safari

Now open Safari on your computer. If you don't see a Develop menu in the top menu bar, then you'll need to turn on the developer settings for Safari. Open the Safari Preferences panel (Safari > Preferences from the top menu) and choose the Advanced tab. At the bottom of the Advanced tab is a box to check to show the Develop menu. Choose it and close the preferences. You should now have the Develop menu showing in the top menu. These steps are shown in figure 9.7.

Now you can start to debug your app on iOS. First, you'll need to get your app running on an emulator or device. I'll run this chapter example in the emulator, so you can see them in the screenshots side by side with the developer tools.

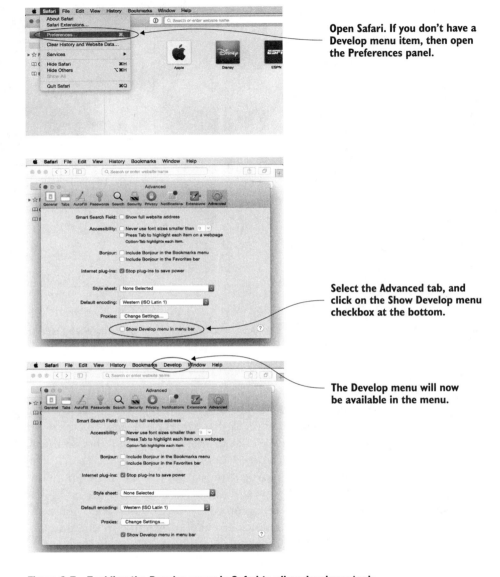

Open Safari. If you don't have a Develop menu item, then open the Preferences panel.

Select the Advanced tab, and click on the Show Develop menu checkbox at the bottom.

The Develop menu will now be available in the menu.

Figure 9.7   Enabling the Develop menu in Safari to allow developer tools

Open Safari when a connected device or emulator
is running. Use the Develop menu to locate the
device, and select the app index.html.

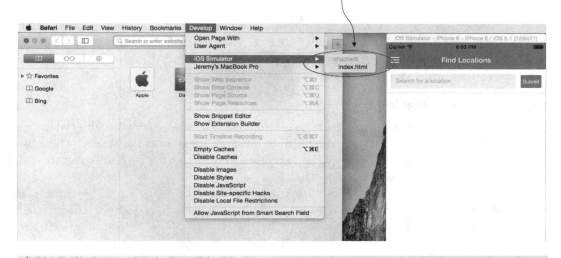

It will open a new Web Inspector
window, where you can interact
with and inspect the app.

Figure 9.8 How to open the developer tools in Safari for an emulator or device

Once the app is running, go to the Develop menu. You should now see either the
device or the emulator listed in the menu, and you can choose the index.html option
for that item as shown in figure 9.8. This will open a new Web Inspector window, and
you should be able to then choose items in the DOM to inspect the styles and content.

The biggest problem I've run into with debugging on Safari like this is that you have to open the app in the device or emulator before you can open the Web Inspector. That means the Web Inspector can't be opened until the app is already started. If you have any bugs or errors happening at the moment the app loads, then the Web Inspector will not yet be open to catch the information. You might have to use a hack like an alert to send messages about JavaScript code on load.

That's all there is to setting up debugging for an iOS emulator or device. Now let's dig into setting up automated tests.

9.5   *Automated testing*

Testing means verifying apps behave as expected. So far, you've been building your app using manual testing by just previewing it and tapping away at the screen. This only works for so long before it becomes cumbersome to manually test every feature, for every platform, for every release.

In a development cycle, you'll use automated testing to help you any time you make a change to your app. You might be fixing a bug you found while debugging or incorporating a new feature that was requested by your client, but you'll want to use automated tests to quickly validate that the app continues to function.

What you want to learn about here is *automated testing*—code that can programmatically verify if your app is working as expected or not. When done well, these tests can execute in mere seconds, which can take a lot of load off the developer's shoulders. When you work in a team, it also allows others to run tests to verify they didn't break the code of another team member. There are so many good reasons to write tests, so why do some projects not have them?

Simply put, writing tests can be challenging at first. Tests themselves are code, so you have to write code to test code. Developers also might think they can manually test faster than it takes to learn and set up automated testing. But the long-term benefits of automated testing are more considerable: stability in your app, easier development without fear of breaking something, and helping teams avoid conflicts in code.

You'll look at two types of automated tests: unit tests and integration tests (also called *end-to-end*). The testing tools you'll use work with Angular because your app is based on Angular.

Unit tests are best for testing individual parts of your code, such as services and controllers, because a unit test is designed to test each individual function (as its own "unit") to assert it returns the expected value.

Integration tests are designed to test the app behavior as a whole by mimicking user behavior, such as tapping on an item in a list to navigate to a detail view, to verify the interface responds as expected. We'll dig into the nuances of each, but most apps will benefit from both types of tests.

I'll help you get started with the foundations of test writing. By the end of this section, you'll be able to start writing tests, and you'll feel encouraged to dig deeper into the world of testing.

9.5.1 *Unit tests with Jasmine and Karma*

Unit tests are automated tests for verifying code executes as expected. The intention is to test the smallest parts of the application, such as a scope method, and check that it returns the correct result.

For example, think about your favorite map app. It probably has a method that takes a pair of latitude and longitude values and calculates the distance between the two locations. It would be best to write a set of tests that checks that if you pass the function different types of values (some might even be invalid values), the method returns the expected result. Here are a few fictitious sample tests that might be written to test this conceptual method:

```
var location1 = [91, 21];                                    Creates two latitude, longitude
var location2 = [82, 32];                                    values for test to use

expect(mapCalculate(location1, location2)).toEqual(123);     Tests that
expect(mapCalculate(location1, undefined)).toEqual(0);       mapCalculate()
                                                             method gives
                      Tests that mapCalculate() method        expected value
                      handles invalid input as expected       with valid input
```

Unit tests are a great way of ensuring the smallest parts of your app work as intended. If you have confidence that the unit tests are running and that your methods are all working as expected, then it becomes easier to make changes in other parts of the application without fear of breaking existing features. I've learned the hard way that without tests it can become very difficult to maintain an app over time.

You'll use the Jasmine (http://jasmine.github.io/) testing framework to write unit tests, and then use Karma (http://karma-runner.github.io/) as the tool that will run them. Jasmine is a popular option for developers who are new to testing, and it's also the primary testing framework used by the Ionic and Angular projects. As shown in figure 9.9, Karma connects a testing framework (in this case, Jasmine), loads all of the

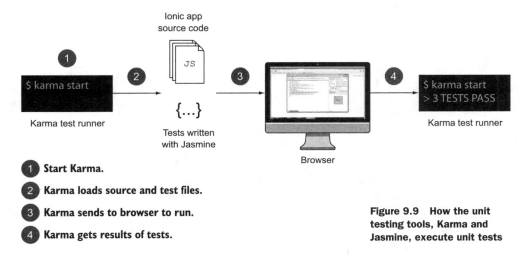

1 Start Karma.

2 Karma loads source and test files.

3 Karma sends to browser to run.

4 Karma gets results of tests.

Figure 9.9 How the unit testing tools, Karma and Jasmine, execute unit tests

tests and application code into a browser, and then runs the tests in a browser (in this case, Chrome). Because your JavaScript runs in the browser, the Jasmine tests are executed in a browser.

You'll start by setting up Jasmine and Karma, and then you'll write some unit tests for the weather app from chapter 6.

SET UP KARMA AND JASMINE

You'll start by installing Karma, which then helps set up Jasmine. Karma has a plugin for Jasmine and Chrome, which you'll install in addition to the core Karma tool. Open the command line, navigate to the project directory you set up at the start of the chapter, and run the following commands to install the tools:

```
$ npm install --save-dev karma karma-jasmine karma-chrome-launcher
$ npm install -g karma-cli
```

The first line adds Karma, the Jasmine plugin, and the Chrome plugin to the project, and saves them as development dependencies. The second line adds Karma globally so you can run it easily from the command line.

Before Karma can run, you need to add a configuration file so it knows what to do. Karma runs just the JavaScript files you specify instead of loading an HTML file and letting the page load (you'll do that in the next section). Make a new file in the project root called karma.conf.js and add the code from the following listing.

Listing 9.1   Karma configuration file (karma.conf.js)

```
module.exports = function(config) {
  config.set({
    frameworks: ['jasmine'],              Declares you want to use Jasmine
    files: [
      'www/lib/ionic/js/ionic.bundle.js',     Tells Karma to load files you include in app
      'www/lib/moment/moment.js',
      'www/lib/moment-timezone/builds/moment-timezone-with-data.js',
      'www/lib/suncalc/suncalc.js',
      'www/lib/angular-mocks/angular-mocks.js',     Adds angular-mocks file, which is used to help write tests
      'www/js/**/*.js',
      'www/views/**/*.js',                  Uses glob patterns to match app and test files
      'test/unit/**/*.js'
    ],
    reporters: ['progress'],              Uses progress reporter option
    browsers: ['Chrome']                  Uses Chrome for testing
  });
};
```

This configuration is what you'll use for your tests. You have to declare the framework you wish to use (in this case, Jasmine) and tell Karma which files to include. Karma will load these files into a browser (in this case, Chrome) and run all of the tests it finds. The results are then reported back to the console, but could be configured to output to a file (several file types are supported, such as HTML or XML). Now you can write a test and execute it. Any files that your app needs to run should be included in the file list, just as you've included libraries such as Moment.js.

WRITING A UNIT TEST FOR THE CHANCE FILTER

Jasmine is a behavior-driven development (BDD) framework. You may be familiar with different agile development methodologies; the primary idea is to help reconcile the difference between technical and management teams during the software development process. When you write tests, you'll *describe* the feature with a list of statements about what *it* should do. I draw attention to the terms *describe* and *it* because they're used as part of the testing syntax.

Jasmine versus other testing frameworks

Jasmine is a very powerful testing framework, but it's not the only option. Several other examples are Mocha, QUnit, and Unit.js. In the world of JavaScript, new frameworks appear all the time, so you might be aware of some other new options.

In short, you should be able to use any testing framework that you desire. The more popular it is, the more likely it's well supported by the tools in this book. Jasmine is the testing framework in use by the Angular project for the 1.x version, so it's a good choice for anyone who's new to testing.

I personally enjoy Jasmine for the most part, but Mocha is another framework I've used. Jasmine provides most everything you need for testing, whereas Mocha is more piecemeal and requires you to add additional tools for certain things. Unless Jasmine is unable to meet your needs or you have more experience with another framework, I recommend it for use with Ionic and Angular apps.

I think the easiest way to get started is to dive in with some examples. The first test you'll write is for the chance filter, which takes a decimal value and turns it into a rounded percentage value between 0 and 100, and rounded to the nearest tenth. For example, you expect a value of 0.36 to be converted to 36 and then rounded to 40%. You want to assert this to be true by writing a test that uses the filter and passing a few sample values. The test can be found in the following listing, and should be created at tests/unit/chance.filter.spec.js.

Listing 9.2   Chance filter unit test (tests/unit/chance.filter.spec.js)

```
describe('Chance Filter', function() {          ◁──① Describes feature, in this case Chance Filter

  beforeEach(module('App'));

  it('should round any decimal percentage to nearest 10 value',
     inject(function(chanceFilter) {            ◁──③
    expect(chanceFilter(0.01)).toEqual(0);
    expect(chanceFilter(0.05)).toEqual(10);
    expect(chanceFilter(0.44)).toEqual(40);
    expect(chanceFilter(0.46)).toEqual(50);
    expect(chanceFilter(0.95)).toEqual(100);
    expect(chanceFilter(undefined)).toEqual(0);
  }));
});
```

① **Using Angular mocks module() method, makes App available** ②

③ **Uses 'it should…' style to declare test, and then starts test by injecting chanceFilter**

④ **Uses assertion library to expect filter to convert some values to expected outputs**

This test has a lot going on, so let's break it down piece by piece. First, look at the describe() method ❶. This is primarily an organizational tool for you to write a test and place all relevant tests inside of this block. The next block is a beforeEach() method ❷, which will run the function inside before every test. This is important because the testing environment is reset between every test, so you can't expect anything to persist between tests. The beforeEach() method uses the module() method to load your app into the test before it executes. The module() method is available because you're using the Angular mocks package, which was included in your configuration file.

The it statement ❸ is where you declare the specific feature requirement. The first argument is a string, typically written to read like "it should do something." The second argument is a function to execute, which will contain the assertions that it actually does do something. Your function uses the inject function to insert the chanceFilter. Normally, you use a filter in the binding expression, such as {{ 0.34 | chance }}, but here you load it directly to call yourself.

Finally, you have six expect statements ❹. These are the assertions talked about earlier, because you basically say that you expect the chanceFilter, given a certain value, to equal the value you specify. In this case, you test six different scenarios to ensure your filter works. You could specify as many of these as you need, including the last one that tests an invalid value to see how well your method handles it.

One of the benefits of Jasmine and the BDD style of testing is the tests are written with a declarative style, so even non-developers can read and understand them. Because you *describe* a feature and declare what *it* should do, it's possible to use tests not just as a way to validate behavior but also as a tool to help plan and clarify features.

RUNNING THE UNIT TESTS

To run the tests, you'll need to use the karma command-line tool. It will start a session where it will watch your files as you edit, so it can automatically run the tests any time you save a file. It will also launch a new Chrome window to run the tests inside of Chrome. Run this command from the root of your project:

```
$ karma start
```

It will start the Karma server, which watches the files and handles running the tests in the browser. It will also execute the tests immediately, and report the output of the tests directly into the command line.

Typically I keep this command-line window open and running my tests the entire time I'm developing. It helps to remind me to write the tests, and helps me see immediately when I might have broken code.

WRITING A UNIT TEST FOR THE SEARCH CONTROLLER

Now you'll create another test for one of the controllers, as shown in listing 9.3. Most of the structure is the same, but you have to do some different setup to test a controller. You'll test the search controller, which is fairly simple, but because it makes an HTTP request, you'll have to do some mocking to test it.

What are mocks, and why do you need them?

During testing you want to isolate the number of conditions that might cause your tests to fail. The problem is most code depends on other code to run—for example, a controller may include the Angular $http service and your code depends on it.

Mocks are special objects that are designed to mimic the behavior of real objects. You don't want to actually make an HTTP request during your tests because this takes time and Angular already tests the $http service before they release a version of Angular, so you don't need to test it again. Angular provides a mock version of $http called $httpBackend, and it's part of the Angular Mocks module included in your tests. Another example would be local storage, where you can create a mock localStorage service that behaves like the real thing. ngCordova also comes with mock services that can be used to mock ngCordova features.

Anything that's not part of your custom codebase should probably be mocked for unit tests. You don't really want your tests to call the real API. Imagine you want to test the user registration for your app. Instead of using the real service, you mock it and avoid the incidental registration. You also want to make sure your tests are fast to increase the likelihood that you'll use them, because you should be running them frequently.

Listing 9.3 Search controller test (test/unit/search-ctrl.spec.js)

❶ Describes search controller feature

❷ Declares some variables to access values inside of child scopes

❸ Before each test runs, adds App module

❹ Before each test runs, injects values for tests

❺ Injects values and makes them available

❻ Uses httpBackend.when() to handle HTTP response for weather API and templates

❼ Instantiates controller with scope and $http services used

```javascript
describe('Search Controller', function () {
  var scope, httpBackend;

  beforeEach(module('App'));

  beforeEach(inject(function ($rootScope, $controller, $httpBackend, $http) {
    scope = $rootScope.$new();
    httpBackend = $httpBackend;
    httpBackend.when('GET',
     'http://maps.googleapis.com/maps/api/geocode/json?address=london')
     .respond({results: [{}, {}, {}]});
    httpBackend.when('GET', 'views/weather/weather.html').respond('');
    httpBackend.when('GET', 'views/settings/settings.html').respond('');
    httpBackend.when('GET', 'views/search/search.html').respond('');
    $controller('SearchCtrl', {
      $scope: scope,
      $http: $http
    });
  }));
```

```
it('should load with a blank model', function () {
  expect(scope.model.term).toEqual('');
});


it('should be able to search for locations', function () {
  scope.model.term = 'london';
  scope.search();
  httpBackend.flush();
  expect(scope.results.length).toEqual(3);
});
})
```

Creates spec to validate
❽ the model.term value is
empty by default

Creates spec for search method, changes term,
calls method, flushes requests, expects results ❾

This test is longer than the controller, and you might be a little concerned about this. Much of what you do in this test is related to setting up the test environment. There's a lot going on here again, so let's walk through it piece by piece.

First, describe ❶ the feature, in this case the search controller. Because the code runs inside of a function, you want to declare some variables here that you'll give values to later ❷. Just like before, start by adding the App module ❸ using the beforeEach() method.

The next beforeEach() method ❹ includes a bit of logic needed to get the controller working. Because you're building isolated tests, you have to do some of the work that Angular normally does behind the scenes. The Angular documentation has more details about how to set up testing for different types of Angular features, such as filters, directives, and controllers. This is often where people start to get anxious about testing, but don't be discouraged!

Create a new scope and get the httpBackend service stored in the variables ❺. You'll need to use these variables in your specs, which is why you made them variables outside of this closure. The first httpBackend.when() call ❻ mocks out the request for the location search. You have to declare the method of the HTTP request (in this case GET) and the URL for the HTTP request, and then chain a response() method and declare a value. You don't have to worry about the response matching the real thing; you just need to ensure the response returns the bare minimum, in this case an array of objects.

The next three uses of httpBackend.when() ❻ all help you mock your templates because those are loaded over HTTP. This is only necessary if you load templates from a URL, which is configured in the states declaration of your app. The last step is to use the $controller service ❼ to register the controller and pass the expected dependencies.

Finally, you get to the two specs where you actually test the controller. The first spec ❽ simply checks that the scope model.term value is blank. It's good to test the default state for a controller. The second spec ❾ changes the model.term value and calls the search() method. This is where the httpBackend mock service takes over.

Instead of making a real HTTP request, it looks at your mock declarations from earlier ❻ and finds a matching request. When it finds a match, it will respond with the value you declared, which is an array of three blank objects. Assert that the scope is updated with the array of objects by checking the length of the array.

If Karma is still running in the command line, then these tests will automatically be added and executed. If you canceled the Karma process, start it again to see the tests passing.

> ### Learning more about Jasmine
>
> Jasmine has a number of features we didn't discuss here that might come in handy in your tests. Jasmine has additional ways to express your tests, such as `expect(value).toBeDefined()` or `expect(value).not.toBeNull()`. To get the most out of your Jasmine tests, be sure to review the documentation at http://jasmine.github.io/ for all possible vocabulary.
>
> One of my favorite ways to understand Jasmine is to look at tests others have written for Angular and Angular modules. You can find the tests on GitHub in the Angular repository or in many of the third-party Angular modules repositories.

The most difficult aspect of testing is understanding how exactly to manually handle many parts of the app that are normally managed by Angular. The Angular documentation has a good set of examples for how to test different parts of the app when you're confused about how to properly organize your test. Writing tests can be a challenge, but the effort to learn and write tests is worth it. You can now modify the application and run the tests anytime to verify that nothing has broken.

9.5.2 Integration tests with Protractor and WebDriver

Some parts of your app are best tested with an integration test that can simulate user behaviors such as tapping or typing values into a form input. Protractor (www .protractortest.org) is a testing framework built specifically for Angular (in fact, by the Angular team), and therefore works for Ionic apps. Protractor is built on top of an API called WebDriver (http://w3c.github.io/webdriver/webdriver-spec .html), which allows you to programmatically interact with an application just like the user would. WebDriver is really just the specification for how programs can programmatically interact with a browser. Selenium (http://docs.seleniumhq.org/projects/ webdriver/) was the project that inspired the WebDriver API spec. See figure 9.10 for an example of how tests are executed using these APIs.

Protractor extends the features of WebDriver and adds better support for Angular apps. By default WebDriver runs as soon as the page is ready, but due to the Angular digest loop, your tests need to run only after Angular is ready. Protractor aids your tests by waiting for Angular to finish rendering the view before running the tests, as well as providing a few unique API calls to target parts of an Angular template. You'll see a few of these in action in the sample test.

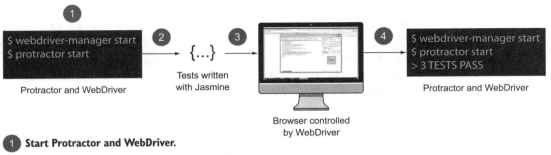

1. **Start Protractor and WebDriver.**

2. **Protractor loads tests from files and sends to browser.**

3. **WebDriver runs the tests, which mimic user behaviors.**

4. **Results are returned to Protractor.**

Figure 9.10   How integration tests are executed using WebDriver/Selenium, Protractor, and Jasmine

During setup, you'll use Selenium (which implements the WebDriver API) and plugins for browsers (Chrome by default) to control the browser to mimic user behaviors. You'll have to have a Selenium server running in the background to run the tests, but this is easily managed by Protractor.

Protractor uses the Jasmine testing framework by default to run tests. Protractor doesn't require you to use Jasmine, so you can choose another testing framework if you'd like such as Mocha or Cucumber.js. Because you used Jasmine earlier, you can write your tests in the same style to make it a little easier.

SET UP AND RUN PROTRACTOR AND WEBDRIVER

First you need to do a one-time setup for Protractor and WebDriver. Start by installing Protractor as a global Node module, just like you did when you installed Ionic and Cordova:

```
$ npm install -g protractor
```

This command will download Protractor and also create a helper tool to easily manage WebDriver. You'll use the tool to download all of the tools for WebDriver to run. The tool will download the Selenium server and Chrome driver, and set them up:

```
$ webdriver-manager update
```

Check that everything is installed by checking Protractor's version number and the WebDriver status. You don't need IEDriver, so you can safely ignore the message about it missing:

```
$ protractor --version
Version 1.6.1
$ webdriver-manager status
selenium standalone is up to date
chromedriver is up to date
IEDriver is not present
```

Any time you want to run your Protractor tests, you need to first make sure the Selenium server (required by WebDriver) is running. To do this you need to have a command-line window open and run the following command:

```
$ webdriver-manager start
```

This will show a lot of diagnostic information about starting the Selenium server. This window must remain open and running any time you want to run your tests. You can stop the server by typing Ctrl-C on your keyboard. You might get a warning about Java not being installed or up to date. To fix this, download and install the latest version of the Java development kit (select the JDK option for your platform, not the JRE option) from http://mng.bz/83Ct.

CONFIGURE PROTRACTOR

Protractor requires a configuration file to run in your project, so you need to add this before you start writing tests. There are many options that you don't usually need, but you can review all of them on the Protractor documentation site listed earlier. Create a new file in the project root called protractor.conf.js:

```
exports.config = {
  seleniumAddress: 'http://localhost:4444/wd/hub',
  specs: ['test/e2e/**/*.spec.js']
};
```

This configuration gives Protractor the address to your local Selenium server (which is set up by the `webdriver-manager` tool) and an array of file paths to look for test files to run. Remember, in Jasmine tests are called *specs*, so in this case it's looking in the test/e2e directory for all files with the ending .spec.js.

WRITING TESTS FOR PROTRACTOR

Because you're using Jasmine, your tests will be structured similarly to the unit tests. The major difference is that you'll be focused on writing tests that mimic the behavior of the user through browser automation.

Protractor and WebDriver provide you a set of methods that you'll use to find an element on the page and interact with it. This is very similar to finding an element on the page in JavaScript using a method like `document.getElementById()`. But with Protractor and WebDriver, you can search for an element on the page by Angular-specific features, such as by the `ngModel` used on the element or the CSS class name.

Start by creating a new spec for your search view. You want to validate that the search page responds when you give it a term and press Search. Your unit tests can validate each piece works, but here you'll be validating that everything works together.

Create a file at tests/e2e/search.spec.js and add the contents of the following listing. These tests will use the same `describe()` and `it()` methods you saw in the unit tests.

1 Uses describe() to declare spec for search view

2 Starts by opening app at initial loading page, which is search view

```
describe('Search View', function() {
  browser.get('http://localhost:8100/');
  var term = element(by.model('model.term'));
  var button = element(by.className('button-search'));
  var results = element.all(by.repeater('result in results'));

  it('should open to the search view', function() {
    expect(term.getText()).toBe('');
  });

  it('should search for a term', function () {
    term.sendKeys('london, uk');
    button.click();
    expect(results.count()).toEqual(1);
  });

  it('should take you to the London, UK weather view', function () {
    results.first().click();
    var title = element(by.tagName('ion-side-menu-
      content')).element(by.className('title'));
    expect(title.getText()).toEqual('London, UK');
  });
});
```

6 First spec to test default term element should be blank

7 Second spec types value into search box, clicks search, and expects it to have four results

8 Third spec clicks on first result and expects weather view to load for that location

5 Creates variable to results list based on ngRepeat value

4 Creates variable to reference button based on class name given to button

3 Creates variable that references input element based on the specified ngModel value

Let's cover what will happen in this test before you run it. First you write a describe() method **1** to create the test for your search view. Then you use the Protractor feature browser.get() **2** to tell Protractor to load the app. This assumes you have ionic serve running in the background to enable the localhost server on port 8100. Protractor is smart enough to load the page and wait for Angular to finish rendering before it starts executing the next steps.

You then create three variables that are references to elements on the page. One is the search box **3**, which finds an element based on the value of ngModel. You had put the ng-model="model.term" on the search input field, and you're able to find that element again using element(by.model('model.term')). Likewise, you're able to set a variable to the search button **4**, but this time you search by the class name of the button. The third variable is the list of results **5**, and this time you find that element based on the value of the ngRepeat attribute. Now that you've assigned variables to the parts of the page you want to test, you can set up the specs.

The first spec ❻ just wants to test that the default value for the search box is empty. It's good to test the default state, and this test is designed to tell you if anything is causing the search box to have a value before it should.

The second spec ❼ actually emulates keyboard input to type the term 'london, uk' into the search box. Then it will emulate a click on the search button, which triggers the actual search to happen. Once that's complete, you check the number of returned items by counting the number of results. There should be four results for the search term.

The last spec ❽ will click on the first result in the list. The item is linked to the weather view, so here you test if the linking between views is correct. It will then check the title of the weather view once the view has loaded, and expect it to match the value of the first list item.

Now that you have an idea of what the test will do, it's time to run it. You'll actually need to have three command-line windows open to run the test. The first will have ionic server running, so the website is available at http://localhost:8100. The second will have the Selenium server running. The third will actually run the Protractor tests. Run the following commands in separate command-line windows:

```
$ ionic serve
$ webdriver-manager start
$ protractor protractor.conf.js
```

When you run the protractor command, you'll notice that a Chrome browser will open and load the app. It will type, click, and change views very quickly; however, you should be able to actually see the interface in Chrome while the test is running.

9.6 *More test examples*

This chapter 9 project contains more tests than we talked about in this chapter. You can use the rest of them as additional examples for how to write different types of tests.

I've added additional unit tests for each of the controllers, filters, and factory services. These tests cover nearly every part of the Angular code you've written. Then I've added a set of additional integration tests to test each of the views. This ensures that the primary features are checked and that the services are returning data as expected.

You can open questions on the GitHub project for this chapter and ask questions or suggest additional tests. You can find the project at https://github.com/ionic-in-action/chapter9.

This brings our discussion on the two primary types of automated testing to a close. The goal of this chapter was to get you started, so you can benefit from spending more time with the documentation sites for Jasmine, Karma, and Protractor.

9.7   *Summary*

Previewing, debugging, and testing are vital parts of the development process, and in this chapter we covered a lot of ways to help you improve the quality of your apps through using different tools and techniques. Let's review the major topics we covered:

- Ionic View and Ionic Lab are two Ionic features that help you to preview your app. Ionic View is great for sharing an app with others without sending it through the app stores, and Ionic Lab is very useful when trying to build cross-platform apps and for previewing the Android and iOS displays side by side.
- We looked at debugging hybrid apps. For iOS, you'll use Safari's Web Inspector tool to connect to a device or emulator and inspect the web view inside of an app. For Android, you'll use Chrome Canary to connect to a device or emulator and inspect the web view.
- Unit tests can be written with the Jasmine testing framework and executed with the Karma test runner. It's possible to test the individual units of code, such as a filter or controller, and verify that the smallest piece works as expected.
- You wrote integration tests with Jasmine, Protractor, and WebDriver. These tests are designed to verify the entire interface behaves as expected by programmatically emulating user events such as clicks and keyboard typing.

In the next and final chapter, you'll learn how to prepare and build your app for production, and how to submit it to the app stores.

10

Building and publishing apps

This chapter covers

- Generating icons and splash-screen images for your app
- Preparing and building your app for production release
- Publishing to Google Play—the submission process
- Publishing to the Apple App Store—the submission process

You're in the home stretch! At this point you have the skills to build a mobile app, but now to reach the finish you need to know how to submit it to the app stores. This important step also includes coming up with icons and loading screen graphics and descriptions of your app.

The app stores are ecosystems that are tightly controlled by Apple and Google. They set the rules when it comes to what's acceptable or not, and those rules can change often. Google is usually able to get new apps on the store in a matter of hours or days. Apple typically takes several days to weeks to review and publish an app as part of their approval process.

In this chapter you'll see screenshots from a submission I've made for an app I call Know Your Brew. I'm an avid home brewer and beer judge, so I wanted to have an app that gives me information in a pinch about the different types of beer. The general process should be the same for your app. There's no example code for this chapter. You'll only go through these steps when you're ready to submit your app; so when you're ready to publish your app, this is your guide.

There are some conditions or situations that aren't covered in this chapter. For example, if you're selling your app or have in-app purchases, you'll need to make sure that your account with Apple and/or Google is set up properly to handle payments. To keep this chapter concise and focused, I'll demonstrate how to upload a free app without any special conditions. For full details for iOS, visit http://mng.bz/z1VP, and for Android visit http://mng.bz/Jzv1.

Remember, the exact steps may change over time, so the screenshots are meant to serve as a guide. Google and Apple change their tools often when releasing a new major platform version, but the basic steps should remain in place.

10.1 Building for production: an overview

Before we dive into the steps, let's take a high-level look at the development process that has gotten you to this point and how it then diverges as you finish your app and publish it to the stores. Figure 10.1 shows everything you've done plus the prepublishing tasks you'll learn about.

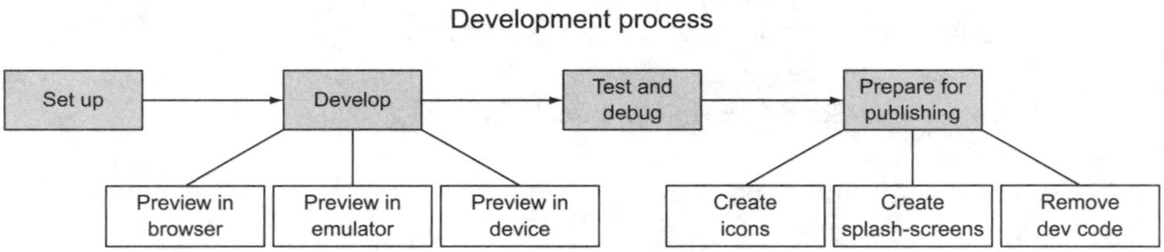

Figure 10.1   Steps you've taken to build your app and prepare it for publishing

You'll learn how to create icons and splash-screen images for your app, and some of the things you should do to remove development code from your app before publishing. Then you'll learn about the steps to build and publish for Android and iOS, as you see in figure 10.2.

We'll cover each step in detail, but this is the general flow to build and publish for each platform. Both platforms have generally the same steps to build an app, but the particulars differ.

For Android you'll use the command-line approach, and with iOS you'll use the Xcode IDE. This is my preferred method, though you can build for iOS from the command line, and likewise you could use the Android Studio IDE to build for Android.

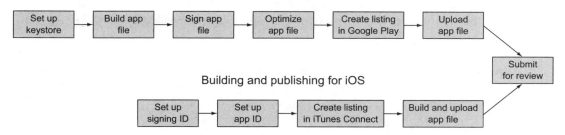

Figure 10.2   **Steps to build and publish an app for Android and iOS**

These are the general steps for both platforms:

- *You need a mechanism to sign your app for both platforms.* For Android this is done with a *keystore*, and for iOS this is called a *signing identity*. But they both do the same thing in the end: they add a signature to the build file that can later be used to verify the author.
- *Both platforms also require you to create a listing in their store.* Let's assume you've already done work to create the marketing material (screenshot images for the listing, description text, etc.), which will make it easier to create the listing. Having good marketing and app descriptions is vital for users to be able to determine if the app is for them or not.
- *You must build and optimize the build file on both platforms.* For Android, you upload the build file through the Google Play developer page, and for iOS, Xcode connects and uploads the file to your account.

At this point, just realize the underlying steps involved are very similar for both platforms, but the nuances about how they work varies and are covered in more detail for each platform.

10.2　*Building icons and splash-screen assets*

As phones have improved over the years, the image quality of the graphics has needed to improve as well. To accommodate this, both Android and iOS require apps to provide a number of different sizes for icons and the loading splash-screen graphic to fit the many different screen sizes and resolutions.

　　For example, the iPhone 6 has a larger screen than the iPhone 5, and apps should provide a loading splash-screen image that fits both sizes of phones. Android devices also have this problem, especially because Android devices have a much greater diversity in size and resolution due to the different phone manufacturers' designs. Creating images for these different situations can easily require dozens of images. You should also consider if you need to make a version for portrait and landscape modes, depending on the device's orientation.

Because it's somewhat painful to create so many images manually, Ionic implemented a feature that takes a single icon and a single splash-screen image and generates the various sizes that are needed for your app. It also will register the images with the cordova.xml file, so when you build the app, the images are linked correctly.

Ionic is able to convert the files by using its remote service, so your images will be uploaded to the Ionic servers for processing. This means there are no other dependencies you need besides the Ionic command-line interface. It supports PNG, PSD (Photoshop), and AI (Illustrator) files.

10.2.1 Creating the primary icons

To begin, you need a single icon graphic that Ionic can use to generate the rest of the sizes from. Ionic requires that you create an icon that's at least 192 pixels square, with no rounded edges. I recommend you make the icon at least 1,024 pixels square so the quality of the icon remains high. Icons are also modified slightly different for each platform; for example, iOS may round the edges of the icon. Ionic has a template for Photoshop that you can use to design your icon at http://mng.bz/2ow0.

There are some design considerations for the icon that you should be aware of. Both Android and iOS have some great documentation details about designing quality icons. iOS guidelines are at http://mng.bz/B3DO, and Android guidelines are at http://mng.bz/N957. Here are a few of the top considerations:

- *Keep the icon simple.* Icons aren't very large, and they should be easy to see.
- *Make it memorable.* The icon should be something uniquely representative of your app and brand.
- *Make sure it looks good large and small.* Don't forget to zoom out and see if the icon still looks clear when it's small.
- *Keep the colors simple.* Avoid using lots of colors or colors that clash.

Once you have your icon created and in a supported format, you need to save it to one of the following locations noted in table 10.1. If Ionic finds a platform-specific icon it will use it; otherwise, it will use the default icon.

Table 10.1 File locations to store icon source images

Target platform	File location
Android	resources/android/icon.png
iOS	resources/ios/icon.png
Default	resources/icon.png

Any time you want to generate the icons, you just need to run the following Ionic CLI command:

```
$ ionic resources -icon
```

This may take a few moments because the files are uploaded to Ionic's servers, converted, and downloaded back into your project. Once it's complete, you should review the generated icons to confirm they appear as desired for all of the different sizes.

10.2.2 *Creating the splash-screen images*

The splash-screen works very similarly to the icon, except there's a little bit more complexity to the splash-screen design. The icons are just resized, but the splash-screen is actually resized and cropped for different resolutions and orientations. You can see in figure 10.3 how the different sizes are cropped from the source splash-screen. If you have Photoshop, you can use the Ionic splash-screen template at http://mng.bz/2ow0 to help you design it to the correct dimensions.

The splash-screen source needs to be at least 2,208 × 2,208 pixels. But you should limit the custom design to a square in the center about 1,200 × 1,200 pixels. Typically this inner square contains some kind of logo branding with a background color. There aren't clear guidelines for the use of splash-screens in iOS and Android, so you should consider what will provide the best experience for your users.

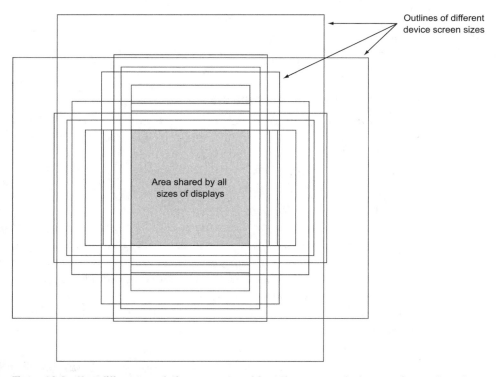

Figure 10.3 How different resolutions are cropped from the source splash-screen image, based on the various iOS and Android device sizes in portrait and landscape modes

After creating the splash-screen graphic in a supported format, you need to save it to one of the following locations noted in table 10.2. If Ionic finds a platform-specific splash-screen image it will use it; otherwise, it will use the default option.

Table 10.2   File locations to store splash-screen source images

Target platform	File location
Android	`resources/android/splash.png`
iOS	`resources/ios/splash.png`
Default	`resources/splash.png`

To generate the splash-screen images, run the following command:

```
$ ionic resources --splash
```

Like with the icons, it will upload to the Ionic servers to process the images, so you don't have to worry about having the necessary software on your machine.

   If you want to generate both icons and splash-screens at once, you can just run the following command:

```
$ ionic resources
```

Now that your icons and splash-screen images are ready, it's time to prepare the app for production.

10.3   *Preparing your app for production*

There are a few things you should check to ensure your app has nothing unnecessary, which can help improve speed and stability, and reduce the app file size. You could run your automated tests to ensure that even when these steps are taken, the application still behaves as expected.

   Here are some steps you should take before a release:

- *Remove the Cordova Console plugin.* This plugin is part of how Cordova allows you to debug your apps, but in production you don't want this. Remove it from your app by running `cordova plugin rm org.apache.cordova.console`.
- *Remove any unnecessary files.* During app development you might install extra third-party libraries or create extra views that you don't end up using. Remove them from the app so you save on file size.
- *Remove unused library files.* Ionic may have installed files in the www/lib directory of your app using Bower, and sometimes those library files also include the sources. You should delete any files that you're not using.
- *Compress your code.* You can run your code through a JavaScript minification system to help optimize the file execution and reduce file size.
- *Compress your graphics.* Images are often what can cause app file size to grow. Try to compress your files and make sure they aren't any larger than necessary.

The main idea here is to ensure everything is ready for widespread use. You wouldn't want debugging code to appear in your app, for example. The more diligent you are about keeping your app clean while you develop, the easier this step is to complete.

10.4 Building Android apps and publishing to Google Play

Now that your app is ready to be built for production, you've got a few steps to run through to build for Android. You'll have to build the app using Cordova, sign the app to verify the source, and optimize the built app. You'll use the command line to run all of the steps for Android, but you could also read about how to use Android Studio at http://mng.bz/T7G4. You'll use the command-line process, as outlined in figure 10.4, because it's simpler for Android.

Building and publishing for Android

Figure 10.4 Review of the Android build and publishing steps

The Google Play Store is the primary place to publish your apps for Android. You'll need to create or link an existing Google account with the Play Store Developer Console. Then you'll be able to create a listing for your app that includes the title, description, images, and other details used to categorize and list the app. Once that's done, you'll upload the built Android app APK file you generated and submit the app for review.

10.4.1 Setting up for signing your apps

Start by setting up a keystore—a file that securely stores the security key that you'll use later to add a signature to your app. With the signature, the author of the app can be verified over time. You can read more about signing at http://mng.bz/T7G4.

To generate a new keystore, you'll use a command-line utility `keytool`. This generates a keystore that's valid for 10,000 days, which should be more than enough to cover the lifetime of your app (and you shouldn't make it shorter, or it might expire!). You'll replace `know_your_brew` with the name of your app (use underscores) in this command:

```
$ keytool -genkey -v -keystore know_your_brew.keystore -alias know_your_brew
    -keyalg RSA -keysize 2048 -validity 10000
```

This generates a new file called, in this case, know_your_brew.keystore, and you can place it anywhere on your computer. Later you'll need to know the location of the file, so make sure you can access it.

You'll reuse the same keystore for the entire life of the app, so you need to keep it for as long as you plan to support the app. You also need to keep it safe and private because it could be used by others for malicious purposes. Every version of the app must be signed with the same keystore or the updates will be rejected. If a team needed to sign an app, the same keystore would need to be used regardless of who builds the app. You should also generate a different keystore for every app you produce.

10.4.2 *Build the release app file*

Next you'll build the app with Cordova. The following `build` command will build a release-ready version of your app:

```
$ cordova build --release android
```

This will generate a new APK file, which is the Android app file type, inside of platforms/android/ant-build/CordovaApp-release-unsigned.apk. The command line should report the exact file path to the APK file. This is an unsigned, release-ready version of your app.

10.4.3 *Signing the APK file*

Now you're ready to use the keystore you created earlier to sign the unsigned version of the APK you just generated. Android comes with a tool called `jarsigner` that will help you with this task.

You'll need to know the file path to both the unsigned APK and the keystore from the previous two steps. I recommend moving them into the same directory so the command is easier to type. In the command you'll replace `know_your_brew` with the same values you used to generate the keystore for your app, and update the name of the app if it's something other than `CordovaApp-release-unsigned.apk`:

```
$ jarsigner -verbose -sigalg SHA1withRSA -digestalg SHA1 -keystore
    know_your_brew.keystore CordovaApp-release-unsigned.apk know_your_brew
```

This takes just a moment, and it will prompt you for the password for the keystore and key. It will modify the APK in place. You can test that the app is now signed properly using `jarsigner` again, and replace the name with your app filename:

```
$ jarsigner -verify -verbose -certs CordovaApp-release-unsigned.apk
```

If you have any signing errors, you might want to rebuild the app using Cordova and try again to ensure you don't have a lingering problem.

10.4.4 *Optimize the APK*

The last step is to optimize the APK file so that it reduces the amount of space and RAM required by the app on a device. The `zipalign` tool is the utility for the job: it will take your signed APK file and create a new optimized APK version that you'll want to use for uploading. Under the hood, `zipalign` will optimize the bytes inside of the package for optimal reading by the operating system processes. The technical details can be found at http://mng.bz/vWfu.

The zipalign tool just takes the name of the signed file (remember, you signed the file in place and haven't changed the filename in this example) and the name of the file to generate. Change KnowYourBrew.apk to the name of your app:

```
$ zipalign -v 4 CordovaApp-release-unsigned.apk KnowYourBrew.apk
```

When the new file is generated, you now have a final version of your Android app that you can use to submit to any Android store. You've finished with the initial build, but let's talk quickly about how to update your app.

10.4.5 *Building an updated version of your app*

Almost certainly you'll eventually want to update your app with new features and bug fixes. The process to build an update to an existing app is the same as building the release, except you don't need to create another keystore. A few details are worth emphasizing:

- You must use the same keystore to sign the app for every update; otherwise, the update will be rejected for not having the same signature and you'll be required to create a new app listing.
- You must update the version and build number in the project config.xml file for the next release. If the numbers aren't changed, then the app will not properly update on your users' devices.
- If you build frequently, you might want to improve the steps by making the commands into a shell script that can be automated.

> **Build troubleshooting**
>
> A couple of problems can happen with a build, typically caused by some tools not being in the system path. Here are a few tips to check or fix if you run into trouble:
>
> Java and Ant must be installed and available in the system path. Android used Ant for its internal building process until it adopted Gradle, but to support older versions Cordova may use Ant.
>
> The android, keystore, and jarsigner commands might not work if you haven't added the path of the SDK to your system path.
>
> The zipalign tool might not work because some of the Android tool builds placed it in the wrong directory. You should search your computer for the zipalign file, and make sure it's in your system path to fix this problem.

10.4.6 *Creating the app listing and uploading the app to the Play Store*

The first step is to make sure you have access to the Developer Console for the Play Store. It requires a Google account. It's recommended that you create a separate Google account for your apps from any personal accounts, so you avoid any situations where your personal account (and perhaps your name) becomes tied to your apps. You can create the Google account at https://play.google.com/apps/publish/ signup/.

There's a one-time US $25 fee to update your account to a developer account. You'll also have to agree to some terms and conditions as part of the registration process. You should walk through the steps and complete the account registration and payment before continuing.

Once you're logged in to your developer account, you can begin the process of creating a listing. You're able to start a listing and finish it later, which is handy when you're trying to track down all of the details for the app. You can review the most up-to-date details about the Google Play publish process at http://mng.bz/6ZDC.

In the process of creating the listing, you'll need to provide the app name and default language, description, title, screenshots, and other metadata. Google Play requires several screenshots, an icon, and a feature graphic. You'll need to use your preferred image editing program to design and size these images accordingly.

Once you've created the full listing, you can upload the app APK file. Google Play has alpha, beta, and production versions that you can use with your app. The alpha and beta versions allow you to push updates before they go into the public Play Store, and get feedback. This can be a great way to roll out updates first to alpha, then beta, and finally to production. Alpha and beta testing might not be very useful until you've gotten a loyal following or have users willing to help you out. But you could be the only member of the beta group so that you can test that your app updates correctly from the Play Store before pushing to production. You can see more details at http://mng.bz/s6s8.

You can also upload an app APK file directly to production mode. This means your app can go live in the Play Store, and anyone is able to find and download it without having to opt-in to the alpha/beta process.

After you have the listing filled in and APK file uploaded, your app should be ready for publishing. Once you've submitted the app, it will be reviewed through both automatic and some manual processes to verify the app doesn't violate any store guidelines. This can take hours or days, but if the app is rejected for any reason, you'll be notified. If you violate any of the Google Play policies, you'll be notified so you can resolve them and resubmit your app.

10.4.7 *Updating the app listing or uploading a new version*

You can modify the app listing details, such as the description, without having to submit a new APK file. For example, you don't have to update the app APK file if you find a typo in your description.

When you update your app APK file, you must update the app version code (which is different from the version number) in the build itself. Cordova generates this value when you create the Android platform files based on the version number in config.xml. This number is built from the version number using this formula (unless you explicitly declare it): PATCH + MINOR * 100 + MAJOR * 10000. For example, version 2.3.6

(MAJOR.MINOR.PATCH) would be 6 + 3 * 100 + 2 * 10000 = 20306. Uploading a new APK file with an updated version code to production will trigger an update for users. The version number is just the value shown to users in the store. See http://mng.bz/0C05 for full details about versioning.

Any changes from updating the app or metadata are usually available within a couple of hours on the Play Store. The status of the changes is shown in the Developer Console, in case you need to verify if the update is still pending or has completed.

10.4.8 Using alternative Android stores

There are other Android stores, such as the Amazon App Store, and the build process is the same regardless of which store you use. There may be different rules or guidelines that you need to adhere to for these stores.

But other stores aren't inherently trusted like the Google Play Store. There is a setting on Android devices in Settings > Security > Unknown Sources that must be enabled to allow apps to be installed from outside of the Google Play Store. This is a major advantage that apps in the Google Play Store have over other stores.

10.5 Building iOS apps and publishing to the AppStore

To build for iOS using this process, you'll need to use a Mac and Xcode, and have your Apple developer account set up for iOS development.

> **Want to build for iOS without a Mac?**
>
> Ionic and other services have features to build an app through their platform. This would allow you to upload your project files to their server and get back the built files ready for submission. As Ionic evolves this feature, you can find details at https://ionic.io.
>
> It's not covered here, but you can leverage some of the CLI tools to build and sign apps that also work on Unix-like environments. These tools run on Unix-based systems such as Linux and Mac. You can review more information about the tools on Apple's site at http://mng.bz/XpsA.

Apple uses iTunes Connect as the way to create a listing in the AppStore and manage the app. You'll add your app listing to iTunes Connect, fill in a lot of details such as screenshots and metadata, connect Xcode to build and upload your app, and submit it for review, as shown in figure 10.5.

Building and publishing for iOS

Figure 10.5   The steps for building and publishing for iOS

If you haven't set up your Apple developer account yet and registered for the iOS Developer Program, you need to do that first. Go to https://developer.apple .com/programs/ to sign up; it costs US $99/year to be part of the iOS Developer Program. You can set up a new account for your apps if you have a personal account with Apple already.

10.5.1 *Set up certificates and ID*

Once you have your account, open Xcode on your Mac and go to the preferences. If you haven't already added your account to Xcode on the Accounts tab, do so now. This will sync Xcode with your account.

Let's start with getting a signing identity (also called *distribution certificate*). This is used to sign an app and verify that the app was built and submitted by the account owner. You can review the official documentation about managing certificates and IDs at http://mng.bz/64k9. The basic steps are these:

1 Log into your Apple developer account in Xcode if you haven't already.
2 In Preferences, manage your account and certificates.
3 Create a new signing identity specifically for distribution (not development).

Once the signing identity has been resolved, it should appear in the list as iOS Distribution. You may already have an iOS Development identity as well from testing.

10.5.2 *Set up an app ID identifier*

Now you'll set up the app ID identifier details through the Apple Developer Member Center. Identifiers are used to allow an app to have access to certain app services, such as Apple Pay or HealthKit. Multiple identifiers might be used in the same app for different services, but in this case you'll use just one.

Go to https://developer.apple.com/membercenter and log in with your Apple ID. Then choose Certificates, Identifiers, and Profiles. You want to set up a new app ID for your app, which is used to keep track of the app throughout the Apple ecosystem. See official documentation about app IDs at http://mng.bz/8hj1. The basic steps are these:

1 Start to register a new app ID.
2 Supply the name of your app, and use the Explicit App ID option. Provide the bundle ID from your app, which is by default the ID in the `<widget>` tag you specified in the Cordova config.xml file of your app (or if you modified the bundle ID value in your Xcode project). *It must match your app bundle ID.*
3 Choose any of the services that need to be enabled. For example, if you use HealthKit in your app, you need to choose that option. Apps often have no additional services, so if you don't think you need it, just leave them as default values.
4 Submit to register the app ID.

That will take care of the ID registration for your app, and it will be used by iTunes Connect and Xcode in the following steps.

10.5.3 *Create listing in iTunes Connect*

You now need to make your listing in iTunes Connect, which is the portal that Apple uses to manage app submissions. You'll use your app ID that you generated to create a new record. Log into iTunes Connect at https://itunesconnect.apple.com to get started. Detailed documentation about iTunes Connect can be found at http://mng.bz/92eZ. The general steps are these:

1 Add a new iOS app.
2 Fill in the app details, and choose the correct bundle ID (the name of the app ID you made earlier) for the app.
3 Create the app listing. You'll fill out more details later.

Now you've generated a new app listing that will eventually be ready to submit to the AppStore. You've taken the app ID you created before and connected it to this app listing. Before you fill out everything in the listing, you'll build your app and get it uploaded first using Xcode. Then you'll come back to finish the listing.

10.5.4 *Build and upload app with Xcode*

Now that you have an app ID and iTunes Connect app listing started, Xcode can help you build and upload the app. You first have to make sure that the Xcode project is up to date with your Cordova project. Run the Cordova `build` task from the project root in the command line:

```
$ cordova build ios --release
```

This will ensure the latest changes from your project are set up in the iOS project. Open the platforms/ios/AppName.xcodeproj file in Xcode. It should allow you to see details about your app in the general view, where you want to confirm things look correct:

- The *bundle identifier* should match the value you specified earlier in the app ID.
- The *version* and *build* numbers should reflect what you intend them to be.
- *Team* should be set to your Apple account.
- *Deployment target* and *devices* should reflect which versions and devices you intend to support.

Xcode is good about prompting you to fix certain errors if you haven't set up something correctly. Review any error messages, and in some cases Xcode can even resolve them for you. You'll also need to make sure you don't have a device connected to the computer.

You can now build the app as an archive (which is the app bundled for uploading), and then you'll upload it. The full documentation is found at http://mng.bz/20m2. The general steps are these:

1 Create a new archive of your app, which will make a build of your app that can be later submitted.
2 Validate the archive you just created, which will ensure the archive can be uploaded correctly and passes validation tests.
3 Submit the app, which will actually submit the file to iTunes Connect.

Now that you've got your app finished and uploaded, you just need to complete the iTunes Connect listing and submit it for review!

10.5.5 *Complete the iTunes Connect app listing*

There are a lot of details to provide for the app listing, which are documented in the app listing form for you. If you try to submit your app without providing some required information, it will let you know what's missing or needs to be fixed.

When you uploaded your archived app, iTunes Connect determined which device sizes it supported. You'll need to upload at least one screenshot image for each of the various app sizes iTunes Connect detected. The easiest way to generate these images is to emulate the app in different versions of the iPhone simulator. The exact sizes and rules can be found by choosing the help icon near the screenshots. You could also upload a short video preview of the app.

Much of the listing is information you'll have to fill out based on your app, such as the description, keywords, support URL, and icon. You can work through these details and consider how to maximize clarity and marketing for your app.

In the build section, you can view the uploaded build versions for your app uploaded from Xcode, and if this is your first app and build, then you'd expect only one. Choose the build from the list and save.

Just like for Android, iOS has the ability to submit an alpha or beta version of your app and release it to that select group. There's a limit to how many users can test a prerelease version, and you can invite them over email. See more details in the documentation at http://mng.bz/1Yp4.

Once you've finished adding the rest of the details to the app listing, you can press Save and then Submit for Review. If any errors are displayed, fix them and you can try again.

Apple has a manual review process, which means it can take several days for your app changes to be fully reviewed and reflected in the App Store. You'll be notified of any issues or updates to your app status.

10.5.6 *Updating the app*

To update an app, start by updating the build and version numbers. This can be done in the Xcode project file, or you can update the Cordova config.xml file and then regenerate the iOS platform files with Cordova by removing the ios platform and adding it again.

With the new version and build numbers, you can then follow the same steps to build and upload a new version to your account. If the numbers aren't updated, then the build will not upload.

Once the new package has been uploaded, you'll see a new number in the top bar for the release. Make any changes to the app listing, such as new screenshots or changing other metadata, press Save, and then press Submit for Review. The changes will go through the same review process, and the existing app will remain in place until the review is complete.

If you choose to release the version automatically, as soon as the review is completed successfully the app will go live. Otherwise, you must manually log in after the review to release a new version. Manual release might be useful if you want to trigger the release of a new version yourself at a certain time.

10.6 Summary

Uploading an app to the stores is the ultimate goal of app development, and this chapter covered the steps to generate icons, build the app, and submit it. Let's review the major topics covered in this chapter:

- Both icons and splash-screens need to be provided in many sizes for different device types.
- You built the app for Android, signed it with your key, and made it ready to be published. You then created and uploaded the Android app to the Play Store using the Developer Console.
- You set up an iOS app with the necessary app ID and iTunes Connect listing, and then were able to build and upload from Xcode. You finished the app listing in iTunes Connect and submitted your app for review.

After going through all of the steps, you'll be able to optimize your app for production and release it to the app stores. Congratulations on finishing your app, and be sure to share what you've built in the author forum!

appendix A
Additional resources

This appendix contains a curated list of additional resources. Resources shared in the chapters are also collected here as a reference.

A.1 Ionic

- http://ionicframework.com—The official Ionic website with documentation, a forum, a blog, and more.
- https://apps.ionic.io/—The Ionic platform where you can manage your apps with Ionic View, Ionic Creator, and other Ionic platform services.
- http://ionicons.com—A preview of all of the icons available in the Ionic icon set, Ionicons.
- https://github.com/driftyco/ionic—The GitHub project to follow the development of Ionic.
- https://github.com/ionic-in-action—The GitHub project for this book.
- http://codepen.io/ionic/public-list/—A list of useful demos for individual features created by the Ionic team.
- http://mng.bz/A24v—The YouTube channel from Ionic containing demos, tutorials, and episodes from the team.

A.2 Angular

- https://angularjs.org—The official documentation and site for Angular 1. It contains links to starter guides, videos, mailing lists, and more.
- http://manning.com/bford—*AngularJS in Action* is a complete book for getting started with Angular and learning the fundamentals.
- http://manning.com/aden—*AngularJS in Depth* is a complete book about digging deeper into how Angular works, which is very useful for improving your Ionic apps.
- http://angular.github.io/protractor—End-to-end testing for Angular is made much easier with Protractor.
- http://karma-runner.github.io—Karma is the popular test runner for executing unit tests built by the Angular team.

- http://jasmine.github.io—Jasmine is the testing library used in this book and by Angular.

A.3   *Cordova*

- http://cordova.apache.org—The official Cordova website with documentation, news, and more.
- http://plugins.cordova.io/npm/index.html—Discover available plugins for Cordova using the official plugin registry.
- http://ngcordova.com—The official ngCordova website with documentation on how to use each of the supported Cordova plugins.
- http://manning.com/camden/—*Apache Cordova in Action*, a great book by Raymond Camden that digs deep into the features of Cordova.

A.4   *Blogs*

- http://ionicinaction.com—The companion website and blog for this book.
- https://blog.nraboy.com—Nic Raboy has many good posts about building mobile apps with Ionic.
- http://www.raymondcamden.com—Raymond Camden blogs regularly about building mobile apps, using Cordova, and also about Ionic.
- http://mobilewebweekly.co—A great weekly email newsletter with carefully curated links to the top posts on mobile development from around the web.

index

Symbols

$ symbol 46
{{ }} double curly braces 38

A

accelerometer 187
action sheet component
        150–153
Amazon App Store 241
Android
    debugging from device 213
    emulators
        previewing apps in 31
        setting up 26–29
    previewing apps on con-
            nected device 33
    publishing apps
        building release version
            238
        building updated
            versions 239
        optimizing APK 238–239
        process overview 237
        setting up for signing of
            apps 237–238
        signing APK 238
        updating app 240–241
        uploading to Google Play
            Store 239–240
        using alternative Android
            stores 241
    recommended versions 25
    supported devices 15
Android Studio 24–25

Android Virtual Device
        Manager. *See* AVD
        Manager
angular.module() method 45
AngularJS
    chapter project setup 41–43
    click events 51–54
    controllers
        loading data using 48–51
        overview 39–40, 45–48
    Cordova plugins and
            191–192
    defined 3
    digest loop 191–192
    directives 54–56
    expressions 79
    filters 51
    form validation using 61
    Ionic framework stack 10
    models
        managing content editing
            using 56–59
        overview 39–40
    ngApp directive 44–45
    online resources 247
    overview 35–38
    prerequisite experience 13
    resources for 62–63
    scope 39–40
    services 41
    templates 38–39
    two-way data binding 41
APK files 238–239
Apple developer account 242
$apply() method 192
asynchronous tasks 50

automated testing
    integration tests
        overview 225–226
        Protractor configuration
            227
        setting up 226–227
        writing tests 227–229
    unit tests
        overview 219–220
        running unit tests 222
        setting up 220
        writing unit tests 221–225
AVD (Android Virtual Device)
        Manager 27

B

back-button component 97
Bitcoin app example
    chapter project setup 96
    charting data
        controller for 118–121
        creating template using
            Highcharts
            component 117–118
        overview 116
        setting up third-party
            libraries 116–117
    detail view 107–111
    loading data service
            content 103–107
    refreshing app using
            ionRefresher
            111–113
    reordering for lists 122–123
    showing help in
            popover 113–115

Bitcoin app example *(continued)*
  tabs
    adding ionNavView for
      each tab 103
    adding tabs container and
      tabs 98
    setting up navigation
      for 96–98
    toggle options for lists
      123–124
Bower 21
browser, previewing apps
  in 22–23
building apps. *See* production
  apps

C

camera
  adding plugin to project 196
  overview 194–196
  using photo book view
    196–198
Cascading Style Sheets. *See* CSS
Chrome 23
CLI (command-line interface)
  9, 19–20
click events, AngularJS 51–54
collection repeat component
  156–159
comma-separated value.
  See CSV
Console plugin 236
content container 72–73
controllers
  data binding using model
    and 76–80
  loading data using 48–51
  loading external data 82–84
  overview 39–40, 45–48
Cordova
  Console plugin 236
  defined 2
  evolution of 187
  installing 19–20
  Ionic framework stack 10–11
  ngCordova 194
  online resources 248
  persistent data storage using
    plugins 179
  plugins
    Angular and 191–192
    considerations for 188
    installing 188–189
    overview 187

platform limitations and
  190–191
testing in emulators 190
troubleshooting 192–193
using in app 189–190
using camera
  adding camera plugin 196
  overview 194–196
  photo book view 196–198
using geolocation
  adding geolocation plugin
    and ngCordova 200
  overview 198–199
  requesting user location
    200–202
$cordovaCamera service 197
CORS (cross-origin resource
  sharing) 140–141
CSS (Cascading Style Sheets)
  components using 74–75
  customizing components 70
  Ionic components for 75
  prerequisite experience 13
  Sass
    custom styling using 167
    overview 164
    setting up 164–165
    using Sass variables in
      Ionic 165
CSV (comma-separated
  value) 116

D

debugging
  from Android device 213
  defined 207–208
  from iOS device 213–218
  overview 212–213
default behavior, overriding
  184–185
dependency injection. *See* DI
$destroy event 115, 155
Developer Console 237, 239
development environment
  Cordova 19–20
  Ionic CLI 19–20
  Node.js 19
  overview 17–19
  previewing environments
    Android emulator 26–29
    Android Studio 24–25
    iOS emulator 25
    previewing in emulator 31

previewing on Android
  device 33
previewing on iOS device
  32–33
setting up connected
  devices 29–30
Xcode 24–25
projects
  adding platforms to 30–31
  creating 20
  folder structure 21–22
  previewing in browser
    22–23
deviceready event 189
DI (dependency injection) 49
digest loop 191–192
directives, AngularJS
  creating 54–56
  overview 38, 56
distribution certificate 242
documentation 247–248
DOM (Document Object
  Model) 40, 44, 156,
  212
double curly braces {{ }} 38
doubletap event 174
drag events 174

E

emulate command 31
emulators
  Android
    previewing apps in 31
    setting up 26–29
  iOS
    previewing apps in 31
    setting up 25
  testing Cordova plugins
    in 190
events, listening for 169–171
Express.js 43, 47
expressions, AngularJS 79
external data, loading 82–84

F

filters 51, 106, 148–150
form validation 61
framework stack
  Angular 10
  Cordova 10–11
  Ionic user interface
    framework 8–10
  overview 7–8

$fromIndex parameter 122
fromTemplateUrl()
    method 155

G

garbage collection 155
Genymotion 213
geolocation
    adding plugin to project 200
    overview 198–199
    requesting user location
        200–202
    searching using Google Geo-
        location API 131–133
gesture events
    listening for events with
        event directives
        169–171
    listening for events with
        $ionicGesture service
        171–173
    overview 169
    supported gestures 174–175
Git 18
Google Chrome Canary
    browser 213
Google Play Store 237, 239–240
Gulp 21, 165

H

--help flag 20
Highcharts component
    controller for 118–121
    creating template for
        117–118
    overview 116
    setting up third-party
        libraries 116–117
hold event 174
HTML (Hypertext Markup
    Language)
    AngularJS templates 38
    prerequisite experience 13
$http service 41, 49, 60, 82, 118
hybrid apps 6–7

I

icons 233–235
import command 166
$index value 52

IndexedDB 178–179
infinite scroll with cards 86–89
installation
    Android Studio 24–25
    Cordova 19–20
    Cordova plugins 188–189
    Ionic CLI 19–20
    ngCordova 194
    Node.js 19
    Xcode 24–25
integration testing
    overview 225–226
    Protractor configuration 227
    setting up 226–227
    writing tests 227–229
ionContent component 72, 74
    ionScroll and 143
    refreshing 112
    tabs and 98
ionDeleteButton component
    138
ionFooterBar component 106
Ionic
    advantages 11–12
    disadvantages 12–13
    framework stack
        Angular 10
        Cordova 10–11
        Ionic user interface
            framework 8–10
        overview 7–8
    online resources 247
    overview 2–3
    prerequisite experience
        13–14
    supported devices 14–15
Ionic Lab 209
Ionic View 210–211
ionic.Platform service 182–183
$ionicActionSheet service
    151–152
$ionicConfigProvider service
    184–185
$ionicGesture service 171–173
$ionicLoading service 80, 85
$ionicModal service 154
Ionicons 75–76
$ionicPlatform.ready method
    189
$ionicPopover service 113–115
$ionicPopup service 160
$ionicView.beforeEnter event
    120
ionInfiniteScroll component

87
ionItem component 123
ionList component 122, 138
ionModal component 153–156
ionModalView component 156
ionNavBackButton
    component 69
ionNavBar component 69, 96
ionNavView component 69, 103
ionPopoverView component
    114
ionRadio component 137
ionRefresher component
    111–113
ionReorderButton component
    122–123
ionScroll component
    overview 142–143
    paging with 143–148
ionSideMenus component
    129–130
ionSlideBox component 89
$ionSlideBoxDelegate service
    90
ionTabs component
    adding ionNavView for each
        tab 103
    adding tabs container and
        tabs 98
    setting up navigation for
        96–98
ionToggle component 123–124
iOS
    debugging from device
        213–218
    emulators
        previewing apps in 31
        setting up 25
    previewing apps on con-
        nected device 32–33
    publishing apps
        creating listing in iTunes
            Connect 243
        process overview 241–242
        setting up app ID 242–243
        setting up for signing of
            apps 242
        updating app 244–245
        uploading 243–244
    recommended versions 25
    supported devices 14–15
isAndroid() method 182
isIOS() method 182
iTunes Connect 241, 243

J

jarsigner utility 238–239
Jasmine
    online resources 225
    overview 219–221
    running unit tests 222
    setting up 220
    writing unit tests 221–225
JavaScript
    Ionic components for 75
    prerequisite experience 13
jQuery 21

K

Karma
    overview 219–220
    running unit tests 222
    setting up 220
    writing unit tests 221–225
keystore utility 239
keytool utility 237

L

lists
    reordering 122–123
    toggle options for 123–124
livereload command 196
loading indicator 84–86
localStorage 175–178
location, searching using
            Google Geolocation
            API 131–133

M

Markdown 54
memory leaks 155
menuClose directive 130
menuToggle directive 130
mobile experiences
    hybrid apps 6–7
    mobile websites (web apps)
            5–6
    native mobile apps 3–5
mocks 223
modals 153–156
models
    AngularJS 39–40
    data binding using controller
            and 76–80

managing content editing
            using 56–59
Moment Timezone 149

N

native mobile apps 3–5
navigation
    chapter project setup 66
    content container 72–73
    CSS components 74–75
    data binding using controller
            and model 76–80
    declaring app states 69–72
    designing for app 67–68
    infinite scroll with cards
            86–89
    loading external data using
            controller 82–84
    loading indicator for view
            84–86
    overview 66–67
    routing vs. 67
    setting up for tabs 96–98
    slidebox component 89–92
    templates for 81–82
    using Ionicons 75–76
ngApp directive 44–45
ngChange directive 118, 120
ngClass directive 52
ngClick directive 52
ngController directive 46
ngCordova directive 11, 194
ngDisabled directive 61
ngForm directive 61
ngHide directive 54
ngIf directive 51, 88
ngModel directive 58, 118
ngRepeat directive 38, 51–52,
            89, 106, 136
ngRoute directive 67
ngShow directive 54
Node.js 19
notification plugin 189
npm (Node Package Manager)
            19, 21, 43, 165

O

online resources
    Angular 247
    blogs 248
    Cordova 248
    Ionic 247

online/offline modes 167–169
otherwise() method 71

P

performance
    improving using collection
            repeat 156–159
    memory leaks and 155
persistent data storage
    Cordova plugins for 179
    overview 175
    using localStorage 175–178
    using Web SQL and
            IndexedDB 178–179
PhoneGap 11
pinch events 175
platform() method 182
platforms
    adding to projects 30–31
    targeting multiple
            adapting behavior
                    182–183
            adapting styling 180–182
            overview 179–180
plugins, Cordova
    Angular and 191–192
    camera
            adding to project 196
            overview 194–196
            photo book view 196–198
    considerations for 188
    geolocation
            adding to project 200
            overview 198–199
            requesting user location
                    200–202
    installing 188–189
    overview 187
    platform limitations and
            190–191
    testing in emulators 190
    troubleshooting 192–193
    using in app 189–190
popovers 113–115
popups 159–161
previewing apps
    in browser 22–23
    in emulator 31
    environment setup
            Android emulator 26–29
            Android Studio 24–25
            connected devices 29–30
            iOS emulator 25
            Xcode 24–25

previewing apps *(continued)*
Ionic Lab 209
Ionic View 210–211
on mobile device
Android 33
iOS 32–33
overview 32
testing vs. 207–208
production apps
Android
building release version
238
building updated versions
239
optimizing APK 238–239
process overview 237
setting up for signing of
apps 237–238
signing APK 238
updating app 240–241
uploading to Google Play
Store 239–240
using alternative Android
stores 241
icons 233–235
iOS
creating listing in iTunes
Connect 243
process overview 241–242
setting up app ID 242–243
setting up for signing of
apps 242
updating app 244–245
uploading 243–244
overview 232–237
splash screen 233–236
projects
adding platforms to 30–31
creating 20
folder structure 21–22
previewing in browser 22–23
promises 50
Protractor
configuration 227
overview 225–226
setting up 226–227
writing tests 227–229
proxy service for CORS
limitation 140–141
publishing apps. *See* production
apps

R

refreshing app 111–113
release event 174

reordering for lists 122–123
required attribute 61
resort app example
home view
content container 72–73
CSS components 74–75
overview 72
using Ionicons 75–76
reservation view 76–80
restaurants view 86–89
slidebox component 89–92
using camera
adding camera plugin 196
overview 194–196
photo book view 196–198
weather view
adding loading indicator
to 84–86
controller for loading
external data 82–84
overview 80–81
template for 81–82
responsive design 6
RESTful APIs 47
$rootScope object 40
rotate event 175
routing 67
See also navigation

S

Safari 23
Sass (Syntactically Awesome
Style Sheets)
custom styling using 167
overview 164
setting up 164–165
using Sass variables in Ionic
165
$scope object 39, 77
scope, AngularJS 39–40
$scope.popover property 114
scrolling content
overview 142–143
using ionScroll with paging
143–148
SDK (software development
kit) 3, 24, 26
serve command 140, 166
services 41, 133–135
settings
controller for 138–139
creating service for 133–135
showing favorites 135–136
template for 136–138

Showdown library 55
show-reorder attribute 122
side menus 128–131
signing apps
Android apps 237–238
iOS apps 242
slidebox component 89–92
software development kit.
See SDK
splash screen 233–236
SQLite 178
$stateChangeStart event 123
$stateParams service 109
$stateProvider service 70, 132,
135
sudo command 19
swipe events 174
Syntactically Awesome Style
Sheets. *See* Sass

T

tabs
adding ionNavView for each
tab 103
adding tabs container and
tabs 98
setting up navigation for
96–98
tap event 174
--target flag 31
templates
AngularJS 38–39
for settings 136–138
for views 81–82
Terminal 17
testing
defined 207–208
importance of 208
integration tests
overview 225–226
Protractor configuration
227
setting up 226–227
writing tests 227–229
overview 218–219
unit tests
overview 219–220
running unit tests 222
setting up 220
writing unit tests 221–225
timezone filter 150
toggle options for lists 123–124
$toIndex parameter 122
touch event 174

transform events 174
troubleshooting 192–193
two-way data binding 41

U

ui.router module 10
ui-router project 66–67
ui-sref attribute 100, 110–111, 133
unit testing
    overview 219–220
    running unit tests 222
    setting up 220
    writing unit tests 221–225
$urlRouterProvider service 70, 132

V

validation, form 61
versioning 240, 243
views
    content container 72–73
    CSS components 74–75
    data binding using controller and model 76–80
    infinite scroll with cards 86–89
    loading external data using controller 82–84
    loading indicator for 84–86
    organizing files by 78
    slidebox component 89–92
    templates for 81–82
    using Ionicons 75–76

Virtual Box 213

W

watch command 166
weather app example
    action sheet component for options 150–153
    chapter project setup 128
    collection repeat for large data set performance 156–159
    current conditions and forecast view
        controller for 141–142
        custom filters 148–150
        getting Forecast.io API key 140
        overview 139–140
        proxy service for CORS limitation 140–141
        template for 141
    current location in 202–204
    custom scrolling content with ionScroll
        overview 142–143
        using ionScroll with paging 143–148
    modals 153–156
    overview 126–128
    popups 159–161
    settings
        controller for 138–139
        creating service for 133–135

    showing favorites 135–136
    template for 136–138
side menu 128–131
using geolocation
    adding geolocation plugin and ngCordova 200
    overview 198–199
    requesting user location 200–202
    searching using Google Geolocation API 131–133
web apps 5–6
Web SQL 178–179
WebDriver API
    overview 225–226
    setting up 226–227
    writing tests 227–229
WebView
    browser previews and 23
    defined 3, 6
$window.navigator.onLine value 168
wireframing 65

X

Xcode 14, 24–25, 241–243

Z

zipalign utility 238–239

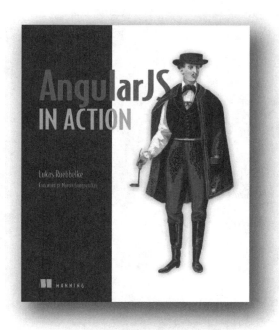

AngularJS in Action
by Lukas Ruebbelke

    ISBN: 9781617291333
    192 pages
    $44.99
    July 2015

Getting MEAN with Mongo, Express, Angular, and Node
by Simon Holmes

    ISBN: 9781617292033
    375 pages
    $44.99
    September 2015

For ordering information go to www.manning.com

MORE TITLES FROM MANNING

Apache Cordova in Action
by Raymond K. Camden

ISBN: 9781633430068
275 pages
$39.99
September 2015

Hello App Inventor!
by Paula Beer and Carl Simmons

ISBN: 9781617291432
360 pages
$39.99
October 2014

For ordering information go to www.manning.com

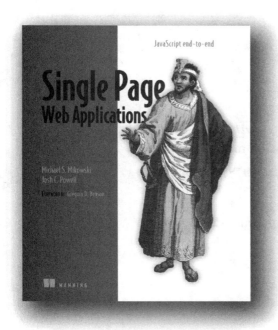

MORE TITLES FROM MANNING

Learn Git in a Month of Lunches
by Rick Umali

ISBN: 9781617292415
375 pages
$39.99
September 2015

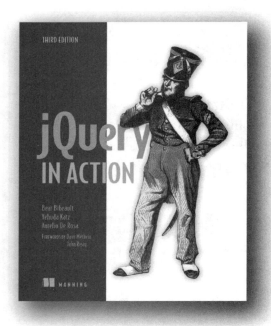

jQuery in Action, Third Edition
by Bear Bibeault, Yehuda Katz, and Aurelio
De Rosa

ISBN: 9781617292071
504 pages
$44.99
August 2015

For ordering information go to www.manning.com